0337224-3

KU-207-444

Current Issues in Economic Policy

Current Issues in Economic Policy

Editors:

R M GRANT and G K SHAW
University of St Andrews

Philip Allan

First published 1975 by

PHILIP ALLAN PUBLISHERS LIMITED
MARKET PLACE
DEDDINGTON
OXFORD OX5 4SE

© PHILIP ALLAN PUBLISHERS 1975

All rights reserved. No part of this publication may be reproduced, stored in a retrieval system, or transmitted, in any form or by any means, electronic, mechanical, photocopying, recording or otherwise, without the prior permission of the publishers.

0 86003 005 9 (hardback)
0 86003 106 3 (paperback)

Reprinted 1977

Set by Computerset (Phototypesetting) Limited, Oxford
Printed in Great Britain by The Camelot Press Limited, Southampton

Contents

603572

Preface

This volume evolved from a growing conviction that most introductory economics courses, as conventionally taught in universities and polytechnics, are predominantly theoretical in approach. To a large extent this is inevitable if the groundwork of the subject is to be laid adequately, especially when many first-year students have no prior contact with economics. Invariably, however, it leads to a situation where the student does not readily perceive how the theoretical structure relates to the policy issues which are at the centre of economic debate and controversy. This is particularly the case when the theoretical framework has been treated as a series of distinct component parts, as an aid to assimilation and comprehension, and its consequences are especially serious when the student does not pursue his economic training beyond the introductory level.

Current Issues is designed to remedy this defect by focussing upon some key areas of applied economics and the role of government in the economy, drawing upon the basic apparatus of elementary micro and macro economic theory. Each author has analysed a current policy issue, primarily although not wholly within a United Kingdom context, invoking no more than the conventional tools of first-year economics. Thus, the book is designed as a complement to an introductory theory text, with the hope that it may bridge the gulf between the abstractions of economic theory and the complexity of economic policy; a gulf clearly and dauntingly perceived by the student and yet a gulf which in reality does not, and should not, exist.

A word of caution is necessary. With regard to content, it was never intended that the book should be exhaustive and the decision on what to include or leave out has been purely a question of personal choice on the part of the editors, who accept responsibility for any glaring omissions. Secondly, for the most part each chapter has been written by a specialist within the field, who has approached the subject matter from his own particular vantage point. There has been no attempt to reflect all shades of opinion on any given topic, even where the subject is highly controversial. Rather, our objective has been to provoke continuing enquiry by introducing the reader to major policy issues and options and indicating how they may be further explored with the aid of contemporary analysis.

The editors wish to thank the participating authors, not only for making the present work possible, but also for their willingness to submit to editorial surgery. We also thank Mrs Joan Reed of St. Andrews University for undertaking the bulk of the secretarial work involved.

R. M. Grant
G. K. Shaw

Foreword: studying economic policy

ALAN PEACOCK
Professor of Economics,
University of York*

The traditional purpose of an introduction is to say nice things
about the authors. Honeyed words will hopefully disarm criticism
and promote sales. This book does not need sponsorship of this
kind. It clearly fills a gap in the undergraduate literature. Books on
basic theory abound and there is a growing number of
undergraduate texts on applied economics displaying
considerable sophistication, but it is difficult to find a *tour
d'horizon* of the main areas of economic policy which is neither on
the one hand too descriptive nor, on the other, too overweighted
with advanced analysis. I have chosen my task as that of trying to
help the reader in using this volume. I attempt to do so by
considering what are the essential ingredients for a study of
economic policy, leaving the reader to consider further how these
ingredients are combined to fashion finished products in the
chapters ahead.

A policy suggests immediately an objective or set of objectives,
chosen by some method by someone. In the study of
macroeconomic policy, the general procedure is to identify
objectives of interest to the policy maker and which are therefore

*The author is presently Chief Economic Adviser, Department of Industry. This
Foreword represents his personal views, which do not commit the Department of
Industry or the Government Economic Service.

1

data to the investigator. The selection of such objectives by the economist is based on observed behaviour of governments.

It may be useful for some purposes to look at objectives singly, but a growing and important field of economic analysis is concerned with the study of macroeconomic policy 'in the round', involving the construction of a government 'utility function' or 'social welfare function' analogous to the individual utility function commonly used in demonstrating the maximising behaviour of consumers or producers. This suggests that objectives must be *quantified* in some way (e.g. the unemployment percentage, the rate of economic growth) and targets set for them. In the likely event that not all targets can be simultaneously reached, the social welfare function can be redefined to indicate how these targets will be 'traded off' against one another. This approach is difficult to implement in examining actual policies because of the problems encountered in acquiring data, not so much on objectives, but on trade-offs. Governments, however formed, may not have precise ideas about trade-offs, and, if they do, may not wish to reveal them unless they are sure that the revelation will support their position (see Chapter 9). What is more, they may change them frequently in the light of the need for support. Both the shape and the position of the government's 'indifference surface' may be indiscernible and, so far as it is revealed, unpredictable. The authors of this volume who have identified targets have been wise to avoid any attempt to calculate the weights attached to individual policies, though the notion of trade-offs provides them with a useful frame of reference.

There is, however, another approach to the problem of identification of objectives and trade-offs. It is often rather misleadingly labelled a microeconomic approach, simply because it derives objectives from the behaviour of individuals faced with the usual economic constraints on resources available to them and on the development of their capacity to alter those constraints. Policy objectives to be implemented by collective action are identified as a logical consequence of individuals' maximising behaviour. The extent and form of collective action by government budgetary and other measures depends on the way in which collective decisions by individuals are arrived at. This approach is used to demonstrate which policies logically follow from individuals' behaviour (Chapter 5), or may be developed into a model which endeavours to explain or even to predict how actual policies emerge (Chapter 2).

There is no logical conflict between these two approaches. Essentially the second approach goes a few stages further back in the political process which governs policy formation than the first approach. Whether or not governments who implement policy decisions take account of individuals' aspirations is a matter for empirical investigation. Where differences and potential conflict between the approaches may arise is in the appraisal of policy decisions, but this is a matter which is considered later.

Once objectives are specified, policy makers must choose instruments in order to fulfil them. In countries with mixed economies, this entails introducing policy measures which are designed to alter the economic environment surrounding private consumers and producers so that they modify their actions in line with the required objective. If it is believed that capital accumulation is the instrument to achieve the objective of growth (Chapter 11), policies will be designed to induce entrepreneurs to increase their rate of investment, for example by lowering tax rates on companies. But policy makers will be interested not only in achieving the correct direction of change but also in the magnitude of change possible within the constraints imposed on their actions, the most important being scarcity of available resources. Thus if increasing investment means reducing consumption— consumption being the rough symbol we might use for alternative objectives — attention is directed towards the problem of tracing the quantitative relationship between the increase in investment and the associated increase in economic growth. The less the increase in investment required to achieve the growth target, the less difficult it will be to achieve other objectives. This argument has been couched in very general terms, but is sufficient to demonstrate what further ingredients are needed in studies of economic policy.

The first requirement, then, is a model which traces the chain of causation between the policy instruments and the objectives. What this model contains will depend on the problem which the economist wishes to illuminate. If it is policy intervention in a single market where one objective is considered, it may be sufficient, particularly at the introductory stage assumed in this volume, to build on simple supply and demand analysis; and there are several examples of the versatility of this simple technique in this work (Chapter 4). Likewise, in examining a single macro-objective such as stemming inflation, the essential relationship between the objective and policy instruments can be`illustrated using either a simple Keynesian-type or Friedman-type (Chapter 10) macroeconomic model.

It is characteristic of the contributions to this volume that objectives are considered singly; though, in contrast, alternative instruments to reach single objectives are frequently considered (Chapter 8). Reference is made in some cases to the side effects of particular instruments used to achieve a single objective on other objectives, so offering a useful reminder to the reader of the complications associated with the pursuit of a unified multi-objective policy. Indeed, the very structure of the work, with single chapters on various aspects of policy, more or less imposes such a framework of analysis. The reader may find it useful to know that there has been a very striking development in economic analysis under the general label of 'the theory of economic policy' in which very sophisticated models are used to show how governments can maximise several objectives simultaneously, given the structure of the economy and the instruments available. Not the least interesting aspect of these attempts to formulate 'optimal decision rules' for government is the way in which, as we have already indicated, the terminology and to some extent the methodology of microeconomic analysis has been deployed.[1]

Most of the contributions deal with the second requirement in marrying instruments to objectives — that of establishing quantitative relationships — either by numerical illustration with reasonably realistic parameter values or by some statistical and/or descriptive background (see the Appendix). The derivation of quantitative relationships is a highly specialised and extremely difficult area of study (econometrics) to which passing reference is made. In essence, statistical techniques are used to calculate the

---

[1]For an extended treatment at a more advanced level see Peston, M. H., *Theory of Macroeconomic Policy*, Philip Allan 1974.

value of parameters — for example, the average and marginal propensity to import and consume, the incremental capital-output ratio — using data from the past. As policy decisions involve consideration of what the quantitative relations between instruments and objectives will be in future time, the question arises as to how far past relationships, hopefully significant ones, can be a guide to future ones and, if this is only likely to be approximately so, what further methods can be used to improve forecasts of expected values.

Here we enter an area of considerable professional controversy. All will agree that errors in estimation of parameters and of lags in adjustment to policy changes have often rendered policies inappropriate. Then the paths divide. There are those economists who maintain that these errors are endemic to any exercise in forecasting and that professional effort should be concentrated more on devising policy measures which dispense with, or at least reduce reliance on, forecasts. There are others who maintain that model building and associated estimation procedures are only in their infancy and that technical progress in economics and econometrics will result in improvements. Sometimes this debate has ideological overtones, for it clearly strengthens the case of those who object to widespread policy intervention on political grounds if such intervention will be ineffective because it must rely on imperfect forecasts. It follows that the nearer one approaches perfect forecasting, the weaker the technical objections become. There is no way of resolving this debate in a satisfactory way, and the practical issue is this: what should economists be doing in the period up to the point when its resolution seems possible? It says much for the intellectual resilience of economics that this issue has been very thoroughly discussed, albeit at an abstract and highly technical level. In broad terms, these investigations endeavour to identify decision rules for government faced with the problem of uncertainty surrounding both the specification of the right economic relationships in the economy and the effects of policy instruments used to attempt to influence these relationships. The rules attempt to distinguish between those situations where the government would be advised to act *as if* the estimated values of parameters will be correct and those where this 'certainty equivalence' approach would not be appropriate. Little of this discussion has so far penetrated the introductory texts in economics and the only purpose in mentioning it here is to underline the importance of uncertainty in decision making, about which perhaps too little is said in expository works in economics.

This suggested framework for studying economic policy is based on purely positive foundations: that is to say, no judgement need be made about the desirability or otherwise either of the policy objectives or the measures which are designed to achieve them. As the reader will be well aware, popular writing on economic policy problems in the financial press is full of references to 'sound' and 'unsound' economic policies and reflects disagreement on policy matters which does little to consolidate the reputation of economics as a scientific discipline, at least in the public eye. These disagreements are inevitable and are healthy if they reflect differing views about the choice of policy objectives and trade-offs between them. After all, there is nothing in a scientific discipline which obliges its members to agree on value judgements. They are perhaps more serious when disagreements concern facts and logic. However, let us assume that the facts and logic are agreed, or at least that there is agreement about how disagreements about them can be resolved, e.g. by statistical and analytical techniques. What then?

Granted the assumption, appraisal of economic policy is possible without recourse to judgement on the policy aims themselves by asking the question: do the instruments achieve the desired ends? In other words, within the limits of our knowledge as economists, policies can be tested for consistency. It should be possible, for instance, to offer at least an informed judgement about whether a particular policy measure will achieve the desired objective, having regard to any possible side effects it may have on other objectives considered relevant. A large part of the time of economists in government is taken up with the task of giving advice, not on whether the objectives are the right ones, but on whether the policy instruments are appropriate for achieving the objectives. Their task may be made more difficult when no known instruments employed in any combination are likely to achieve what their political masters would wish. Thus the 'objectives/ economic model/instruments' logic may help to achieve consistency in policy making, both through the choice of instruments and the adaptation in policy aims which may be a necessary consequence of the constraints on the effectiveness of the instruments themselves. It may also point in the direction in which instrumental innovations might be sought. There are several examples in this book which introduce the reader to the problem of consistency of ends and means (Chapters 12 and 13) and with the related question of minimising resource use in the process (the discussions of cost-benefit and cost-effectiveness in Chapters 6 and 7).

It would do less than justice to the authors of this volume to let the matter of appraisal end at this point.

Economists frequently judge policy measures by reference to the postulates of welfare economics (which are expounded in Chapter 1). Broadly speaking, and with due regard to circumstances in which competitive markets may not conform with their interests, a very large proportion of the economics profession would judge any policy measures in terms of their effects on the welfare of individuals. They would have to admit that, in the last analysis, the famous Paretian axioms are value judgements. They justify support for them on various grounds, the principal one being that the informed judgement of 'reasonable men' would lead to a consensus view that individuals must be the ultimate judges of their own welfare. Practical expression of the application of these axioms is exemplified (Chapter 3) by such devices as showing the effect of government measures on consumers' surplus. The implicit conclusion of this approach is that if consumers' surplus is reduced by some policy measures then, whether or not governments act consistently in achieving their own stated objectives, Paretian welfare criteria pronounce these measures as inappropriate because individuals' welfare is decreased. Furthermore, this approach employs a model of the economy in which governments act completely independently of individual decision makers, who appear to have no part in the political process. Its relevance depends on whether such a model is consistent with the political decision making system actually in existence. If it is, and political decisions are beyond the control of individuals, then it is difficult to reconcile Paretian welfare economics with the condition that individual preferences are sovereign. If, as 'liberal Paretians' believe, the implications for political decision making of the Paretian welfare axioms must be fully explained, appraisal of policies must depend on which policies are sanctioned by political arrangements consistent with these axioms. Individual decisions through the market place and through the political process cannot then be segmented.[2]

The analysis of the ingredients which form a study of economic policy tempts me to conclude as follows.

Firstly, there is obviously no fundamental difference between a macroeconomic and a microeconomic approach to policy questions. Both require the delineation of objectives, the use of economic models, the specification of parameter values and the identification of policy instruments. The macro/micro distinction simply emphasises in a rough-and-ready way the scale of policy operations.

Secondly, the conventional distinction between 'theory' and 'applied' wears thin when policy issues, as in this volume, are properly analysed. All that one can say is that different policy issues may require different degrees of abstraction in explaining them properly and different degrees of technical input, though this is less obvious at an introductory level. Such statements that an economist is a good theorist but not a good applied or policy-oriented economist are thoroughly misleading, suggesting a false dichotomy between the creative innovator and the plodding tool-user. Apart from the fact that several contributors to this volume move easily between different levels of abstraction, the creative mind can find plenty to test it in the design of policy instruments as well as in improving the models in which their effects are manifested.

Thirdly, it is possible to offer an appraisal of economic policies, allowing for human frailty, without the author having to pass judgement on policy objectives. Policies can simply be tested for consistency between objectives and instruments. Despite this, many members of the economics profession are still committed to Paretian axioms, which are used to judge policy measures

[2]For a discussion of these issues and other difficulties associated with the application of Paretian axioms to political questions see Rowley, C. K., and Peacock, A. T., *Welfare Economics: A Liberal Re-Statement*, Martin Robertson 1975.

independently of the objectives to which they are directed. But whether objectives are treated as data or as axioms to which the economist is committed, they must be made explicit if rational discussion of policy issues employing economic analysis is to proceed.

Alan Peacock
January 1975

1. Economic problems, economic theory and the role of government in the UK economy

R M GRANT
Lecturer in Economics,
University of St Andrews

For two centuries the British economy has experienced almost continuous and unprecedented expansion. A growth of population from 8 millions in 1771 to 54 millions in 1971 has been outstripped by the increase in output. The result has been an increase in per capita national income of tenfold from about £72 in 1671 to £777 in 1971 (at constant 1971 prices). The rise in the nation's living standards is reflected not only in terms of consumption and wealth but also in the doubling of life expectancy, the near elimination of starvation, malnutrition and illiteracy and the enormous reduction in the scale of poverty.

Yet despite this increase in affluence and lessening of hardship, economic problems are as evident today as at any time during our history. The public's preoccupation with economic matters is evident from the contents of newspapers and Parliamentary debates and from the central issues in all the post-war general elections. The paradox between growing affluence and the increasing awareness of economic problems is not difficult to understand. Fundamental to the failure of growth to eliminate society's economic problems is the recognised fact that human wants are insatiable. While at any point of time an individual's economic desires are limited, as his wants become satisfied so the horizon of aspiration recedes: the progression being from the goods necessary to provide the nutrition and warmth essential for survival to the more sophisticated goods required to satisfy the

11

desires for luxury and status; as material wants become satisfied so consumer demand extends to services — recreation, travel, education and better medical treatment.

Not only has economic growth failed to solve the basic problem of scarcity, but economic growth tends to create new problems. Increasing output per head has been achieved through technological advance and capital accumulation. These involve the replacing of simple, small-scale production methods by complex, large-scale methods and necessitate specialisation — by labour, by institutions and by geographical areas. The result is an increased interdependence of the whole economy and vulnerability of the economy to malfunctioning in any one part. The disruptive effects of strikes by relatively small numbers of the country's workforce clearly illustrate the extent of economic interdependence. Nor is interdependence limited to countries' internal economies. The Great Depression of the 1930's, the acceleration of inflation during the 1970's and the impact of the recent rise in the price of crude oil have all been world-wide economic problems which demonstrate the ability of international trade and monetary relationships to transmit globally the economic problems of any one country.

In so far as economic growth in the past has failed to solve the problem of scarcity and has tended to expand rather than narrow the range of economic problems faced by society, so it offers only limited hope for the future. Increasingly economists and natural scientists are being forced to recognise the problems of reconciling the economic expansion of the industrialised world with the constraints imposed by the natural world. The more pessimistic forecasters have suggested that the depletion of natural resources and increasing pollution and urbanisation pose a threat to the very existence of civilisation. Thus even if the high rates of economic growth unsuccessfully sought after by successive British governments were attained in the future, there seems little likelihood that the investments in knowledge made by today's students of economics will be rendered obsolescent by the elimination of economic want.

Current concern with economic problems is a reflection not only of the existence of economic problems but also of the movement of economic affairs to the centre of the arena of political debate. Concern with the problems of poverty and unemployment in 18th century Britain was limited by the acceptance of these problems as part of society's natural order. Moral philosophers who concerned themselves with these problems looked to their solution in the reform of human nature rather than to reform of the economy. The gradual recognition by government of responsibility for economic affairs is a result of the development of economic science and pressure from public opinion. As our knowledge of the operation of the economic system has increased, so the progressive democratisation of the political process has encouraged government to take an increasingly active role in the economy. The relationship between economic theory and economic policy has been close: the economic problems facing society have stimulated the formulation of economic theory which in turn has provided a framework for government action. It is the application of the basic tools of economic analysis to the solution of problems facing the British economy through public policy that is the subject matter of this book.

As a background to the analysis of specific areas of government policy and the particular issues facing the UK economy at the present time which follow in subsequent chapters, the concern of this introduction is with the general role of the state in the UK economy. The approach is mainly historical: we trace the transition of the economy from a primarily free enterprise capitalist system to a mixed economy comprising both private and public sectors which has been the dominant feature of 20th century economic development. By relating the expanding economic role of the state both to the nature of economic problems emerging in the British economy and to the development of economic theory we shall be in a position to examine the sources of current economic problems and understand the present position of government as a regulatory and decision-making force. Finally we shall investigate the relationship between economic theory and economic policy emphasising the usefulness and limitations of economic theory as a practical tool for the improvement of social welfare.

Our starting point is the development of capitalism in Britain. It was the rise of Britain as an industrialised capitalist country that accelerated the development of economic science and it was the recognition of the virtues of capitalism in generating growth followed by the awareness of the problems confronting the capitalist economy that was responsible for the changing role of government in the economy during the 19th and 20th centuries.

The Rise of Industrial Capitalism

By the middle of the 19th century Britain emerged from the period of economic and social transformation referred to as the 'industrial revolution' as the most powerful economic and military power in the world. The contrasts between 1700 and 1850 are startling. At the beginning of the 18th century the British economy showed many of the characteristics of a present day less-developed country: an agrarian based economy with a low rate of growth of output and population, techniques of production that had changed little over the previous 400 years and the bulk of the population living close to subsistence level. By 1850 population had trebled, output increased eightfold and the basis of the economy had shifted from agriculture to manufacture. W. W. Rostow calls this transition from a static traditional economy to a dynamic growing economy a nation's 'take-off' — the point at which the residual of savings over consumption is sufficient to finance the investment in capital equipment and innovation which puts the economy on the path of self-sustaining growth. Rostow suggests that Britain's take-off occurred between 1783 and 1802 (Rostow 1960).

Economic expansion was only one aspect of the industrial revolution. The most fundamental economic development was the change in the system of economic organisation from a tradition-based economy chiefly at subsistence level to a complex market economy. Expansion of manufacturing industry and the use of capital intensive production methods resulted in a shift in production from small-holdings and home based handicraft industries to factories located in new urban areas. As self-employment and self-sufficiency gave way to wage earning and specialisation, so the importance of the market increased. While the peasant farmer's consumption needs were met largely by his own production, the urban working classes were dependent on market purchases for almost all of their consumption. Improvements in transportation enabled the expansion of local markets into regional and national markets, thus widening the scope for further specialisation and increasing society's dependence on the efficient operation of the price mechanism. Indeed, it was the market that provided the organising force for the industrial revolution. It was the desire for profit that motivated the innovations of Watt, Arkwright and Stevenson and the investment in the expanding engineering, textile and transport industries. The changing distribution of population, in particular the drift from the countryside into the towns, was in response to wage incentives and employment offers from expanding industry. In contrast to the later industrial development of Germany, Russia and Japan the role of the state in encouraging and directing economic development was negligible.

Classical Economics and Laissez-faire

The rise of industrial society during the late 18th and 19th centuries was paralleled by the development of the scientific study of economics. The publication of Adam Smith's *An Inquiry into the Nature and Causes of the Wealth of Nations* in 1776 coincided with the initial phases of the industrial revolution. Smith's popular and influential book provided the foundation for the analysis of the market economy and the process of economic development, an analysis which was extended by the economists of the 'Classical School' — notably David Ricardo and J. S. Mill.

Smith's most exciting and influential discovery was the mechanism of the 'invisible hand' — the process by which individual decisions of self-interest are co-ordinated by the price mechanism to promote the common good of all. While firms operate to maximise their profits and households make their decisions of labour supply and income expenditure so as to maximise their benefits from consumption, the price mechanism ensures perfect compatibility between these independent decisions. Consumer preferences for goods and services are signalled by price adjustments which provide profit incentives for

firms. The switching of resources into the most desired areas of
production is then achieved through firms offering wage and
interest incentives to workers and investors. The result is an
allocation of resources which maximises social welfare.

It was the belief in the perfection of this mechanism that was
responsible for the dominant intellectual climate of thought
concerning the correct role of government in the economy. If
market competition can be relied on to maximise the efficiency of
production and distribution and provide an automatic adjustment
mechanism to take account of changes in consumer tastes and
changes in production techniques, then there is no need for the
government to intervene in the economy other than to maintain
the forces of competition. This policy conclusion of non-
intervention is referred to as 'laissez-faire'. A typical laissez-faire
viewpoint of the period is expressed in Frederic Bastiat's account
of his visit to Paris in 1845:

How does each succeeding day manage to bring to this gigantic market
just what is necessary — neither too much, nor too little? What then is the
resourceful and secret power that governs the amazing regularity of such
complicated movements? ... That power is ... the principle of free
exchange. We put our faith in that inner light which Providence has
placed in the hearts of all men, and to which has been trusted the
preservation and the unlimited improvement of our species, a light we
term 'self-interest', which is so illuminating, so constant and so
penetrating, when it is left free of every interference. Where would you be,
inhabitants of Paris, if some cabinet minister decided to substitute for that
power contrivances of his own invention? ... Although there may be
much suffering within your walls ... it is certain that the arbitrary
intervention of the government would infinitely multiply this suffering
and spread among all of you the ills that affect only a small number of
your fellow citizens. (Quoted in Kohler 1970.)

The extent to which the Classical economists supported a policy
of laissez-faire has not been entirely settled. Even Smith's
unshakeable faith in natural self-interest and man's 'propensity to
truck, barter and exchange' did not lead him to advocate a policy
of complete laissez-faire and later economists also envisaged a
limited role for government. But in the hands of political pressure
groups anxious to further their economic interests, the doctrine of
laissez-faire lost all its qualifications. The issue of free trade
provided the focal point for the more radical espousals of the

laissez-faire doctrine by businessmen and polemic economists in their attack upon the mercantilist restrictions on trade that had proliferated during the 17th and 18th centuries. The success of this movement is seen in the repeal of the Corn Laws (1846) and Navigation Acts (1849) and the progressive lowering of tariffs throughout the 19th century.

Problems of the Capitalist Economy

The performance of the British economy during the 19th century clearly demonstrated the dynamism of the free enterprise economy. The pessimistic forecasts by Ricardo of stagnation through diminishing returns and by Malthus of poverty through over-population were discredited, and the ability of the profit motive operating through competitive markets to stimulate innovation and capital accumulation was realised. The annual rate of growth of real output averaged 2.8% during the century compared to under 1% in the 18th and 2.0% in the 20th century. The position of Britain as the world's strongest military power for most of the century was based on economic prosperity, and it was trading interests that spearheaded the drive for overseas possessions.

But expansion was only one aspect of economic development. As the general level of prosperity increased, the extent of economic hardship and social problems became increasingly apparent in Victorian Britain. The poor living conditions in many of the new urban areas were revealed in Friedrich Engels' descriptions of working class life, but it was not until the more thorough social surveys of Seebohm Rowntree in York and Charles Booth in London at the end of the 19th century that the full extent of urban poverty was realised. Problems of low wages were compounded by the lack of social provision against sickness, unemployment and old age.

The most noticeable cause of poverty and the greatest threat to the security of working class families was unemployment. Unemployment had long been a feature of British society. But while pre-19th century unemployment was mainly a result of the lag between the displacement of population from the land due to increasing agricultural efficiency and their absorption into the towns, it became clear during the 19th century that the nature of unemployment was changing. Throughout the century oscillations of industrial production around the upward trend became increasingly pronounced and the 'business cycle' became an accepted feature of the industrial economy. Downturns in the business cycle occurred in the 40's, 50's and 70's, but it was the deep depressions of 1884-87 and 1892-93 that first created large-scale mass unemployment and revealed the inability of family support, private charity and the Poor Law system to cope with the resulting hardship.

While it was the working classes who directly suffered the problems of poverty and urban squalor, some defects of the operation of the economy had a wider impact. The expansion of the output of manufactured goods highlighted the inability of free enterprise to provide essential services. The lack of social and sanitary services and the problems of pollution and uncontrolled urban development affected the better-off as well as the poor. In particular the failure of free enterprise, the churches and private charity to provide a basic education to all members of society was a central issue in the pressure for a widening of the responsibilities of government.

It was the increasing awareness of these economic and social problems to which the market economy provided no solution that was responsible for the popular disillusionment with laissez-faire. While working class socialist movements of the 19th century never posed a serious threat to the status quo, the extension of the franchise to all adult males gave the poorer members of society the political influence to demand a more active government role in the economy. Social reforms no longer reflected the humanity of the ruling classes but resulted from the need for the Establishment to appease the working classes in order to maintain its own position. This democratic pressure was effective in encouraging the expansion in local and central government services in the late 19th and early 20th centuries and in demanding more comprehensive programmes for greater equality of income and opportunity after 1945.

Concern for, and protest against, the inequity of the capitalist economy was one source of pressure for a more active

governmental role in the economy; the second influence behind
the growth in government intervention was the developments in
economic theory of the late 19th and 20th centuries. It was the
undermining of the theoretical basis for laissez-faire that was to
broaden the scope of state intervention from humanitarian
considerations for society's least fortunate to acceptance of overall
responsibility for the state of the economy. It is to the analysis of
these two forces that we now turn.

Value Judgements as a Basis for Government Intervention

The policy of laissez-faire was based, as we have seen, on the belief
in the ability of the competitive market economy to maximise the
efficiency of production and distribution and so to maximise the
economic welfare of society. We have noted how the growing
recognition of the problems that accompanied capitalist economic
development placed increasing doubt on this proposition. From
an analytical viewpoint we can identify two sources of this doubt:
scepticism of the inherent efficiency of the market economy
(illustrated in particular by periodic large-scale involuntary
unemployment), and protest against the inequality of income
distribution in society. The separation of considerations of equity
from considerations of efficiency is vital for the analysis of
economic problems and policy. To explain this distinction we
must examine the sense in which social welfare is maximised in the
perfectly competitive economy.

   Our basic premise in welfare considerations is that the only
meaningful concept of welfare is an individual one; economic
satisfaction (or utility) is perceived only by individual human
beings. Thus when talking about social welfare we are concerned
with the welfare of all the individuals in society. Since utility is a
subjective experience, it cannot be measured objectively. Hence
we cannot sum together individuals' utilities as believed by the
Utilitarians. Though social welfare cannot be measured
quantitatively, the condition for an increase in social welfare can
be identified where the utility of at least one member of society
increases while the utility of all others is unchanged. A maximum
of social welfare is reached where no further increase in any

individual's utility can be made without a loss in someone else's occurring. This maximum is called a 'Pareto Optimum'.

If resources are initially distributed between individuals we can show that so long as decisions are rational and are based on a complete knowledge of the alternatives available, then the perfectly competitive economy reaches a Pareto Optimum. Optimisation is achieved through the price mechanism: consumer preferences for goods and services are expressed through their relative prices, the allocation of resources according to these preferences is then achieved through price incentives to factors of production, the productivity of these resources being maximised by firms choosing the least-cost methods of producing the desired outputs. At the equilibrium set of prices we are unable to redistribute final goods between consumers so as to make any one consumer better off without making someone else worse off; we are unable to redistribute resources between products so as to produce any more of one good without producing less of another, and we cannot redistribute resources among products so as to produce a more preferred collection of goods.

A Pareto Optimum equilibrium in the economy is not unique, for every initial distribution of resources in society there will correspond a Pareto Optimum with a different distribution of income. Since interpersonal comparisons of utility are not possible on the basis of any objective criteria, welfare economics does not enable us to rank different Pareto Optima. Thus by either redistributing resource ownership or redistributing final income among consumers, the government can achieve a range of different income distributions all of which are welfare maximising in the Pareto sense. The decision between alternative distributions of income lies outside the scope of positive economics and any choice must be based on a value judgement by society. Thus we have two criteria for evaluating social welfare: a positive criterion which enables us to identify an efficiency maximisation in the economy (a 'Pareto Optimum') and a normative criterion for evaluating the impact of redistribution of income.[1]

On the basis of this distinction, it is clear that the supporters of

[1] It is now generally accepted that the Pareto criterion is not value free; however the ethical values implicit in the concept of Pareto Optimum are relatively uncontroversial.

the laissez-faire doctrine confused economic efficiency with normative considerations of equity. A redistribution of income by government will cause the economy to move to a new point of general equilibrium; so long as redistribution does not involve artificial adjustments in prices, then the new equilibrium will also be Pareto Optimal. Normally, however, taxes on income and goods will affect market prices and so cause the economy to depart from the Pareto Optimum. In this case government must balance an increase in social welfare resulting from a more desirable distribution of income, against a fall in social welfare resulting from a decline in efficiency.[2]

In a democratic society value judgements by government are made by society as a whole through the electoral process. As we have seen, it was the extension of the electorate that changed the government's value judgements regarding the optimal distribution of income, and it was this belief in the desirability of a more equal distribution of income than that arising naturally from the market economy that provided the most powerful motivation for an increase in government intervention in the economy during the 20th century.

Government efforts to achieve a redistribution of income began modestly with the establishment of the principle of progressive taxation and the introduction of National Insurance, which was to be the foundation of the post-war 'welfare state'. The framework for income redistribution was established by the 1906 to 1914 Liberal government which introduced surtax, old age pensions and sickness and unemployment benefits and raised income tax to the unprecedented level of 6 new pence in the £. The redistributive effect of these measures was slight: progressive income taxation only offset the regressiveness of indirect taxation, and benefits to those in situations of special need represented only very modest payments designed to supplement local authority 'poor relief'. While governmental redistribution of income increased in the inter-war period, this was largely a result of the expansion of public expenditure increasing the burden of taxation on the better

---

[2]A frequent example of this conflict is where government wishes to increase income equality by increasing income tax, but has to contend with a fall in the quantity of labour supplied which may reduce the rate of growth of national income.

off rather than any major departure in policy. The attempt by government to achieve a major re-ordering of incomes is a feature of post-war government policy and particularly of the 1945-50 Labour government, which expanded the scope of National Insurance, introduced National Assistance and family allowances, and instituted free medical services and free education right up to the tertiary level.

Income redistribution has not been the only area where normative judgements by government have provided the motivation for intervention in the economy. A second value judgement which has justified state intervention is the belief that in certain instances governmental decision making is superior to private decision making. An essential condition for the attainment of maximum efficiency in the allocation of resources and distribution of products in the competitive economy is the ability of consumers to take decisions that maximise their welfare. This requires not only that consumers are rational but also that they are informed of the whole range of choices available and the consequences of these choices. Legislation restricting the free choice of individuals was one of the most important areas of government intervention during the 19th century and was a response primarily to pressure from social reformers. Examples are the Factory Acts limiting hours of work and prohibiting child employment, the licencing laws restricting the opening hours of public houses and the Education Acts which made schooling up to a minimum age compulsory. The justification for these limitations on freedom of choice must lie in the inability of some individuals to make choices that maximise their long-term welfare due to short-sightedness or lack of adequate information. Similar arguments are heard today from the advocates of prohibition of the sale of cigarettes and tobacco.

Imperfections of the Market Economy

What we have shown is that, even if we accept the ability of the competitive free enterprise economy to allocate resources and output in such a way as to reach an equilibrium point where no one can be made better off except at the expense of someone else, then it is possible to justify government intervention either to redistribute income in accordance with the democratically expressed wishes of society, or to use governments' superior access to information to prevent individuals from making sub-optimal decisions. Intervention on the basis of these principles was responsible for much of the humanitarian state intervention in the economy during the late 19th and early 20th centuries and income redistribution has been one of the most important areas, and certainly the most controversial, of government economic policy in post-war Britain.

Considerations of equity and justice are only one source of stimulus for the rapid 20th century growth of state economic intervention. The most important developments of economic theory this century have been directed at revealing the assumptions implicit in the conclusion that the competitive economy maximises efficiency and so reaches a welfare optimum in the Pareto sense. The refinement of the neo-classical competitive market model laid the basis for an analysis of the economy where the assumptions of perfection were dropped. It was these developments in economic theory that pin-pointed the sources of imperfection in the working of the market economy and exposed the fallacy in the doctrine of laissez-faire. We proceed by identifying some of the major sources of imperfection of the market economy, indicating the types of problem to which they give rise and outlining government policies that have attempted to remedy these problems.

Imperfection of Competition

The maximisation of efficiency by the market economy is dependent on the existence of perfect competition. Perfect competition requires that buyers and sellers in markets are so numerous that no individual buyer or seller can influence market price, buyers and sellers all have full knowledge of the alternatives open to them, and there is complete mobility of resources. In practice, of course, these conditions can never fully be met. Moreover there is always an incentive among sellers and buyers to co-operate so as to limit competition. As Adam Smith noted:

"People of the same trade seldom meet together, even for merriment or diversion, but the conversation ends in a conspiracy against the public, or in some contrivance to raise prices." (Smith 1910, p.117.)

Thus while the price mechanism automatically allocates resources according to the preferences of consumers, there is no mechanism that ensures the maintenance of competition. While the dangers of monopoly have long been recognised, government policy to preserve competition has been haphazard. The policy of free trade, which was directed towards the lowering of tariffs and the removal of other impediments to domestic and foreign trade, certainly had the stimulation of competition as one of its objectives. On the other hand legislation explicitly directed against monopoly and collusion was enacted only in the post-war years.

More complex problems are posed in industries where economies of scale are present. For the government to prevent the emergence of monopoly in such industries will involve inefficiency through sub-optimal sized firms. One solution for the problem of these 'natural monopolies' is a government regulated monopoly which enables exploitation of economies of scale without monopoly pricing. In Britain the problem of natural monopolies such as airlines, railways, postal services and public utilities has been dealt with by nationalisation of these industries.

Externalities

The attainment of a Pareto Optimum under the market system requires that individual welfare maximising decisions by consumers and firms simultaneously maximise social welfare. Individual decisions are made so as to maximise the difference between the costs and the benefits of any action. For this individual maximisation of welfare to maximise the welfare of society requires that the costs and benefits of any action to the individual (private costs and benefits) are identical to those of society (social costs and benefits). This identity will not hold where one individual's action affects the welfare of another individual and the external welfare effect is not taken into account in the individual's cost-benefit calculation. Externalities may be external costs — when a factory's smokey chimneys impose higher laundry and cleaning bills on neighbouring residents; or external benefits — when the eradication of insect pests on one farmer's land leads to higher crop yields for surrounding farmers.

The presence of externalities prevents the attainment of a Pareto Optimum in the economy due to non-optimal output levels of different goods[3] and the adoption of inefficient techniques of production.[4] Two solutions to the problem of externalities are available to governments. Firstly, externalities can be internalised so that private costs and benefits are made equal to social costs and benefits. This can be achieved either by legislative change forcing those responsible for external costs to provide compensation to others and allowing the propagators of external benefits to charge the beneficiaries, or by the adjustment of market prices by taxes and subsidies to take externalities into account. While the law of liability has not undergone any major changes as a result of the economic analysis of the problem of externalities, adjustment of market prices by taxes and subsidies has been a growing area of government intervention. The imposition of petrol tax and road tax ensure that the motorist bears some of the cost of highway maintenance, pollution and congestion for which he is responsible. One area where external benefits are particularly important is innovation. To encourage the optimal quantity of productive resources into research and development, the government boosts the rewards from invention by the granting of patents, and reduces the cost of research by subsidies and research grants.

Secondly, the government can calculate what is the socially optimal level of output to an activity where externalities are important and choose the socially least-cost technique of production and, by taking charge of the production of the good or

[3] In the above example of the farmer with crop-ravaging insects, the consumption of pesticide is too low. If the farmer could be induced financially by his neighbours to use more pesticide, then both the farmer and his neighbours could be made better off.

[4] In the case of the factory's smoke emissions, if the extra cost of a smokeless production technique is less than the cost savings in laundry bills to the local residents, then the existing technique is inefficient. The residents could pay the factory owners to use the smokeless method and both groups could be made better off.

service, directly determine the allocation of resources to the activity. The most important and long established direct state provision of a private consumption good is education. Because of the contribution of education to the productivity of industry and to cultural enrichment, the social benefits of education far outweigh the net private benefits. The principle of universal, free, compulsory education was recognised in the 1870 Education Act and since then the sphere of public education has expanded into secondary and further education. The establishment of the National Health Service in 1948 is a more recent extension of the public sector into an area where external benefits are large.

A major problem of state provision of goods and services is determining the optimal allocation of resources to the activity. It is this problem that the technique of cost-benefit analysis attempts to solve by evaluating the desirability of public investment in new projects through the calculation of the social costs and benefits of the expenditure involved. Since almost all public investment projects generate benefits to some members of society and losses to others, cost-benefit analysis cannot unambiguously show that a project represents an increase in social welfare in the Pareto sense. Judging the net welfare effect in these cases invokes the *compensation principle*: are the gains of the beneficiaries sufficient to compensate the losers? If so, then the project represents a *potential* Pareto improvement. However, use of the compensation principle to justify the aggregation of costs and benefits necessitates inter-personal comparisons of utility which leads us from the path of positive economics into the field of value judgements.

Public Goods

A special case of externalities relates to public goods. These are goods whose benefits are spread evenly over the whole community irrespective of who actually purchases the good. For this reason public goods are sometimes called 'collective goods', meaning that they are consumed collectively by society as a whole rather than by individuals. Because an individual can benefit as much from other peoples' purchases of public goods as his own, there is little incentive for anyone to provide himself with public goods and consequently the market economy will under-allocate resources to these goods. For goods that are consumed collectively, provision must also be made collectively — since the market mechanism does not effectively operate for these goods, provision must be by the state.

The most important example of a public good is defence. An individual cannot protect himself from attack by a foreign power without at the same time providing protection to the other members of his community. Consequently defence can only be effectively provided by the state and this activity has always been the primary function of government. Prior to this century defence was the only significant item of public expenditure, and despite the vast expansion of the scope of the public sector, defence remains the largest single item in the government's budget. The size of defence expenditure is a function largely of the state of Britain's foreign relations. During the First and Second World Wars, when defence was the overriding national priority, the direction of national resources to this single objective meant that Britain was virtually a planned economy.

General Equilibrium Problems

The imperfections of the market economy we have dealt with so far, although important in terms of particular problems, are of limited scope: monopoly, externality and public goods cause misallocations of resources, but they can be rectified by limited government intervention and call for the qualification rather than the abandonment of the concept of the invisible hand. By far the most important problem of the market economy, however, is not inefficiency in the employment of productive resources, but the inability of the market economy to reach an equilibrium where all resources are employed.

As we have seen, unemployment in 19th century Britain was a major source of poverty and government policy towards unemployment in the early years of the 20th century was directed at alleviating the hardship of unemployment rather than tackling the problem itself. In fact, any policy to deal with the problem of unemployment was impossible due to the lack of understanding of the problem. The existence of large-scale involuntary unemployment was difficult to explain within the framework of price theory, for it implied a failure to reach equilibrium in the labour market. Explanations of unemployment during the first three decades of this century suggested that economic change combined with a lack of labour mobility (both occupationally and geographically), or a lack of wage flexibility due to trade union monopoly power, were to blame. Such explanations of unemployment were difficult to maintain during the inter-war years when the experience of the period not only created widespread disillusion over the usefulness of the neo-classical model in explaining the operation of the economy, but also finally discredited laissez-faire as a tenable basis for the role of the state.

Between 1921 and 1938 the unemployment rate never fell below 9% and it reached a peak of 22% in 1932. Failure to understand the causes of unemployment resulted in the government resorting to a policy of attempting to maintain confidence in the pound and in the monetary system. Such a policy involved supporting an overvalued exchange rate by domestic deflation and a paranoiac concern with balancing the public budget. The irrelevance of a theory that assumed the automatic adjustment of the economy towards a full employment equilibrium and the failure of policies to deal with the crisis created an atmosphere receptive to new ideas. The breakthrough came with the publication of *A General Theory of Employment, Interest and Money* by John Maynard Keynes, a book that laid the structure of modern macroeconomic theory. While the extent of Keynes's contribution to economic theory has yet to be fully assessed, the basic message for policy makers was clear: the market economy cannot be relied upon to adjust automatically to a full employment level of output; where demand from the private sector is insufficient to call forth an output that will employ all of the nation's resources, then it is up to the government to stimulate aggregate demand by expanding public expenditure to take up the slack.

Acceptance of Keynes's ideas was delayed both by the resistance of politicians and Treasury officials to the major re-orientation in their ideas on economic policy demanded by the 'General Theory' and by the intervention of war. The Second World War replaced the market economy by a centrally planned economy where resource allocation and product distribution was controlled physically by the government, and the war effort eliminated the problem of unemployment. Although the 1944 White Paper on Employment Policy declared that "The Government accept as one of their primary aims and responsibilities the maintenance of a high and stable level of employment", it was not until the 1950's that a contra-cyclical budgetary policy was consciously practised by Chancellors of the Exchequer.

Post-war Directions in Economic Policy

The effect of the Keynesian revolution on the development of post-war economic policy is far wider than the encouragement it gave to macroeconomic management. Most important was the change in the attitude of both politicians and the general public to the significance and scope of economic policy. If the government could ensure economic stability and prosperity ˙ by the manipulation of its budget, there seemed few limits to the power of government to provide solutions to economic problems. Growing confidence in the government's ability to improve the operation of the economy has resulted in the abandonment by most sections of informed opinion of laissez-faire views of a narrowly defined economic role of government.

Yet despite the general consensus in favour of a mixed economy, political debate in post-war Britain has been dominated by differences of opinion over the extent and methods of economic intervention. The Labour Party, which embodies the democratic socialist tradition in British politics, has consistently favoured a transfer of ownership and decision making from the private to the public sector. This preference for direct public control over the economy stems from a distaste for private profit as a form of remuneration and a distrust of profit incentives as reliable indicators of the public interest. The Conservative Party, on the other hand, has traditionally viewed government intervention in the economy as an infringement of individual liberty. The minimisation of this loss of individual freedom requires that the government's discretionary powers are limited; as a result the

Conservative Party has tended to favour government policy operating impersonally through the market mechanism, rather than replacing the market system by centrally planned decision making.

These differences in the approach to economic policy, though moderated by administrative pragmatism and the necessity for both parties to appeal to the middle ground of political opinion, are clearly revealed in the policies of Labour and Conservative administrations. The Labour government of 1945-50 was responsible for the most rapid extension in the size and scope of the public sector of the economy ever to take place in peacetime. The following Conservative government, while not undoing the work of the Labour government, was less enthusiastic over the administration of such a large public sector and revealed its preference for indirect over direct economic intervention in its emphasis on monetary rather than fiscal policy as a means of demand management, in the belief that monetary policy was neutral in its impact — it influenced neither relative prices nor the distribution of income.

Since 1960, however, government under both parties has increasingly relied on direct intervention to achieve economic goals. The convergent trend of the economic policies of Conservative and Labour administrations has reflected not so much a narrowing of the ideological differences between the parties as the ineffectiveness of traditional tools of economic management in dealing with the problems which have afflicted the post-war economy. The most important of these problems have been a balance of payments weakness, a persistent tendency towards inflation and an inability of the British economy to match the rates of growth of other industrialised countries.

The unresponsiveness of these ailments to fiscal and monetary manipulation, combined with an inflexibility in the use of these instruments resulting from the commitment of successive governments to full employment, has encouraged experimentation with more direct means of economic intervention. Most ambitious have been the attempts by government to achieve policy goals through co-operation and consultation with private industry and trade unions. Attempts to stimulate Britain's rate of economic growth through joint action by government, industry and unions were initiated by the founding of the National Economic Development Committee in 1962, but the potential of 'indicative planning' to achieve major results lost credibility with the conspicuous failure of the National Plan, which was wound up in 1968 only three years after its introduction. In attempting to control inflation, the quest by the government for co-operation with other economic interests continues — the voluntary price restraint agreed by the CBI in 1972 and the 1974 'social contract' with the TUC being examples.

The intensification of the problem of inflation during the late sixties and the seventies has resulted in the government increasing its direct intervention by controls over prices and incomes. Though attempts to limit the rate of increase of wages and prices have been made throughout the post-war period, comprehensive statutory controls over prices and incomes have been a feature only of the past decade. More direct forms of intervention have also been associated with policy towards private industry. While it has been Labour governments which have introduced the most far-reaching measures to restrict and control private industry through the Industrial Reorganisation Corporation and the National Enterprise Board, the Conservative government of 1970-74 was also responsible for an increase in public involvement in industry, particularly in the finance of individual companies under the 1972 Industry Act.

Conclusion: The Role of Economic Theory in Policy Making

In this chapter we have examined the growth of the role of government in the economy and related this growth to the development of economic theory. It has been the advances in our knowledge of the workings of the economic system that has enabled the identification of ways in which the government can intervene in the economy to increase social welfare — the most notable example of this being the success of policies based on Keynesian economics in solving the problem of large-scale unemployment. Yet despite the successes in economic policy in some areas, the failure of policy to remedy the persistent post-war problems of low growth, inflation and recurrent balance of payments crises have shaken the faith of both economists and the public in the ability of economic theory successfully to direct public policy. The failure of economists to agree on the causes of these problems, let alone the remedies, has encouraged a bout of pessimism within the economic profession. Professor Phelps-Brown has emphasised the limited nature of the recent advances made in economic theory (Phelps-Brown 1972), while the Director of the National Institute for Economic and Social Research has asked "Is progress in economic science possible?" (Worswick 1972).

While the directions of development of modern economic theory are open to criticism, to blame the failures of economic policy solely on the weaknesses of economic theory is to misunderstand the role of theory in policy making. Theory can identify the range of options open to a government in its attempt to achieve desired changes in the magnitude of economic variables, but the choice of policy objectives and the choice of policy tools to achieve these objectives is the responsibility of the political authorities.

Severe limitations on the usefulness of economic theory in designing specific policies result from the ability of theory only to predict qualitative and not quantitative relationships between economic variables. Knowledge that the demand for a commodity is inversely related to its price is of little value in deciding by how much the tax on petrol must be increased in order to achieve a 2% fall in its consumption. Further problems result from the inability of theory to predict the time that an economic variable takes in moving from one equilibrium position to another. Clearly macroeconomic 'fine-tuning' is of little use if the government has no knowledge of the time it takes for changes in public expenditure, taxation and the supply of money to achieve desired changes in output, employment and the rate of inflation. Estimation of these quantitative relationships between economic variables is the primary objective of econometrics. Accurate empirical estimation in an economy where almost all economic variables are changing simultaneously and where information is a costly resource is problematic. Even the seemingly straightforward task of comparing the validity of the contradictory predictions of rival hypotheses is usually fraught with difficulties.

We see therefore that economic theory is only the starting point in the designing of economic policy. The scope of policy choices is closely constrained by the social and political environment in which policy is implemented and, so long as our knowledge of the quantitative relationships between economic variables is vague, policy making will be a process of trial and error and must inevitably include elements of common-sense and guesswork.

References

Kohler, H., *Economics: the Science of Scarcity*, Dryden Press 1970.

Phelps-Brown, E. H., The Underdevelopment of Economics, *Economic Journal*, 82, 1972.

Rostow, W. W., *The Stages of Economic Growth*, Cambridge University Press 1960.

Smith, A., *The Wealth of Nations*, J. M. Dent 1910.

Worswick, G. D. N., Is Progress in Economic Science Possible? *Economic Journal*, 82, 1972.

Suggestions for Further Reading

On Western economic development:
Heilbroner, R. L., *The Making of Economic Society* (4th edn), Prentice Hall 1972.

On the relationship between economic policy and economic thought in Britain and America during the 20th century:
Winch, D., *Economics and Policy*, Hodder & Stoughton 1969.

On welfare economics in general:
Nath, S. K., *A Perspective of Welfare Economics*, Macmillan 1973.

On the analytics of Pareto Optimum achievement under perfect competition:
Lancaster, K., *Introduction to Modern Microeconomics*, Rand McNally 1969, Chapter 10.

2. Industry, labour and public policy

KEITH HARTLEY
Senior Lecturer in Economics,
University of York

British government policy towards industry and labour has been both extensive and controversial. Recent industrial policy has involved debates about the desirability of state support for companies in financial difficulties, the extension of state ownership of industry, the control of prices and profits, and whether mergers are in the 'public interest'. Public concern over the conduct of private industry has never been greater, focussing in particular on the profit levels of oil and drug companies (e.g. Roche) and the degree of industry's 'social responsibility'. Labour market and industrial relations policy has been dominated by conflicting views over the role of government and law in the regulation of trade union behaviour and the desirability of an incomes policy. Frequently controversy has centred on the agencies established by government to implement its industrial and labour policies; the Industrial Reorganisation Corporation, the Monopolies and Mergers Commission, the Industrial Training Boards, the National Enterprise Board and the National Industrial Relations Court have all been the subjects of political debate. In this chapter, rather than attempt a chronological description of recent British industrial and labour market policy, it is proposed to identify the contribution of economic theory to current policy debates.

Methodology

The economist has to identify the general theoretical issues which are all too frequently concealed in the detailed controversy surrounding a particular government decision. Consider the example of government aid to such firms as Upper Clyde Shipbuilders (UCS), Harland and Wolff, British Leyland, Ferranti and the British Aircraft Corporation (Concorde). Each is an example of a more general issue, namely, what is the economic 'logic' of state support for private firms and industries? A similar set of general questions can be formulated for other policy issues. On mergers and competition, does economic analysis suggest any policy 'rules' for the formation of mergers and for the control of monopolies? Are these 'rules' applicable to both industry and labour (trade unions)? Within the labour market, what are the economic arguments for government intervention in industrial training and geographical mobility and for the provision of a state employment service?

To show how economic theory provides a set of generalisations which can be applied to specific policy issues, two groups of questions will be considered. First, why does the state have an industry and labour policy? Second, what is the contribution of economic theory to the formulation and appraisal of policy measures? Detailed consideration will be given to four recent policy developments, namely government support for the private sector, especially the Industry Act 1972; policy towards the labour market, including the employment and training services operated by the Manpower Services Commission established in 1974; and policy on mergers, monopoly and competition in the product and labour markets as reflected in the Fair Trading Act 1973 and the Industrial Relations Act 1971-74.

Why do Governments Need an Industry and Labour Policy?

British governments have usually pursued a set of macro-policy objectives relating to economic growth, full employment, price stability, the balance of payments and income distribution. These targets can be regarded as a means of contributing to, and ideally of maximising, the utility or welfare of individuals in the community. On this basis, government intervention in product and labour markets forms the microeconomic foundations of macro-policy objectives. For example, the Industrial Training Act (1964) and the Selective Employment Tax (1966-73) were both designed as tax-subsidy measures to raise the growth rate: the former operated through increasing the supply of skilled labour whilst the latter promoted a re-allocation of labour from services to the higher productivity manufacturing sector. To achieve employment objectives, governments have supported (e.g. through subsidies, loans and defence orders) firms which would otherwise go out of business and industries which would otherwise contract; Harland and Wolff, UCS, Rolls Royce and the shipbuilding industries are examples. To assist the re-allocation of unemployed labour, grants are available for geographical mobility and training opportunities are provided in Government Training Centres. For the price stability objective, micro-policy has included investigations of monopolies (Monopolies Commission) and the general abolition of restrictive trade practices (1956 Act) and resale price maintenance (1964 Act). More recently, various prices and incomes policies have introduced price controls with the National Board for Prices and Incomes (1965-71) and the Prices Commission (1971) as 'policing' agencies. The balance of payments objective has involved state intervention in industrial structure through the Industrial Reorganisation Corporation (1966-70), which aimed to create larger firms (via mergers) capable of obtaining scale economies and so competing in world markets. Similarly, government support for British projects such as aluminium smelting plants (1968) and civil aircraft have been explained in terms of their import-savings and foreign exchange contributions. Finally, a variety of existing industry and labour policies contribute to income distribution objectives. Examples include policies towards industrial training and re-training, grants for geographical mobility, earnings-related unemployment benefits, the introduction of equal pay and price and profit controls.

In this simple model, governments are regarded as agencies for improving and, ultimately, maximising the welfare of the community. Thus the model suggests that state intervention in industry and labour markets is a means of contributing to social welfare. This immediately raises the question of why intervention is required in private markets: why cannot markets be left alone? In practice, actual industry and labour markets may 'fail' to operate satisfactorily in the sense of failing to respond to the preferences of the community, with adverse effects on the utility or welfare of individuals. Market failure can arise from two sources. First, markets might be imperfect due to monopoly, restrictive practices and entry barriers. Second, externalities might be present so that markets provide 'too much' (e.g. pollution) or 'too little' (e.g. research and development) of a commodity. Both sources of market failure might provide a rationale for state intervention in a private market. On this basis industry and labour policies are a means by which governments aim to maximise social welfare.

Policy Instruments

Policy objectives are achieved through policy measures or instruments. Within the field of industry and labour, governments have available a whole range of policy instruments. Using the market failure analysis, industry and labour policies can be classified as market-improving or market-displacing, the choice of policy depending on the value judgements of the decision maker. Market-improving policies aim to improve the operation of private markets and promote opportunities for consumer choice. Examples include the provision of more labour market information to individuals and a vigorous anti-monopoly policy to expand competition. Such policies are likely to be preferred by those who favour consumer sovereignty and the dispersion of economic and political power in a society. In contrast, those who believe that individuals are not the best judges of their welfare might favour market-displacing policies which aim to restrict, replace or even prevent the operation of private markets. British examples include nationalisation, the state education, employment and health services, as well as policies on prostitution, drugs, abortion and immigration. An advantage of this market classification scheme is that it separates the positive

and normative issues in policy debates: a distinction is made
between the *technical issues* concerned with the causes of market
failure and the *policy issues* relating to the most appropriate
solution.

Whilst policy instruments are the means of achieving objectives,
difficulties frequently arise because of conflicts in aims. A policy
which sites firms in their least-cost locations or which aims to
maximise the gains from international trade might conflict with
regional employment objectives. Concern with the balance of
payments might require larger firms capable of competing in
world markets; but mergers might result in domestic monopolies
and so conflict with competition policy. Conflicts in objectives
imply 'sacrifices', with the inevitable controversies over the
relative importance of policy goals. The existence of conflicts has
been recognised in a well-established principle of economic policy
which maintains that to achieve a stated number of objectives, a
government requires at least an equal number of different policy
instruments (Tinbergen 1952). Applied to industry and labour
policy, the principle suggests that if, say, a government retains
'lame ducks' to achieve its employment objective, some other
policy instrument such as price controls will be required for its
price stability goal, and a further policy measure such as a floating
exchange rate, wage subsidies or mergers will have to be used for
the balance of payments objective.

An Alternative Explanation of Industry and Labour Policies

The analysis of British governments as social welfare
maximisers is not without its critics. Basically, the approach seems
to ignore the existing voting and political party arrangements in a
democracy. Difficulties inevitably arise in compiling a social
welfare function which reflects the individual preferences of
British voters and which contains no 'dictatorial' decisions. Also
elections are based on equality of voters so that voting is not
'weighted' by the strengths of individual preferences. Nor can an
individual reveal his feelings for any single item within the mix of
issues presented to the electorate. Furthermore, the social welfare
model of British governments implies that politicians have no

private motives and faithfully respond to the will of the majority.
Since the assumptions are so unrealistic, the model is likely to fail
to explain and predict the behaviour of British governments and
their industry and labour policies.

An alternative economic theory of democracy has been
constructed by Anthony Downs using different assumptions and
deriving alternative explanations and predictions (Downs 1957).
The Downs model assumes that voters are utility maximisers and
that political parties are vote maximisers. Politicians are assumed
to be motivated by self-interest and the desire to hold office, so
that policies are formulated as a means of achieving office. From
these assumptions Downs derives a number of testable
propositions, two of which are especially relevant to explaining
the industry and labour policies of British governments. First, in a
two-party democracy both parties agree on any issues favoured by
a majority of voters. In such a system, party policies tend to be
vague and similiar (consensus politics). Second, government
policies tend to favour producers more than consumers. Producer
interest groups (i.e. management and trade unions) are dominant
because they have the most to gain from trying to influence
government policy in their favour. Since most men earn their
incomes in one activity but spend in many, the area of earning
(producing) is much more vital to them than the area of spending
(consuming). Producer interest groups can afford substantial
investments in information to influence governments (on the
employment effects of cancelling Concorde, for instance) and the
potential returns are likely to make the investments worthwhile.
Consumers are in a different position. They cannot afford major
investments to acquire information on the price effects of, say,
monopoly, tariffs, agricultural support schemes and industrial
location policy, and there are substantial transactions costs in
organising consumer groups. Thus, with the Downs model, the
industry and labour policies of successive British governments are
a means of maximising votes. Such vote maximisation will not
necessarily result in maximum welfare for the community; votes
could be maximised at a sub-optimal Paretian welfare position.

The economic model of democracy is widely applicable, an
obvious example being defence and the military-industrial
complex. Since defence is frequently an election issue, vote-

maximising politicians have an incentive to be well-informed about public opinion. However, median preference voters are likely to be uncertain in their assessment of defence. On the one hand, voters will favour civil goods and 'free-riding'; on the other, they will probably require some minimum level of protection. For vote-conscious politicians, the collection of information on diverse and uncertain voter preferences is costly. In addition, the citizens who are best informed on any specific issue are likely to be those whose incomes are directly affected: producer interest groups in the form of weapons firms (management, scientists and unions) tend to be dominant since, with their relatively favourable earnings, they have the most to gain from trying to influence government policy in their favour. The influence of weapons contractors will be reinforced by the budget-maximising aims of the Ministry of Defence and the Services, with the result that government policy is likely to favour producers rather than consumers. Similarly, British government support for advanced technology projects such as Concorde and the RB211 jet engine is more appropriately explained by an economic theory of politics. With such projects there exists a readily identifiable producer interest group with employment, relatively favourable earnings, technology and other vote-winning attributes supported by a Ministry with a major budgetary involvement.

The Downs model also explains the form and extent of state intervention in the British economy. In the two-party democracy of Britain, where the mass of voters seem to have been concentrated at the centre rather than the extremes of the political spectrum, the model predicts consensus politics and hence similar industry and labour policies between the parties. This was evident, for example, in the late 1960's when both major political parties developed similar policies towards industrial relations and training and, more recently, towards state support for the private sector. Parties do, of course, attempt to differentiate their policies, but movements towards the extremes of the political spectrum are likely to be constrained by the potential losses of moderate voters. On this basis, neither party is likely to move towards the industry and labour policy extremes of, say, complete laissez-faire or total collectivism.

Economic Theory and Industry and Labour Policy

The emphasis, so far, has been on the analysis of industry and labour policy using alternative models of government behaviour. It remains to be shown how economic theory can be used to assess current policy issues. The examples selected are topical and questions arise as to whether economic theory offers any policy guidelines for state intervention and whether it can be used to analyse policy measures.

Public Money in the Private Sector: Why Should the State Support Private Firms?

In recent years the state has become increasingly involved in providing financial assistance to private firms and industries, this commitment being incorporated in the Industry Act 1972. The Act allows the government to provide finance where it is likely to benefit the economy of the UK or any part of it, and where it is in the national interest that financial assistance should be provided. This is contrary to the alternative view that private industry should stand on its own feet and that 'lame ducks' can be left to market forces — a view which suggests that private markets, if left to themselves, will work satisfactorily. However, actual markets frequently 'fail', so that market failure could provide the economic logic for state intervention. Theory suggests two general arguments for intervention in the specific form of subsidies to private industry. First, if society wishes to achieve an optimum allocation of resources, private firms will have to introduce marginal cost pricing for their products. For firms in decreasing cost activities, such a pricing policy will require subsidies. Second, markets might fail because of externalities and subsidies are a means of correcting any divergence between social and private costs and benefits. Needless to say, the marginal cost pricing argument was *not* used in the classic examples of state support in the early 1970's (i.e. UCS, Concorde, Rolls Royce). Instead, subsidies were generally justified on the grounds of social benefits (i.e. the national interest). It was frequently claimed that state support for a firm or industry was required for reasons of advanced technology, balance of payments, defence or employment (HMSO 1972). Such arguments need to be critically assessed. The alleged social benefits have to be identified and measured and the resource costs involved have to be estimated. In assessing costs, consideration has to be given to the possibilities of alternative and lower-cost methods of achieving the same ends. State support for the British aircraft industry provides an example of the possibilities for a critical appraisal of current subsidy policy.[1]

Traditionally, British governments have supported the domestic aircraft industry because of its contributions to advanced technology, the balance of payments and defence (Hartley 1974). The technology argument maintains that aircraft work advances the frontiers of knowledge and results in benefits or spin-off to the rest of British industry. Examples of technological fall-out from the UK aircraft industry include electronics, radar, radio, gas turbines, digital computers and the development of alloys. On this basis, subsidies to the domestic aircraft industry provide benefits to the community, so that fall-out is an external economy. Certainly, there is analytical support for the general proposition that competitive markets will tend to under-invest in invention and research simply because it is difficult to establish complete property rights in marketable ideas and information. The under-investment is reinforced by the risks of research and by increasing returns in the use of information. Using this analysis Arrow concluded that "for optimal allocation to invention it would be necessary for the government or some other agency not governed by profit-and-loss criteria to finance research and invention" (Arrow 1962, p.623). The resources to be devoted to research and their allocation between competing research activities can be determined by the standard marginal calculation. For optimum allocation, resources would be devoted to research until the expected social benefit at the margin equals the additional expected social benefit in other uses. But general economic principles can take us no further. The ultimate allocative decision by governments will depend on evidence and judgement,

[1]This section concentrates on the general arguments for state support. The issue of public ownership is analysed in the chapter on Nationalised Industries. In addition, some of the employment arguments for state intervention are considered in the next section on manpower policy; see also the chapter on Regional Policy.

influenced by scientific interest groups in the Ministries and industry.

None of this necessarily constitutes a *prima facie* case for state support of the British aircraft industry. The analysis simply suggests under-investment in research and hence a case for state intervention to correct the market failure. Whether the current size of the aircraft industry represents the best use of scarce technical resources is a judgement which might be partly based on the evidence of *past* results. At first glance, the evidence is impressive. New techniques and products developed in aviation have been applied in industries such as engineering, vehicles, building, chemicals, machine tools, nuclear power and medicine. However, the available evidence is qualitative, with no indication of the value to the economy of the technological fall-out. To constitute a case for state support, it has to be shown that the current volume of aircraft work results in a *net* contribution to the economy's stock of technology. In the early 1970's the British aircraft industry employed over 200,000 people, including some 7,000 scientists, engineers and technologists and government expenditure on aircraft research and development was about £160m. Questions arise as to whether some of the technical resources used in aircraft work would yield similar or larger technological benefits if they were employed elsewhere in the economy. One school of thought maintains that during the 1960's Britain's scientific and technical resources were over-committed. Compared with the USA, Britain lacked scientific and technical manpower in the chemicals, electrical, instruments, machinery and vehicle industries. During the period a substantial proportion of this scarce manpower was allocated to the aircraft industry and the competitive performance of the industry left much to be desired. A US study concluded that "fall-out of benefit to the commercial sector may occur from time to time (generally farther in the future than is commonly supposed), but these by-product benefits should not be adduced as a major justification for support of the aerospace programme. Where stimulation of the civilian economy is an important objective, fall-out from aerospace technology cannot be relied upon as a principal stimulant except in isolated instances. Broadly speaking, such stimulation can be achieved more effectively by other forms of supporting civilian research and industrial innovation" (HMSO 1965). It is this type of analysis and evidence which raises doubts about the technological fall-out benefits from the British aircraft industry and the present level of state support.

The balance of payments case for state support maintains that the British aircraft industry contributes foreign currency through exports and import savings. British government concern with the balance of payments has traditionally been associated with a desire to maintain a fixed exchange rate. Once the rate becomes over-valued, British industry will 'fail' to export or reduce imports to a sufficient extent to avoid a balance of payments deficit. In such a situation market failure, if it can be called such, arises because for the economy as a whole a pound earned abroad has more value to society than a pound earned at home. If a government wishes to remove the deficit whilst maintaining the exchange rate, state intervention to expand exports or reduce imports by firms and industries is a possible policy solution. For this to be used as a case for the current level of state support, it has to be shown that the industry results in a greater contribution to the balance of payments than alternative uses of the resources. A study of civil aircraft showed that there are some UK industries (e.g. vehicles and mechanical and instrument engineering) which make a larger contribution to the balance of payments than the civil aircraft sector (Hartley 1974). In addition, there are more general objections to the foreign currency argument for support, namely that there are real income gains from international trade based on comparative advantage and that where a nation has a continuing balance of payments deficit changes in the exchange rate are an appropriate policy instrument.

The defence benefits from the aircraft industry are a further source of the divergence between social and private costs and benefits. Without state support, it is maintained that the aircraft industry will be too small for the country's defence needs. To assess this argument, evidence is required on the value of the defence benefits and their associated costs: are the alleged benefits from an independent domestic aircraft industry of the current size really worth the costs of support? In recent years, state support in the form of purchases of higher-cost domestic aircraft has been substantial. By not purchasing from the least-cost source of supply (USA), state support for the British aircraft industry was probably

£1,200m during the period 1950-70. This is a substantial sacrifice of defence and civilian goods (e.g. schools, hospitals) and the sum indicates the value which policy makers must be implicitly placing on the defence benefits of a domestic aircraft industry. Whilst individuals will differ in their views about the definition and valuation of benefits, economists can contribute to the policy debate by quantifying the costs of existing policies.

The various arguments for state support of any domestic industry are usually aggregated to form the basis for debates about the appropriate or optimum size of the industry. The cost-benefit framework which has been used for the appraisal of current policy suggests the criterion for optimum size. The industry's optimal size occurs when, at the margin, the benefits which accrue to society are equal to the costs. However, the issue of optimal size can be complicated by the existence of a budget-maximising state agency responsible for the industry (Department of Industry, Ministry of Defence). Budget maximisation enables bureaucrats to create large organisations and so satisfy their preferences for power and prestige. To maximise its budget, a state agency can under-estimate the costs of a project for a given demand or it can attempt to increase or over-estimate demand. Over-optimistic cost estimates have frequently occurred with advanced technology projects and, on the demand side, the possibility arises that budget-maximising agencies together with producer interest groups may have combined to persuade vote-conscious governments that the alleged (over-estimated) social benefits of a project are sufficient to make it worthwhile. The claims of technological fall-out from aerospace projects is a conspicuous example of alleged external benefits. In addition to over-estimating the social benefits of a project, budget-maximising agencies have every incentive to confuse total costs and benefits with marginal costs and benefits. By concentrating on total costs and benefits, programmes are likely to exceed their optimal size.

Similar analyses may be applied to the state support of other private sector industries. In the seven years up to the end of 1974 state aid to the ship-building industry (principally to the Upper Clyde yards and to Harland and Wolff) has totalled £133m, while between 1970 and 1974 the machine tool industry has received £16m of special grants and loans[2]. Though such expenditure may be justified in terms of the imperfection of the market mechanism in achieving national economic goals, the possibility remains that this support has been a response by government to the weight of producer interests operating through the political system — the result being that government has supported oversized industries and prevented the desirable movement of resources out of the supported industries into more productive areas of the economy. Inevitably questions are raised about the adequacy of existing public policies to facilitate a re-allocation of resources. Manpower or labour market policy is obviously central to any adjustment measures designed to promote a transfer of resources between industries and regions in the economy.

Manpower Policy

Manpower policy embraces all aspects of public policy towards the factor of production, labour, and the operation of the market for labour. It includes the state provision of labour market information, together with policies towards training and re-training, mobility and regional development, as well as provision for such special groups as the unemployed and redundant, the disabled, the older worker, women and immigrants. Under the Employment and Training Act 1973, a Manpower Services Commission was established to promote "the efficient working of the labour market in Great Britain" (HMSO 1973, p.1).

Improvements in the efficiency of the labour market can contribute to the securing of macroeconomic policy objectives. Policies on training, re-training, mobility and labour market information can reduce frictional and structural unemployment and assist in the re-allocation of labour from declining to expanding industries, so contributing to employment and growth objectives. In addition, in so far as there exists a trade-off between price stability and employment, both theory and evidence show that manpower policies (e.g. training and more information to aid job search) which reduce imbalances in labour markets will move the policy frontier in a favourable direction (Thirlwall, vol. X). However, there are sources of conflict in policy objectives.

[2]See Samuel Brittan, Economic Viewpoint, *Financial Times,* 13 December 1974.

Measures to promote labour mobility for growth aims can conflict with regional 'balance' objectives. Similarly, increases in unemployment benefit tend to raise the length of unemployment, so leading to a conflict between social and employment objectives. Evidence shows that in the late 1960's an increase in unemployment benefit of £1 per week probably increased the length of unemployment by about one-half of a week and that in 1968 earnings-related benefit probably contributed to a rise in unemployment of about 12,000 men (MacKay 1972).

To improve the operation of the labour market, the Manpower Services Commission acquired the employment and training services previously operated by the Department of Employment. These are now separate agencies and form the executive branches of the Commission. The Employment Services Agency operates the state employment service, including the professional and executive register, the occupational guidance service and financial assistance for mobility. The Training Services Agency is responsible for policy towards training in both the public and private sectors, including the Government Training Centres and the Industrial Training Boards. To understand policy in this area, consideration has to be given to the economic justification of a state employment service and of government intervention in training.

The Employment Services Agency performs a market clearing function through bringing together employed and unemployed workers searching for new jobs and employers seeking new workers. On past evidence, employers have notified about two million vacancies to the Service and it has filled about 1½ million jobs or some 20% of total job changes in Britain. Recent changes in the Service have aimed to improve its market clearing function by bringing together more buyers and sellers in the labour market. For example, to remove the 'dole queue' image, a separate administration has been created for the payment of unemployment benefit. Computerised job banks and the extensive circulation of vacancies throughout large city areas will aid the matching of jobs and job seekers. Modern, purpose-built job centres and the extension of self-service centres displaying local vacancies are designed to encourage more employers and workers to use the Service. To extend the market clearing function from unskilled and semi-skilled manual labour to white-collar workers, the Service's professional and executive register has been completely re-styled and employers are now charged for this service. Through these various changes, the Employment Services Agency will contribute to an improvement in the adjustment and clearing operations of the labour market. In effect, the Service can be regarded as an information exchange (c.f. stock exchange). It provides information about jobs and labour to large numbers of buyers and sellers, so reducing the costs of transactions in the labour market. As a result of such lower costs, more transactions are likely as buyers and sellers take advantage of increased opportunities for mutually beneficial exchange. Apparently, a state-employment service is justified on the grounds that without government involvement "a national network for information about vacancies, special teams to help with major redundancies, an occupational guidance service . . . are not likely to be provided" (HMSO 1971, p.6). Since these are aspects of labour market information, the source of market failure requires consideration.

In the competitive model, the efficient operation of the labour market partly depends upon the extent to which the system transmits information about relative scarcities in the economy. If, for example, individuals are completely unaware of income and employment prospects in various jobs, this will impair the extent to which labour will respond by acquiring new skills and moving from the declining to the expanding sectors of the economy. In the circumstances, both firms and labour in the UK find it worthwhile to invest in the acquisition of market information. The result is an extensive private sector information market. Advertisements in newspapers and trade journals, specialist job agencies together with learning-by-experience and informal contacts with friends and relatives are all methods of searching the labour market. Such methods frequently involve substantial costs in the form of time and money outlays. Even though firms and workers are willing to pay for information, private competitive markets are not likely to provide as much of the 'commodity' as consumers require. Under-provision arises because of the difficulty of establishing property rights in information. If a firm sells job information to an individual, how can it prevent such knowledge being given to others who might otherwise be willing to pay for the service? In addition, with information which is of general value, the costs of informing people are largely independent of the number to whom the information is transmitted (low or zero marginal costs), so that private provision might produce conditions of technical monopoly. Thus, state intervention in the information market for labour can be rationalised on grounds of externalities and technical monopoly.

The existence of market failure does not, however, indicate the most appropriate policy solution. A variety of alternatives are feasible, including the state subsidisation of private information agencies, the state provision of grants and loans to individuals for investment in job search, as well as the public ownership or regulation of technical monopolies. Additional criteria are required for the selection of the state Employment Services Agency as the preferred form of government intervention. For example, there might be a general community preference for public ownership of technical monopolies and such a preference is likely to be reinforced by the budgetary aims of government departments. In addition, state involvement in its present form can be justified because much labour market information is generated within government. Because of the public social security system, it is likely that for certain kinds of information the state is potentially the lowest-cost organisation for collecting and distributing information.

The Manpower Commission's involvement in the labour market is not restricted to the Employment Services Agency. The market clearing function of the Agency involves the state in training and mobility, the aim being to provide labour with marketable skills in areas of relative scarcity. The Commission's Training Services Agency has general responsibility for providing training for employment. Part of its task involves co-ordinating the work of the Industrial Training Boards (ITB's) established under the Industrial Training Act 1964 (ITA). Since the Act has been operated by both Conservative and Labour administrations, it can be regarded as an example of consensus politics. There are now almost 30 Training Boards covering about 15 million workers in agriculture, manufacturing industry, construction, gas, electricity, water and several service industries. The Boards represent a substantial state involvement in private sector training and have inevitably attracted criticism. Doubts have been expressed about the economic logic of the 1964 Act and the general policy presumption in favour of training, despite the absence of evidence on the costs and benefits of existing commitments. The supporters of the 1964 ITA defend the Boards and state involvement by maintaining that in industrial training "private enterprise had not done all that was required" (HMSO 1972, p.13). For the economist, the task in analysing such policy controversies is to distinguish between the *technical issues*, concerned with the potential sources of market failure, and the *policy issues*, relating to the alternatives and the selection of the most desirable solution.

The underlying philosophy of the 1964 ITA was that Britain's growth performance had been adversely affected by shortages of skilled manpower and that inadequate industrial training was the cause of the 'bottlenecks'. Furthermore, it was believed that the market failure in training (shortages) arose from externalities in the form of poaching: many firms did not train but poached skilled labour from others. Accordingly, the 1964 ITA aimed to ensure an adequate supply of properly trained men and women at all levels in industry; to secure an improvement in the quality and efficiency of industrial training and to share the cost of training more evenly between firms. The policy instruments to achieve these objectives were the ITBs together with their levy-grant and advisory systems. The levy usually takes the form of a payroll tax imposed on most firms in an industry, whilst grants are earmarked subsidies paid to firms for approved training. In this way, the Boards have used tax-subsidy policy to re-distribute training costs between poachers and trainers, so correcting for externalities (poaching) in the market. Although the 1973 Employment and Training Act introduced some amendments allowing exemption from levy for small firms and those whose training is adequate, the basic philosophy of the original ITA remains unchanged.

The failure of private markets to provide adequate investment in the training of skilled manpower arises from two major sources. Firms are unwilling to train the skilled manpower they require because of the fear of poaching. The difficulty arises from the fact that the property rights in any investment in labour (human capital) lie with the individual and not with the employer. While the employer will be willing to provide training in skills which are of value only in that firm, general skills which have value to a number of employers are highly marketable and hence poachable, so that the firm will be reluctant to cover their costs. The tendency will be, therefore, for the costs of general training to be borne by the individual. Individuals, however, will be unable to provide for the optimal level of investment in training because of their limited access to finance. A major obstacle to the emergence of a private capital market providing funds for training (and other labour market investments such as job search and mobility) arises because skills or expected future earnings are not acceptable security for a loan in the same way that a machine would be. Private sector attempts to solve the problem through voluntary contracts are likely to be restricted by the high administration and enforcement costs resulting from labour mobility. In the circumstances, it is likely that the relatively high transactions costs for private investors will lead to under-investment in training and other forms of human capital. Since technical monopoly is likely to be a lower-cost method for administering any national scheme for financing human investments, it follows that state intervention to create such a monopoly (e.g. a state manpower bank) will substantially reduce transactions costs and remove this potential source of under-investment in training.

There are other imperfections which are likely to contribute to shortages of skilled labour. For example, unions can contribute to skill shortages through entry restrictions for specific trades. A Royal Commission stated that where the only method of entry into a craft is "via an apprenticeship, supply will respond slowly and inadequately to demand. Where expansion is required it will be delayed." (HMSO 1968, p.87.) The Training Boards are aware of the apprenticeship problem and some successes have been achieved, notably by the Engineering ITB. However, the problems of monopoly, entry barriers, imperfections in the capital market and under-investment in information and mobility — each of which can contribute to skill shortages — are outside the remit of the ITB's. In the circumstances, the analysis of shortages and market failure in training indicates reservations about the original economic logic of adopting a training solution for what are basically labour market problems. The newly-formed Manpower

Services Commission which combines employment and training services suggests that policy now recognises the basic unity of the labour market with correspondingly less emphasis on a 'piece-meal' approach to manpower. There remain, though, more general questions about public policy towards monopoly and market imperfections in the British economy.

Competition Policy

Casual empiricism shows that in Britain departures from competition are extensive and are not confined to industries and product markets. Monopolies and imperfections exist in the factor markets for capital, labour and land. Monopoly is also present in government bureaucracies. Further state involvement in competition policy occurs with public sector purchases from private industry and the associated 'rules' for competitive and non-competitive tendering for government contracts. If society wishes to achieve an optimal allocation of resources, then welfare economics theory concludes that monopoly results in a mis-allocation of resources and is undesirable. This suggests that in private enterprise economies public policy should generally favour competition in product and factor markets. Departures from the competitive ideal occur when buyers or sellers in a market exist in small numbers, where they are large in relation to the size of the market and where there are barriers to entering the market. Although the departures from competition are numerous, policy in Britain has not adopted the guidelines of welfare economics and condemned monopolies and imperfections as undesirable.

Traditionally, British policy has been concerned with single firm monopolies, mergers and restrictive practices in product markets. There has been no general policy ruling that monopolies and mergers are undesirable and each case has been examined on its merits. Policy appears to recognise that mergers and single firm monopolies involve not only costs (e.g. welfare losses due to reduced competition), but possible benefits in such forms as scale economies and technical progress through research and development. Inevitably, there has been criticism of the vagueness of the public interest criterion, of inconsistencies in policy and of government reluctance to act against monopoly situations. Such criticisms can be understood by applying the Downs model of vote-maximising governments to explain monopoly legislation in the UK.

The Downs model suggests that democratic governments will favour producers more than consumers. The model predicts that any pro-competition or vigorous anti-monopoly policy is unlikely to be introduced and enforced simply because of opposition from producer interest groups. In addition, in formulating anti-monopoly policy, vote-maximising governments find it difficult to assess the preferences of the median voter, who is likely to be undecided between the benefits of large firms and the 'unacceptable face of capitalism'. A possible outcome is that a vote-maximising government which wishes to avoid risks will introduce inconsistent legislation (Rowley 1973); this occurs where a government accepts a recommendation of the Monopolies Commission and then fails to implement it. A further example occurred in the late 1960's when the government simultaneously pursued policies for controlling monopolies and mergers (1965 Act) and policies for promoting mergers in the economy (Industrial Reorganisation Corporation 1966). It might be argued that the policies of the Monopolies Commission and the Industrial Reorganisation Corporation (IRC) were not inconsistent since it might be deduced that for all mergers supported by the IRC benefits exceeded costs, whereas mergers condemned by the Monopolies Commission would be those where costs exceeded benefits. This is a far from satisfactory rationalisation of apparent inconsistencies in policy. With a discretionary policy, two regulatory agencies are unlikely to have identical preference functions, so that differences can arise in the specification and, more especially, in the valuation of costs and benefits.

The Fair Trading Act 1973 is more difficult to explain since, at first sight, it appears to refute the Downs model. The 1973 Act established a Director-General of Fair Trading with responsibilities for the control of monopolies, mergers and restrictive practices and with a new emphasis on consumer protection. It is the emphasis on the protection of the consumer which seems to refute the Downs prediction that democratic governments will favour producers in their actions. Two possibilities suggest that a refutation is premature. First, the proconsumer emphasis can be regarded as the response of vote-maximising governments to the growth of the consumer movement as a new interest group (e.g. Naderism). This movement has established specialist consumer 'firms', which have organised consumers into an integrated group able to afford investments to acquire information on unfair trading practices and so influence governments (as well as clarifying the preferences of voters). Second, the emphasis on consumer protection might be a further example of inconsistent legislation in this area. Time will show whether the 1973 Act will be an example of government legislating in favour of consumers but subsequently limiting any effective implementation.

Monopoly is not confined to product markets. Imperfections exist in labour markets and, in recent years, the promotion of equal employment opportunities — the Race Relations Act 1968 and the Equal Pay Act 1970 — can be regarded as policy measures to remove some of these imperfections. Monopoly unions have raised more controversial policy issues. During the 1960's, owing to the increasing concern with unofficial strikes which imposed costs on the rest of the economy, with inefficiencies due to restrictive labour practices and with wage inflation, the Donovan Commission was established to examine "the role of trade unions and employers' associations in promoting the interests of their members and in accelerating the social and economic advance of the nation with particular reference to the law affecting the activities of these bodies" (HMSO 1968, p.1). The Commission's recommendations reflected a preference for the traditional British system of voluntary collective bargaining and for its reform by publicity and persuasion rather than by comprehensive changes in the law. The general belief seemed to be that good industrial relations depend on voluntary associations and the freedom of individuals, with the right to strike as a basic liberty. It was also felt that legal sanctions would be ineffective since, in the Commission's view, they could not be related to the basic causes of unofficial strikes. The Commission placed the responsibility for changes in industrial relations on employers. To induce employers to change, the Donovan Report recommended an Industrial Relations Act requiring companies to register collective agreements with the Department of Employment. Failure to register or to report the absence of an agreement was to render a firm liable to a monetary penalty. The Report also recommended an Industrial Relations Commission to investigate registered agreements and problem areas referred to it by the Department of Employment. This Commission was to work through publicity and persuasion and there were to be no penalties for non-compliance with its recommendations. In some ways the recommendations of the Royal Commission were similar to the policies adopted in the 1948 and 1956 legislation on monopolies and restrictive practices in product markets. The original Monopolies Commission was very much an inquiry agency, whilst the 1956 legislation required the registration of restrictive trade agreements. However, the similarities with the 1956 Restrictive Trade Practices Act were superficial. After considering the 1956 model, the Royal Commission asserted that it would be "out of the question to list all restrictions on the use of labour and say that these were to be assumed to be against the public interest, unless the contrary were proved . . . It is in any case mistaken to think that it is possible to deal with practices which are part of a worker's way of life in the same way as specific and clearly identifiable trading practices . . . This is essentially a situation in which only educative processes and reasoning can lead people to revise their attitudes." (HMSO 1968 pp.81-2.) The quotation is typical of much of the general methodological approach to industrial relations. A single preferred policy recommendation (education and reasoning) is somehow derived from a belief that labour is 'different' (not explained) and that it is 'out of the question' to list restrictive labour practices (a testable hypothesis) and relate these to the public interest (not defined). Such difficulties of methodology arise because industrial relations is an inter-disciplinary area which lacks a logically consistent analytical framework, so that the approach to the subject has been predominantly descriptive. In complete contrast, the more specialised approach of, say, economics provides a body of well-established theory and testable predictions about the operation of labour markets and the behaviour of trade unions and firms. Welfare economics also provides a *starting point* for assessing the welfare effects of both market failure and policy measures designed to improve the utility of individuals in the community. For example, if the public interest were identified with optimum resource allocation, then welfare economics suggests that collective bargaining and 'closed shops' can restrict individual choices and so adversely affect utility levels in the labour market. Similarly, for optimum resource allocation, welfare theory suggests the policy 'rule' that labour should be paid the value of its marginal product (c.f. marginal cost pricing rule), which would be the outcome under competition.

Following the Report of the Royal Commission, the Labour and Conservative administrations attempted to introduce legislation on industrial relations and both encountered opposition from the trade unions. The Conservative government's Industrial Relations Act 1971-74 introduced a comprehensive legal framework for industrial relations and was a major departure from the voluntary philosophy of the Donovan Report. The 1971 Act established a system of voluntary registration for trade unions, a Commission on Industrial Relations and a National Industrial Relations Court. The voluntary registration system gave legal benefits to unions in return for which their rules had to conform to certain standards. Only registered unions were legally allowed to strike. Even so, constraints were placed on the right to strike which affected official and, especially, unofficial strikes. Also, in an emergency situation, the state could apply to the National Industrial Relations Court for an order requiring a cooling-off period or a strike ballot. Under the 1971 Act the Commission on Industrial Relations investigated and made recommendations on such issues as trade union recognition and general industrial relations problems and some of its recommendations could be legally enforced. The National Industrial Relations Court was responsible for the legal decisions (e.g. restraining orders, compensation awards) taken under the Act. In some ways the NIRC resembled the Restrictive Practices Court established in 1956. The Industrial Relations Act created a legal framework for regulating 'unfair industrial practices'. Such unfair practices included the breaking of a legally binding agreement, forcing an employer to sack a worker who is not a union member and secondary boycotts where workers in dispute with a firm induce their colleagues to withhold supplies from the enterprise. In this way, the 1971 Act resembled a non-discretionary policy which established a general presumption that specific unfair industrial practices were against the public interest. However, unlike the restrictive practices legislation, union registration was voluntary, there were no exemptions or 'gateways' and the initiative for the legal enforcement of the 1971 Act rested with employers and unions and not with the Registrar or the NIRC. Similar comparisons can be made between the Commission on Industrial Relations (CIR) and the Monopolies Commission. For example, it is an interesting exercise to speculate on the policy implications of applying existing fair trading legislation to trade unions.[3] If unions were treated in the same way as monopolies in the product market, then a monopoly situation would arise where a single union or group of unions acting together controlled one quarter of a market's labour supply (including local labour markets). Actual or proposed mergers between unions would also be subject to the market share criterion as well as to the £5m value of assets criterion. Following an investigation of a union monopoly situation, the Monopoly and Mergers Commission would be required to decide whether the monopoly or merger was contrary to the public interest. Under the 1973 Fair Trading Act, the public interest guidelines were modified to include specific references to the desirability of maintaining and promoting competition and of using competition (including new entrants) as a means of reducing costs and developing new techniques and products. The 1973 public interest guidelines also required the Commission to consider the balanced distribution of industry and employment as well as "all matters which appear to . . . be relevant." Presumably, if it were to examine the behaviour of union monopolies and mergers, the Commission would consider such performance indicators as the rate of return on human capital (skills) and union membership, scale economies in unions, entry conditions, tariff protection and the unions' contribution to technical efficiency including innovation. In view of recent history, this is obviously a sensitive area for vote-conscious politicians!

Trade union opposition to the Industrial Relations Act 1971-74

[3] The 1973 Act contains a provision for the investigation of restrictive labour practices by the Commission, but there is no power for the Minister to make an order.

is now a classic example of the influence on legislation of a dominant interest group. Applying the Downs model, union opposition arose because the 1971 Act was interpreted as a policy measure which would adversely affect the market power of a major producer pressure group. The opposition was no different from that of, say, the military-industrial complex to the proposed cancellation of weapons projects, or that of the academic-scientific-student complex to proposals for reductions in expenditure on higher education. In other words, "the specialised groups in society, whose articulateness is fortified by their relatively favourable earnings, are major constitutents of political decision-makers" (Stockfisch 1972, p.18).[4]

The record of recent legislative attempts to reform industrial relations is likely to lead governments to accept the existing organisation of trade unions as a policy-created constraint (second-best). An alternative would be to formulate a more vigorous and active anti-monopoly and pro-competition policy in the *product market*. The logic of such an indirect approach to labour market imperfections is suggested by recent developments in the concept of organisational slack or technical inefficiency. Such inefficiency tends to arise where competitive pressures are absent. Competition eliminates relatively high-cost producers and also "tends to discipline managements *and employees* to utilise their inputs, and to put forth more effort, more energetically and more effectively than is the case where this pressure is absent" (Comanor 1969, p.304). In other words, restrictive labour practices and other sources of inefficiency are likely to arise where the absence of competition allows both labour and management to pursue their own utility functions (e.g. on-the-job leisure). A similar outcome is likely when governments introduce maximum profit controls (e.g. defence and prices and incomes policy). Certainly the available evidence indicates that many British firms operate with a substantial amount of 'slack'. For example the National Board for Prices and Incomes frequently made recommendations for improved efficiency and also attempted to 'shock' firms into increased efficiency by refusing requests for a

---

[4]To some extent the election of February 1974 might be interpreted as a desire by median preference voters to return to consensus politics and avoid (costly) movements to the extremes of the political spectrum.

rise in prices. Thus, opportunities exist for using competition policy to reduce restrictive labour practices and other sources of technical inefficiency in the British economy. Since the proposed policy would involve costs, it would not be worthwhile to eliminate all restrictive practices; but the outcome would be an optimal (smaller) amount of inefficiency. More significantly, changes would be required of established groups in the economy and ultimately the acceptability of the proposal to governments and political parties would depend on its vote-winning attributes.

References

Arrow, K.J., Economic Welfare and the Allocation of Resources for Invention in *The Rate and Direction of Inventive Activity*, NBER, Princeton University Press 1962, p.623.

Comanor, W. S., and Leibenstein, H., Allocative Efficiency, X-Efficiency and the Measurement of Welfare Losses, *Economica*, August 1969, p.304.

Downs, A., *An Economic Theory of Democracy*, Harper & Row 1957.

Hartley, K., *A Market for Aircraft*, IEA Hobart Paper 57, 1974.

MacKay, D. I., and Reid, G. L., Redundancy, Unemployment and Manpower Policies, *Economic Journal*, December 1972, p.1268.

Pencavel, J. H., Relative Wages and Trade Unions in the United Kingdom, *Economica*, May 1974.

Rowley, C. K., *Anti-Trust and Economic Efficiency*, Macmillan 1973.

Stockfisch, J. A., *The Political Economy of Bureaucracy*, General Learning Press 1972, p.16.

Thirlwall, A. P., Government Manpower Policies in Great Britain, *British Journal of Industrial Relations*, Vol. X, No. 2.

Tinbergen, J., *On the Theory of Economic Policy*, North-Holland 1952.

Employment and Training: Government Proposals, Cmnd 5250, HMSO 1973.

People and Jobs, Department of Employment, HMSO 1971.

Public Money in the Private Sector, HC 347, HMSO 1972.

Report of the Committee of Inquiry into the Aircraft Industry, Cmnd 2853, HMSO 1965, p.135.

Report of the Royal Commission on Trade Unions and Employers' Associations, 1965-1968, Cmnd 3623, HMSO 1968 (Donovan).

Suggestions for Further Reading

References to further reading on particular areas of industrial and labour policy are indicated in the chapter. On the analysis of the role of government in the economy see:

Downs (1957).

Niskanen, W. A., *Bureaucracy: Servant or Master? Lessons from America*, Institute of Economic Affairs 1973.

Friedman, M., *Capitalism and Freedom*, University of Chicago Press 1962.

3. The nationalised industries

M H PESTON
Professor of Economics,
Queen Mary College, University of London

What is a nationalised industry? This is by no means a simple question, as the House of Commons Select Committee on Nationalised Industries discovered in 1968 when it enquired as to whether the Bank of England was a nationalised industry in a sense which enabled them to examine it. When the Committee was set up in 1956 its terms of reference were defined as follows: "to examine the Reports and Accounts of the Nationalised Industries established by Statute whose controlling Boards are appointed by Ministers of the Crown and whose annual receipts are not wholly or mainly derived from monies provided by Parliament or advanced from the Exchequer." What this amounts to is (a) that the industries are wholly owned by the state or sufficiently owned by the state to be controlled by it; (b) that the industries operate in such a way as to gain most of their revenue other than from direct Parliamentary or Treasury subsidy; and (c) that they are run by Boards of Directors. The obvious examples, British Airways, the National Coal Board, the Electricity Council, the Central Electricity Generating Board, the North of Scotland Hydro-Electric Board, the Gas Council, British Rail, the British Airports Authority, the Post Office, the British Waterways Board, the British Transport Docks Board, the British Steel Corporation, come pretty easily within the heading of nationalised industries. In addition London Transport did, before it was taken over by the Greater London Council. On the other hand, the BBC is not a

nationalised industry because it receives its income directly from
the Exchequer as is voted by Parliament. Similarly the Stationery
Office does not operate with an independent Board, although it
does get most of its income from sales to the public.

It is interesting to note that the Select Committee did decide that
the Bank of England was also a nationalised industry. Indeed, it
would have been extraordinary if it had come to an opposite
conclusion, since the government in 1946 was under the
impression that it had nationalised it. Similarly, they decided that
the Independent Broadcasting Authority, and quite a number of
other small corporations and firms, were also nationalised
industries. A full list of these can be found in the Report which the
Select Committee published.

In recent years there have been a great many changes. Some
parts of Rolls Royce have been taken into public ownership as well
as some parts of Court Line Limited. The state management
districts around Carlisle and Thomas Cook Limited have been
sold back to the private sector. More to the point, a great deal of
public money has been put into a wide variety of private
enterprises without necessarily obtaining a controlling interest.
For the purposes of the present discussion we shall assume that the
Select Committee's definition is appropriate, and that the basic list
that we have given is broadly what one is talking about when one
comes to discuss the economics of nationalised industries.

Nevertheless, while there is a basic list of nationalised industries
which we shall be referring to, much of what we have to say is of
broader applicability and, in particular, the fact that London
Transport is no longer defined as a nationalised industry in a legal
sense does not mean that the same economics is no longer relevant
to it. On the other hand, most of the mixed enterprises which are
only partially owned by the state and in which it does not
necessarily have a controlling interest may be regarded as
commercial in the ordinary sense of that term, and are not the
subject of the present essay.

There is a further complication to be mentioned concerning
definition. In the National Accounts Statistics of the United
Kingdom which are referred to below, reference is made to the
public corporations and a great many tables of statistics are
published with data on their operations. The public corporations

define a wider variety of institutions than the nationalised industries, including, for example, the BBC. It is also worth noting that such bodies as the Royal Ordnance Factories and other trading bodies are neither defined as nationalised industries nor as public corporations because they lack even the indépendence to borrow, or to retain their own trading surpluses. They are therefore a part of central government, and are defined as government trading bodies.

In sum, there is therefore an extraordinary range of related activities which come into the public sector which are of interest to the economist. There is a spectrum from the well-defined nationalised industry right across to things like the Royal Ordnance Factories, the selling of postcards in the National Gallery, etc. The important thing to bear in mind is that statistics are published under various headings which look as if they must refer simply to the nationalised industries, but may not. Great care must be exercised in interpreting the figures that are published.

Reasons for Nationalisation

The extent of nationalisation differs between nations. In almost all countries of Western Europe and in North America the postal services are nationalised; but it is not necessarily the case that the telephone or the telegraph services are in public ownership. They are certainly so in the United Kingdom and in France, but they are under private ownership in the United States. Railways are publicly owned in a great many countries of Western Europe; they are not publicly owned in the United States, and they are only half publicly owned in Canada. The electricity industry and the gas industry are publicly owned in almost all of Western Europe, but not always as complete public monopolies. In Sweden, for example, some electricity is generated by private enterprise and some by local municipal enterprise. Coal mining is a state monopoly in Austria, Great Britain and France, whereas in Italy, Sweden, Norway, Finland and West Germany the state merely owns a large share. Similar remarks can be made about iron and steel. The aluminium industry is to a large extent state owned in Norway, but not in many other countries. The firms producing cigarettes and tobacco and matches are state owned in a number of countries but not in the United Kingdom. We can find examples of state ownership of cars, aircraft, oil, armaments, alcoholic beverages, salt and forestry in different countries, but none of these are nationalised in all the countries of Western Europe. In other words, with the exception of the Post Office it is impossible to find any industry which is a state monopoly in every country of Western Europe and North America. It is also impossible to find an important industry in which there is not some degree of public ownership in one of these countries.

This heterogeneity of experience suggests that there have been many reasons for nationalisation, and that some of them may be peculiar to the countries in question. In the United Kingdom and in Austria and to some extent in Italy, nationalisation has taken place in order to fulfil explicit political programmes. In Austria again, in Italy and also to a considerable extent in Germany, nationalisation has happened by chance and is often a left-over phenomenon from a previous era. Bank failures on the continent of Europe in the inter-war period, together with the fact that the banks were important financiers of industry, meant that when government stepped in to rectify the situation they often found themselves as owners of particular industrial or commercial enterprises. Public enterprise has emerged in some countries not as a political programme, or at least not as a consequence of one party's political programme, but simply as a commitment to planning. Electricité de France is in the public sector and is part of the French commitment to a very special planning procedure. Despite the fact that right-wing governments very sympathetic to free enterprise have been in power in France for almost two decades, there has been no attempt on the part of the central government to give up these commanding heights of the economy or to abandon the planning process. The public transport system in Paris is in public ownership; and again this is not for ideological reasons, but simply as part of the commitment to plan Paris transport.

Although in many countries of the Western world nationalisation is connected with state interference in industry, other methods of state interference exist as well. It would therefore be wrong to identify the mixed economy simply with state ownership of particular enterprises. In many countries there is a wide variety of other methods of controlling industries, including those in private ownership. In several Western European countries wage and price controls are well established and are applied to private enterprise as well as to public enterprise. In Italy there is a central government National Holding Company which owns outright, or nearly outright, a wide variety of different industrial enterprises; and there is a great deal of other government interference with the rest of the economy. Governments can interfere and plan the economy without 100% nationalisation, although it can still be argued that planning and control is much assisted by public ownership.

The chance element in nationalisation is exemplified by the state management districts in Carlisle, which were nationalised simply as a result of the attempt to cut down alcoholism in World War I. They remained in public ownership for 50 years until the Conservative administration of 1970 sold them back to the private sector for what were alleged to be purely doctrinaire reasons. At that point there may have been no particular reason why they should have been in state ownership, but equally there was no particular reason why they should have been sold back to private enterprise. Of course, nationalisation must be regarded to a considerable extent as an ideological matter, connected with some theories of the decline of capitalism and the growth of socialism. Marx identified the public ownership of capital as the distinguishing mark of socialism. It is not apparent from Marx himself whether a process of nationalisation would in fact represent a method of getting from capitalism to socialism, but certainly other left-wing thinkers, notably democratic socialists in Western Europe and the United Kingdom, did see gradual nationalisation as the procedure by which socialism in some form would be reached. Amongst economists this view was emphasised by Schumpeter (1942).

Ideology apart, a number of reasons have been put forward to justify nationalisation in terms of economics. Firstly, it was seen as a method of dealing with monopoly. In certain industries, largely because of economies of scale, the most successful economic unit gives rise to monopoly, which is regarded as politically undesirable and economically inefficient. Various methods have been suggested to deal with this, notably the introduction of taxes of different kinds and public regulation. The trouble is that the taxes would have to be adjusted to the particular industries, which is likely to be administratively impossible and unfair. Similarly, public utility regulation, as occurs in the United States, may also be seen as administratively extremely difficult and open to corruption. The nationalisation approach, if it is based on laying down general rules of behaviour for the industries within which management may proceed independently, enables the evils of monopoly to be avoided while at the same time allowing sufficient entrepreneurial effort to keep the industries efficient and up-to-date.

A second and related case for nationalisation concerns the problem of industries which are liable to go out of existence in conditions of free enterprise, but which the government wishes to preserve. It could happen that simply as a result of chance forces or miscalculations on the part of private entrepreneurship a concern that is inherently viable becomes bankrupt, but free enterprise and free financial markets are unwilling to provide new finance in order that it may continue. The government may then provide the finance itself, and feel that the best way of doing this, especially when extremely large sums of money are involved, would be by taking the concern under its own wing. The obvious example in recent years is Rolls Royce, but there have been plenty of other examples in many countries over a long period of time. The question then arises of what meaning can be attached to the industry or the firm being economically viable but private enterprise being unwilling to risk its own finance. The answer may lie in a difference of view about the likely risks involved, and also a difference in attitudes to risk. The government can decide quite simply that private enterprise or finance is too cautious. Economic viability is not an objective thing to be determined solely by the estimates of private decision makers in free capital markets. They can be mistaken, and governments can be correct in their estimation of economic prospects. Of course, the reverse is also possible; namely that governments are mistaken and free enterprise correct in their estimates of economic viability.

The cases we are discussing here would not necessarily involve a public interest in the enterprise as such. In others, such as Rolls

Royce, there might be national prestige or strategic advantage necessitating that the firm should stay in existence, either by nationalisation or state subsidy.

More generally, what we are discussing are the workings of the economy and the problems of planning. If industries are subject to random shocks of one kind or another, it will happen sometimes that they contract rapidly or go out of existence altogether. Most economists do not believe that free markets always adjust quickly or efficiently enough to be able to cope with this kind of problem. That is why national planning procedures are introduced. The easiest way of introducing planning is via public ownership, especially if the planning structure of the economy is fairly primitive. In the United Kingdom we are still far from being able to cope easily with the decline of individual enterprises and the transfer of the labour force to new enterprises. This process may then be slowed down a little and managed via the public ownership of the declining firm. Advocates of free enterprise argue that this is inefficient compared with letting the declining firms go out of existence and allowing the labour force to become temporarily unemployed. It is difficult to lay down general principles in this area of discourse. The free market solution may be correct in some cases; public ownership will be correct in others. The trouble with the latter is that, setting all ideology apart and concentrating solely on the economic arguments, the subsequent adjustment process may not occur. Nationalisation can become a means simply of keeping particular enterprises in existence for no purpose other than maintaining the labour force in full employment. It is worth emphasising, therefore, that to a large extent this has not been true of public enterprise in recent years in the United Kingdom. In coal mining and the railways, for example, strong efforts have been made to increase efficiency in the physical sense and reduce the labour force. Under purely free enterprise the industries' labour forces might have declined more rapidly still, but it is not true that they have failed to decline rapidly by national or international standards. Anyway, the pure free enterprise of economic theory exists in few industries in few countries. If the coal industry had remained in private hands it would still have had to be subsidised, and there would have been very strong calls to keep so-called uneconomic pits in existence for social reasons. At the present time, although the Conservative Party is opposed on ideological grounds both to nationalisation and to state subsidy of private enterprise, in specific cases it advocates the use of public funds to preserve particular firms in aircraft manufacture, motor vehicle manufacture, and certain enterprises in the defence field.

Other arguments in favour of nationalisation may be mentioned briefly. A curious one popular 50 or more years ago is that employees had a bias on moral grounds against working for private enterprise. They were happier in the public service and in the public sector. It follows that the costs of operation of public enterprises would be lower since they could pay lower salaries than private firms. A second argument concerns industries where inspection is of significance. If they were in private operation, a public inspectorate would have to be set up, adding to their costs; with public operation, the inspection function can be built into the concerns themselves. It is suggested that various sanitation operations come into this category.

At the present time an important argument concerns the role of worker participation in particular enterprises and labour relations generally. It used to be believed 30 years ago that labour relations would be improved enormously if industries were nationalised. Industries such as coal mining were nationalised partly to please the miners. Today, while it is true that nationalised industries take a leading role in improving labour relations, no one could argue that their labour relations are overwhelmingly good or superior to all private enterprise. Similarly, worker participation, while it may be easier in nationalised industries, is not incompatible with private enterprise.

To summarise at this point, there is a need for state interference, for anti-monopoly purposes, to maintain standards, to deal with external economies and diseconomies, to improve the adjustment mechanism of the economic system, to take risks which private enterprise wishes to avoid, and to improve labour relations. These together comprise an explanation of why nationalisation occurs or may be justified. Equally, in almost all cases alternative measures exist, making it a matter of judgement and ideology why a particular solution is or is not adopted.

What is interesting as far as the UK is concerned is that it used to be assumed that public ownership implied public monopoly. The great nationalised industries of Britain are, indeed, as close to being monopolies within their technical field of operation as they could be; but in the economic sense of monopoly — to mean the absence of competition or close substitutes — most are not monopolies at all. The National Coal Board may have a monopoly of the production of coal, but in relevant markets it is not coal that matters but fuels. The coal industry, therefore, is subject to strong competition, frequently from other nationalised industries, namely gas and electricity, but also from private enterprise, i.e. oil. Similarly, the electricity and gas industries and the railways may be technical monopolies, but they are not insulated from real competition.

Future nationalisation may not be entirely in the form of technical monopoly. The extension of public enterprise may be by the purchase of individual firms, especially those in economic difficulties. The projected National Enterprise Board must be seen partly as a means of extending public ownership and, therefore, of nationalisation, but without taking over the whole of an industry. It may even be that the aircraft industry, which is on the agenda for nationalisation, will finish up partially in public ownership but not wholly.

It is also worth noting that partial public ownership may itself mean one of two things; the complete public ownership of a firm within an industry, leaving the remaining part of the industry in private hands; or the purchase of part of a firm or industry by the government, leaving the remainder in private hands. It may be thought that the latter procedure, of public shareholding, is not a full form of nationalisation, but the acquisition of some of a firm's equity is surely an extension of public ownership.

The Operation and Efficiency of the Nationalised Industries

I turn now to the problem of the efficient operation of the nationalised industries. Table 1 provides figures of the scale of investment and the gross trading surpluses of the public corporations.

There are two points of interest here. Firstly, the sheer size of the public corporations, of which the nationalised industries comprise

Table 1.

	Gross trading surplus £m	(a)÷ Gross revenue %	(a)÷net capital stock %	Gross investment at 1970 £m	(d)÷total investment %	(d)÷total public sector investment %
	(a)	(b)	(c)	(d)	(e)	(f)
1963	881	18·9	8·2	1,500	20·4	52
1964	969	19·6	8·2	1,816	19·8	54
1965	1,037	19·8	8·0	1,864	20·1	54
1966	1,094	20·0	7·8	2,000	21·2	54
1967	1,187	19·4	7·2	2,267	22·3	54
1968	1,419	20·0	7·8	2,397	20·0	57
1969	1,515	19·8	7·7	2,397	17·5	60
1970	1,521	18·2	6·9	2,427	18·1	59
1971	1,604	17·8	6·4	2,370	18·2	59
1972	1,805	18·2	6·4	2,402	15·5	62
1973	2,164	19·2	6·6	2,389	14·6	61

by far the largest part, is indicated by the scale of their investment activity. Although as a share of national investment this has fallen somewhat over the past decade, it still comprises 15% of the total and in 1967 was over 20%. Within the public sector it has risen from about 50% to about 60%. Secondly, the industries earn a gross trading surplus of some magnitude equal to approximately one-fifth of their gross revenues. As a ratio of their net capital stock the figure has fallen from 8.2% in 1963 to 6.6% in 1973. A comparable figure for the private sector would be about 20%. It would be a mistake, however, to infer from the declining ratio of gross surplus to net capital stock that efficiency was falling. The industries' capital stock expanded pretty rapidly at the beginning of the period in accord with the National Plan. Demand did not expand so rapidly, and to support anti-inflation policy prices were being held back by the end of the period.

What is clear is that because of their size, their level of investment and their central position in the economy, the operation of the nationalised industries is of primary importance to the performance of the economy as a whole. But the establishment of objectives for nationalised industries or criteria for measuring their performance is no easy matter. While private industry has the relatively unambiguous objective of maximising the return on its owners' capital, the fact that the nationalised industries have been transferred from private into public ownership is indicative of the belief that the profit motive is an unsatisfactory guide for these industries. The simple answer to the question "How should the nationalised industries conduct their affairs?" is that they should operate in the public interest by seeking to maximise their contribution to social welfare. Such an objective is so vague as to be useless and could be used as a justification for almost any action by a nationalised industry — including gross inefficiency. In a democratic society the direction of the public interest can only be interpreted by our political representatives, yet the detailed control by government over the affairs of the nationalised industries has been implicitly rejected in the organisational structure of public corporations, which is designed to give considerable autonomy to the board of directors.

Up to 1960 government policy showed considerable uncertainty as to the appropriate objectives of public enterprise and the optimal degree of ministerial control. Since then, however, some measure of reconciliation has been achieved between the conflicting objectives of government's need to interpret the meaning of the public interest and the desirability of autonomy for the nationalised industries in their day to day operation, through the laying down by government of general criteria for their conduct. Of considerable importance has been the investment and pricing policies of the nationalised industries and government policy towards these has been expressed most clearly in two White Papers (HMSO 1961, HMSO 1967). Initially, the concern was with the problem of financing the industries' investment, and the desire to meet more of this from the trading surplus rather than from the budget and central government borrowing. Rapidly, however, horizons were widened to include incentives to managerial efficiency and considerations of overall resource allocation. A major publication by the House of Commons Select Committee on Nationalised Industries *Ministerial Control of the Nationalised Industries 1967-68* (1968) stressed the need for explicit rational control by the central government leading to efficient resource allocation. It was in favour of broad ground rules being set by the government, within which the industries would operate while not being subject to day-to-day *ad hoc* interference from on high.

About the time this report was published, it looked as if the nationalised industries were entering a new era of efficiency and enterprise. Since then there has been a degree of backsliding so that now managerial morale is lower than it might be, and microeconomic considerations are not being given the priority they deserve.

Pricing Policy of Nationalised Industries

Let us now turn explicitly to the economics of pricing. Even before the great wave of nationalisation in 1945, there was considerable debate about what the correct pricing policies for nationalised industries should be. One point of view was that they should engage in average cost pricing; namely, that they should bring in sufficient revenue just to cover their costs. A different point of view, related to optimisation theory and welfare economics, was that they should engage in marginal cost pricing policies. Many industries did for a long time pursue policies of average cost pricing, especially as the nationalisation acts imposed the duty on Boards that, taking one year with another, they should break even. Most economists, however, regarded this as an accountant's criterion and could see no reason why it should be met.

It is not well founded in welfare economics. There is also the question of whether average cost pricing policies are to mean simply that the total revenue of the whole organisation should equal its total cost, or whether the rule should be applied to every good and service produced by the particular industry. The legislation threw no light on this, and there was little justification within economics why the organisation should break even. It was perfectly possible for total revenue to equal total cost, but for the industry to earn surpluses on some activities and make deficits on others. One of the early problems that worried students of the nationalised industries, quite apart from the marginal cost controversy, was the justification of the phenomenon of 'cross-subsidisation'. In the case of the railways, for example, what reason was there for profitable lines in certain areas to subsidise unprofitable lines in other areas? In the coal industry certain sorts of coal were easily mined and were much demanded. Did it make sense to earn profits on those in order to subsidise other coal from difficult mines which was not as much demanded?

Another problem that arose in connection with average cost pricing (although it applied equally to marginal cost pricing) concerned the definition of cost. Many of the advocates of average cost pricing assumed that these would be the costs as reported in the accounts of the nationalised industries, but this was not something that economists could make sense of. Much of the capital in the accounts was valued at original cost or purchase price rather than replacement cost. The interest element was at the rate of interest that the industry had contracted to pay at a given date. That particular rate itself could be regarded as arbitrary, not necessarily reflecting the value of capital at the time of the investment decision or at the time that the accounts were being constructed. Even current costs may not be costs in an economic sense. If, for example, some workers would be unemployed if dismissed by the industry, it could be argued that their wages were greater than the true cost of employing them and that the accounts of the firm exaggerated its costs.

An argument in favour of average cost pricing was that if an industry failed to balance its books by taking in sufficient revenue, other means would have to be found to make up the difference. A deficit in the nationalised industries would require an offsetting surplus elsewhere in the system. This would be generated by business or personal savings, or taxation would have to be raised. If we were exactly at full employment, a move towards a deficit in a nationalised industry would not differ from a deficit in the ordinary accounts of the central government. It would be expansionary in a macroeconomic sense and, if demand inflation were to be avoided, some other item of expenditure would have to be reduced or taxes increased. Of course, this does not mean that the correct policy for the nationalised industries would be to break even. It would be perfectly possible to argue that welfare would be maximised by a deficit in a nationalised industry, taxation being higher than it otherwise would be. Anyway, we might not be at full employment equilibrium with the nationalised industries just balancing their books. The appropriate form of deficit finance to achieve full employment might then be in those industries rather than in the budget as usually conceived.

Altogether, a policy of simple breaking even requires rather more justification than saying that it is obvious that that is what nationalised industries ought to do; but, once the policy of average cost pricing is brought into question, all sorts of difficulties arise and one is immediately led to consider what the general principles of pricing policy ought to be.

The correct pricing policy is one which maximises welfare. The problem is then to lay down some welfare criteria and see what pricing policy follows from them. In essence the criteria that the economist has applied in deriving the marginal cost pricing rule assume that, broadly speaking, preferences of individuals as reflected in demand for goods and services and supply of factors of production are a correct basis for the measurement of welfare. He then discusses whether demands for and supplies of goods and services at prices quoted in the market are correct measures of those preferences and, therefore, of welfare. If they are, namely if demand at the market price is a correct measure of marginal benefit received, and if supply at the market price is a correct measure of marginal benefit forgone, then it follows that welfare is maximised when demand equals supply; the supply curve of the firm in competitive conditions being its marginal cost curve. To maximise welfare, therefore, it follows that the nationalised industry should act as though it were a perfectly competitive firm, treating its marginal cost curve as its supply curve and pricing at marginal cost for every level of output. Figure 1 explains the optimality of the marginal cost pricing rule.

The line DD represents the consumers' demand schedule for the output of a nationalised industry. It shows the price that consumers are willing to pay for different quantities of the product, the price equalling the additional benefit derived from the final unit of the product consumed (the marginal utility). The marginal cost schedule MC shows the addition to total cost of extra units of output. The addition to total welfare resulting from the production of an extra unit of output X is the difference between marginal benefit and marginal cost — the vertical distance AB. The optimal output of the product occurs where, for the last unit of production, marginal cost just equals marginal

Figure 1.

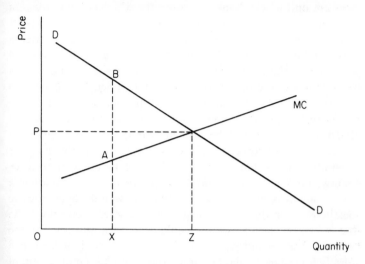

benefit — an output of Z. If the nationalised industry prices at marginal cost for every level of output, MC is its supply schedule and equilibrium in the market is reached at a price of P and an output of Z — the welfare maximising output.

There are, however, many reasons why neither the demand curve nor the supply curve are correct measures of marginal benefits received or marginal costs forgone. Firstly, there are phenomena of external economies and diseconomies. In the production, sale and consumption of many goods and services benefits may be received by people who do not pay for them, or costs incurred by those who are not compensated for them. The list of possible external economies and diseconomies which are not dealt with through the market is enormous. Included would be the penalties of noise, dirt and other consequences of industrial and commercial activity. It has been argued that the marginal cost of a railway line as measured by British Rail is less than its marginal social cost, because account is not taken of the suffering of people who live near the railway. A similar and more pertinent comment could be made about the marginal costs of British Airways. It might be considered a little more difficult to think up examples of external economies in the case of the nationalised industries. A possible example is the installation of telephones; the more people there are on the telephone, the more the whole community gain who wish to communicate by telephone.

A second modification of ordinary marginal cost pricing policies requires the identification of the particular consumers and producers of the product and the recognition that attention may be paid more to the welfare of some than to others. An increase in the price of electricity falls to a disproportionate extent on the poorer sections of the community. If there were no other way of offsetting this, it could be argued that the demand curve for electricity did not correctly reflect social welfare, but that a higher demand curve would. Similarly, if some of the labour force employed in the industry would be permanently out of a job at a lower scale of operation, the supply curve would exaggerate the social cost of production of the goods or services in question. The first of these considerations would lead to a subsidy for the product. The second might do the same, or it might lead to a subsidy for the particular factor of production, the employment of which was considered socially advantageous. In both cases modification of the simple nationalised industry pricing rules would depend on whether there were other means of achieving the desired social objective. In other words, to go back to the desirability of subsidising electricity for poor people, it might be easier to do this directly by the issue of electricity vouchers or special adjustments to their electricity bills. Alternatively, the objective might not be to subsidise their electricity but to subsidise them more generally, by raising various transfer payments such as old age pensions, social security, etc.

Another modification of simple marginal cost pricing policy arises from so-called second best considerations. Ignoring both external economies and diseconomies and distributional aspects of the problem, it could still happen that demand did not represent marginal social benefits and supply marginal social costs, because of distortions elsewhere in the economy. The obvious example concerns the existence of monopoly pricing policies. A nationalised industry may use as an input a commodity produced by a monopoly in the private sector. Included in its price would be an element of monopoly profit which was not a true social cost. It could then be argued that public enterprise ought to adjust its own costs downwards to allow for this.

Let us consider what happens if the industry in question increases its output by one marginal unit: the price it charges will measure the resulting increase in benefit. It will require resources to an extent measured by marginal costs, so that some other industry's output contracts by this amount divided by its marginal cost. The value of the contraction in the other industry's output is obtained by multiplying this quantity by its price. There will be an increase in net benefit as long as the price charged by the first industry exceeds the value lost, as given by the formula just described. Thus, the welfare maximising formula would be price equal to marginal cost, divided by marginal cost in the other industry times price in the other industry. It can then easily be seen that if price elsewhere exceeds marginal cost (because, for example, of the exercise of monopoly power), then the correct pricing policy would be for price to exceed marginal cost in the nationalised industry. More generally, it could be stated that price in the nationalised industry should be related to marginal cost by a formula which reflects the extent to which prices in other industries are related to marginal costs. An approximation then would be to allow prices to exceed marginal costs by the average extent to which they exceed marginal costs in the economy at large. A better approximation would be for price to exceed marginal cost to an extent determined by the relationship between price and marginal cost in industries closely related to the nationalised industry.

It is worth remarking that, although all the foregoing discussion modifies the marginal cost pricing rule, it does not make the case for average cost pricing. Rather, what it amounts to is the proposition that price should be related to marginal cost. The second-best procedure also throws some light on the question of public sector surpluses and deficits. If a marginal cost pricing policy were to lead to the industry being in deficit or to producing a smaller surplus than would otherwise be the case, its marginal costs can be adjusted to take into account the way in which other prices and taxes would have to change. If, for example, an industry engaged in a marginal cost pricing policy caused the government to have to raise some indirect taxes, the welfare loss due to those indirect tax changes must itself be included in the marginal cost pricing rule.

Criteria for investment decisions can be similarly derived from basic premises concerning social welfare, the principle being that an investment project is worth doing if it increases the present discounted value of social welfare. A particular problem in establishing investment criteria for nationalised industries is determining the optimal rate of discount to apply to their future returns. As in the case of the marginal cost pricing rule, simple investment rules become much more complex once the issues of externalities, income distribution and second-best are raised.

Despite their deficiencies, however, the use of general operating rules such as marginal cost pricing and the test discount rate for investment evaluation are valuable, since they allow the nationalised industries more freedom to use their commercial judgement while still being subject to overall central control. Ministers remain able to bring social and other non-commercial considerations to bear, but should do this explicitly and, if possible, on the basis of cost-benefit appraisal. The extent of progress along this path of rationalisation of control procedures is difficult to judge. While the White Papers of 1961 and 1967 clearly outlined general operating rules for the nationalised industries, in recent years departures from these rules have been increasingly frequent, as concern over inflation and unemployment has encouraged increasing *ad hoc* intervention by Ministers in the decision making by nationalised industry Boards. Evidence is provided in the most recent report of the Select Committee on Nationalised Industries (HMSO 1974); a relevant concluding quotation is the following: "To sum up, your Committee believe that the evidence which has been presented to them shows that in the last five years the impetus towards a more rational control of the nationalised industries has tended to decrease. Departments, including the Treasury, have paid insufficient attention to the more general problems of the industries. Your committee are, therefore, led to the conclusion that government has been far from successful in its self-imposed role, as set out in the 1961 and 1967 White Papers and considered by your committee's predecessors, of exercising its control publicly and according to well-defined ground rules, without interfering with the management functions of the industries themselves." (para. 108.)

References

Schumpeter, J. A., *Capitalism, Socialism and Democracy,* Harper & Row 1942.

House of Commons Select Committee on Nationalised Industries, *Capital Investment Procedures 1973-74*, HMSO 1974.

House of Commons Select Committee on Nationalised Industries, *Ministerial Control of the Nationalised Industries*, HMSO 1968.

Nationalised Industries: A Review of Economic and Financial Objectives, Cmnd 3437, HMSO 1967.

The Financial and Economic Obligations of the Nationalised Industries, Cmnd 1337, HMSO 1961.

4. The economics of agricultural policy

DAVID COLMAN and JOHN McINERNEY
Senior Lecturers in Agricultural Economics,
University of Manchester

Introduction

In the eyes of many people, farming is a rather unique kind of
production process. With land as its dominant input, its
dependence on biological processes and climatic factors in
production, and the variety and widespread geographical
distribution of its producing units, agriculture seems to have little
in common with what is generally termed 'industry'. However, all
industries have their own special characteristics, and from the
overall standpoint of national economic policy, there is really no
fundamental distinction between that sector of the economy which
is concerned with food production and those such as the
manufacturing, service or other sectors. All consume some
proportion of the nation's limited resources of land, labour and
capital, make a particular contribution to GNP in the economy,
and generate an income for a certain section of the community.[1]
With continuing economic growth and development, and changes
in incomes, tastes and technology, all sectors are subject to a series
of economic pressures which demand a continual adjustment in
the level and pattern of their outputs and resource inputs, and in

---

[1] Indeed, even though employing less than 3% of the working population,
agriculture ranks as one of the largest single industries in the UK, having an annual
gross output of some £4,000m.

their whole structure of production. Agriculture is no exception to this rule, and societies at all stages of economic development have found it desirable to establish specific policies towards the agricultural sector for either (or both) of two reasons: (a) to mould and direct these adjustments along desired lines so that they follow some acceptable equilibrium progression for the economy as a whole, and (b) to correct or modify some of the side effects that result from these changes. Partly because of the central importance of food supplies to a nation's existence, partly because of a traditional political interest that agriculture retains and partly because of the special characteristics of agricultural production and the technical and social problems that are created in the adjustment process, questions of agricultural policy have come to adopt a particular significance which justifies them as a specific subject of study.

It is the object in this chapter to identify those economic pressures that impinge on the agricultural sectors of both developed and developing nations, to examine their effects, and to analyse the various policy objectives that governments assume and the instruments they adopt in response to these pressures. The free market for agricultural products, both nationally and internationally, is usually viewed as closely approximating the classic model of perfect competition and it will be seen that a great deal of understanding of the economics of agriculture can be generated merely by the use of elementary demand-supply analysis.

The Background to Contemporary UK Agricultural Policies

The situation in the agricultural sector has long been an issue of interest to national governments, and remains so today — as witnessed by the international concern over world food supplies, the thrust towards economic change in the predominantly agricultural Third World, the recent controversies over farm policy in the EEC, and the political significance of the rising level of food prices in an era of severe inflation.

In the UK the main direction of current agricultural policies was determined at the end of the Second World War, but has evolved from measures instituted long before that time and still retains elements originating in the 1920's and 30's. From the Repeal of the Corn Laws in 1846, British agriculture developed in an era of free trade and growing industrialisation, which resulted in a steady erosion of its competitive position as the North American and Australasian continents developed as sources of imported food. A collapse of farm prices and incomes after the 1914-18 war resulted in a mild acceptance of government responsibility to subsidise farmers, which gathered strength with the depression of the 1930's. During that period tariffs and quotas were imposed on certain imported commodities, monopsonistic Producer Marketing Boards were established under government sponsorship (of which the Milk Marketing Board is perhaps the now most familiar example) and a range of specific price subsidies were introduced. The outbreak of war in 1939 saw Britain still heavily dependent on imported food and vulnerable to blockade; all food prices were brought directly under the control of the Ministry of Food; farmers were exhorted greatly to expand domestic food supplies, being given assurances about the prices they would receive. In the post-war situation of severe deficit in world food supplies and the weak position of the pound sterling, the Agriculture Act of 1947 formalised the war-time arrangements and made provision for "promoting and maintaining, by the provision of guaranteed prices and assured markets . . . , a stable and efficient agricultural industry capable of producing such part of the nation's food . . . as in the national interest it is desirable to produce in the United Kingdom, and of producing it at minimum prices consistent with proper remuneration and living conditions for farmers and workers in agriculture and an adequate return on capital invested in the industry".

The twin pillars of 'stability' and 'efficiency' were fostered by the provision of free advisory services, production grants for key inputs, and an annual Price Review at which the government and farmers' representatives negotiated guaranteed prices for a wide range of products for the year ahead. Further Agriculture Acts since that time, while still subscribing to the aims of a stable and efficient agriculture with proper remuneration for farmers, have seen the emphasis shift gradually away from direct support for farmers' incomes, first towards greater flexibility in domestic price and supply management, and later more towards engendering the kind of desirable technological and structural change that would move the agricultural sector in the direction of adjustment to its long run equilibrium position in the economy. More recently, Britain's membership of the European Community has required a further and marked change in the style of its agricultural policies, from farm income support via Exchequer payments to price support through market intervention. The workings of the various policy instruments will be analysed later in the chapter.

The Characteristics of Agriculture which Shape Agricultural Policy

Since food is one of the main basic necessities for human existence, the earliest forms of economic activity tend to be centred around agricultural production. In the process of economic growth and development, however, other industries become established and the emphasis in economic life progressively moves away from the agricultural sector towards first the industrial and later the service sectors of the economy. Not all national economies follow an identical route in this direction though and there are some exceptions to the general pattern: Denmark and New Zealand for instance are 'developed' economies which are also heavily dependent in international trade on their highly productive agricultural sectors.

The essential determinants of this basic pattern of change can be summarised in terms of the income elasticity of demand for agricultural products. At very low levels of income, which can only support biological subsistence, the income elasticity of demand for food is close to unity and any rise in income is largely spent on food to effect an improvement in the diet. As per capita incomes rise above subsistence, enabling a higher level and progressively more varied pattern of consumption, the income elasticity of demand for food inevitably falls, until eventually it approaches zero in the most affluent sections of the community.[2] This occurs because

---

[2]In the UK the income elasticity for all food products taken together is now in the region of 0.2.

there is a limit to consumers' capacity and willingness to consume food, and in consequence the rate of increase in demand for food products in industrial nations falls over time until it approaches the rate of population growth. Once basic food demands have been met, additional income will be increasingly spent on products from the industrial and service sectors of the economy — clothing, housing, consumer goods and services, and leisure, etc. Thus, in the absence of any direct interference by government, agriculture is steadily being 'pulled' into a new pattern in relation to the rest of the economy, merely by the pressures arising from the continuing process of economic growth.

In the richer societies we must even be careful to distinguish between the demand for 'food' as purchased by the consumer and the demand for the basic output of the farmer. Much of the additional expenditures on food that come with higher incomes represent purchases of an increasing service element in the product — frozen, pre-packaged, processed foods, restaurant meals, etc — which generate income for the food processing and associated service industries, but include no greater component of agricultural output nor income to the farm producer.

This relative decline in the role of agriculture, whether viewed as a necessary condition for economic development or an inevitable consequence of it, is an inexorable process which has given rise to the so-called 'farm problem' characteristic of the advanced economies such as the USA and the UK, and it provides both a social and an economic basis for establishing policies directed specifically at the agricultural sector. For if agriculture's share of the rising national income declines, then the returns to resources in farming will become progressively lower than those prevailing in the rest of the economy; per capita incomes earned by people working in agriculture will steadily fall below the national average and the agricultural population will show a continuing tendency to form a low income group.[3] Clearly the market signals indicate that there should be a shift in resources out of agriculture into the more rapidly expanding areas of consumer demand. The obvious

[3] The current minimum wage rates for agricultural workers are among the lowest in the country.

remedy, of course, is for labour to move out to these expanding sectors of the economy (for the possibility of land use transfers is limited, while the capital inputs can hardly change their use), and to a certain extent this will occur automatically once the earnings differential becomes sufficiently marked to act as a spur. But for two major reasons the state may feel it desirable actively to intervene and mould the long-run agricultural adjustment process, rather than leave it to the uncertain hand of free market forces.

Firstly, if agricultural output is not to decline as a result of losing labour — indeed from society's point of view it needs to grow at least as fast as the rise in population[4] — then some other inputs (specifically capital since the land stock is fixed) must be substituted in its place. But a situation of declining resource returns in agriculture does not provide adequate funds for those farmers who remain in agriculture to adopt more productive technology and to invest in the necessary labour-saving machinery. Given these circumstances, plus a general desire to keep food prices low, governments often pursue policies to encourage the generation, adoption and exploitation of new technologies (new inputs and new production methods), and to foster changes in the size structure of farms in the search for potential economies of scale.

Secondly, the loss of labour must involve farmers as well as farm workers. The progression from a labour-intensive towards a capital-intensive and modern farm sector involves the adoption of relatively large and indivisible capital items — efficient buildings, powerful tractors, larger machinery — which carry with them economies of minimum size. The smaller farms cannot efficiently utilise this technology, and must either gradually disappear for their land to be amalgamated into larger farm units, or their occupiers must find an additional source of income and thereby resort to part-time farming. Since the farm is also the family home and the rural existence a rather specific 'way of life', the occupational transfer completely out of agriculture is especially difficult for the farm family. In consequence, the adjustment of

[4]Note that there is current concern about the situation in various Third World countries, where population has increased faster than food supplies in the last few years.

agricultural labour (and hence other resources) to the changing needs of the economy is a very slow process, with many farmers hanging on in the face of very low incomes and creating a tendency for agriculture to become a depressed sector. The low income situation may become a regional problem of some social importance in those dominantly rural and agriculturally more marginal areas — the poorer farming areas and uplands in Britain for example — where alternative employment opportunities are severely limited. The state often therefore sees a need to involve itself in the agricultural sector for social reasons, much as it does for other disadvantaged groups or depressed regions, in order to cushion the harsh impact of economic forces by supporting the level of farmers' incomes.

Given the approximately perfectly competitive conditions of agricultural production and the inelastic demand for food products, the continual adoption of new technology causes the agricultural supply curve to shift outwards more rapidly than the demand curve; which we have already seen tends to expand slowly over time. The lower food prices which result are beneficial to consumers (and welcomed by governments), but intensify the pressure on the farmer and the need for agricultural adjustment. Indeed, it is arguable that, in countries such as the UK and USA, the mass of consumers have benefited greatly at the expense of the farming community and society appears to accept some responsibility to compensate farmers accordingly. In the face of the prevailing economic pressures too many farmers have attempted to remain in agriculture. But in order to maintain their incomes, these farmers have struggled to obtain funds for investment in the more productive inputs and methods as they became available, thereby accelerating the rate of supply growth. But while for each individual farmer this type of response is both rational and necessary if his real income is to be maintained (or increased), paradoxically the aggregate effect of all farmers adopting new technology may be a worsening of the farm income problem, for the reasons indicated above.

This situation to a greater or lesser extent has characterised the agricultural sectors of developed nations ever since the Second World War. It has only been since 1972, when a combination of political and climatic events combined with certain cyclical phenomena conspired to raise world food prices dramatically, that the underlying theme of low farm prices and incomes has been markedly changed.

There are, however, a variety of other economic and technical characteristics associated with the farm sector that give rise to situations calling for state interference on a more short-run basis. Because of the fact that there are no technical substitutes for food as a component of consumer expenditures, the demand for agricultural products as a whole is relatively price inelastic. In the face of a demand curve of this nature, prices are extremely sensitive to variations in supply — as the most elementary market analysis makes clear. Yet the supply of agricultural output is inherently unstable because of its dependence on the uncontrollable climatic inputs of rain and sunshine in the biological production process. Despite the fact that much technological advance — in the form of irrigation systems, crop harvesting and drying equipment, and measures to control pests and diseases — serves to insulate the farmer from some of the vagaries of nature, the output that is achieved at the end of the production process still may deviate markedly from that which the farmer expected when he made his initial resource allocation plans.

The resulting tendency for agricultural product supply and prices to vary from year to year is disadvantageous both domestically and internationally — as recent experience with grain and livestock prices has shown. For the consumer, whether in a developed or developing nation (but particularly the latter, where food expenditures occupy a high proportion of the household budget), fluctuating food prices automatically bring fluctuations in real income and the need for the adjustment of expenditure patterns. For the farmer, especially one who is a specialist producer in one or two products, unstable prices make forward planning of production hazardous, and represent a disincentive for appropriate investment in productive capacity. Furthermore, a price inelastic demand can bring about the somewhat paradoxical situation whereby farmers' revenues and incomes are lower in years of high output than in the seasons of 'unfavourable' production conditions. Finally, for a developing country whose economic fortunes depend on an exported agricultural commodity, the price fluctuations on world markets resulting from variations in world supply can play havoc with attempts to foster a programme of economic advance.

As well as random variations in agricultural product prices over time, the relatively long lag between resource commitment and saleable output (at least one year for cereal crops, over two years for fat cattle, and up to seven years for certain perennial tree crops) can give rise to cyclical price fluctuations as epitomised in the classic 'cobweb' manner.[5] An initial disequilibrium price, but unrecognised as such, can cause farmers to commit an inappropriate amount of resources to production, with the result that the level of output which ultimately comes on to the market causes price to overshoot equilibrium and arrive at an equally transient level; revision of production plans in the light of this new price again merely serves to establish another disequilibrium market situation, and so the process continues.

This inherent instability in agricultural product prices, both random and cyclical in character, provides yet another focus for government intervention through policies of price or market stabilisation; though whether these policy goals are primarily designed with the well-being of the consumer or the producer in mind is often a debatable point.

Finally, agricultural intervention in the short run may be initiated as a result of international trade considerations. The agricultural policy of one particular nation may well result in a modification of its trading pattern, and this may justifiably stimulate counter measures by the countries with which it trades.

The Choice of Agricultural Policy Objectives and Instruments

The package of agricultural policies pursued by any one nation is typically moulded by a set of forces, not always harmonious. Some of these forces originate from the general characteristics of

---

[5]See for example Lipsey (1971, Chapter 12). The price of beef in the EEC seems currently to be suffering from just such a phenomenon.

agriculture referred to above, and to a greater or lesser extent shape the long-run policies of the majority of nations. These general characteristics are (a) that the agricultural sector declines in importance as nations become wealthier, and (b) that there are inbuilt tendencies for instability in agricultural prices, farm incomes, and the supply of individual commodities. The policies of most countries therefore include some measures to promote the efficient 'adjustment' of the agricultural sector, and some to improve the stability of agricultural markets. Instruments to achieve the first of these objectives typically include incentives or legislation to encourage the migration of labour out of the agricultural sector, the amalgamation of small farms, and also schemes designed to accelerate the development and uptake of improved agricultural technology. A variety of different market intervention instruments, such as minimum import prices and intervention buying, are employed to promote the second general objective of market stability, and such policy devices are in widespread use.

Agricultural policies are also shaped by the specific characteristics of each country's agricultural sector. Perhaps the most significant of these is the size of the agricultural sector relative to that of the economy as a whole. Developing nations such as Bangladesh or Thailand, with more than 80% of their economically active populations engaged in agriculture, are clearly constrained in the type of agricultural policy they can pursue. The revenue requirements of their government programmes must clearly be fulfilled in significant measure by taxing the dominant agricultural sector, thereby ruling out large-scale subsidisation of farmers. It is also obvious that in countries where the agricultural sector is large it is not feasible to adopt an expansionary fiscal policy towards agriculture whilst trying to deflate the economy as a whole; thus in developing countries agricultural policy is controlled by the direction and needs of overall economic management. Another aspect of the size problem is that in poor nations a very large proportion of total personal expenditure is on agricultural products. This creates pressure to keep down the price of foodstuffs and to refrain from policies of encouraging agricultural expansion via higher product prices. Instead it leads to expansionary policies based upon the

development of cheaper agricultural inputs, improved
management abilities, and more efficient marketing.

Because of the relatively small size of the agricultural sector in
the UK and other industrial nations, agricultural policy is freed
from many of the constraints operating in poorer countries. It is,
for example, feasible to subsidise farm incomes if thought
desirable, because the cost of such support is relatively minor to
the taxpayers or consumers who foot the bill. It is also possible for
rich countries to pursue agricultural policy to some extent
independently of the economic policy directed to other sectors of
the economy. In the UK, for instance, it has often been argued —
and also practised, for example in 1968 (HMSO 1968)—that in
balance of payments crises, when general deflation of the economy
was considered desirable, agriculture should have increased
Exchequer support to expand output and hence reduce imports.

This freedom in agricultural policy matters was important to the
post-1930 development of farm support policies in North America
and Western Europe. For reasons enunciated later, the economic
justifications for such policies are unconvincing, and their
development owes much to local political considerations. This
primacy of political over economic considerations is obviously
favoured where agriculture is a small sector of the economy.

While the list of special considerations influencing agricultural
policy could be extended to a great length to include such factors
as location, climate and the pattern of agricultural trade, it will be
more instructive to concentrate on a summary of major objectives
of agricultural policy and the main types of measures for achieving
them. Four principal aims of agricultural policy can be discerned.[6]
These are: to secure orderly resource *adjustment*; to *stabilise* farm
prices, incomes and supply; to *support* farmers' incomes; and to
tax away resources from agriculture for national development.
Perhaps we should also add a fifth objective, that of national
agricultural self-sufficiency, which has received powerful political
support in such countries as the UK and Japan.

---

[6]A slightly different taxonomy of major objectives is presented by Johnson
(1973, p.29). This book provides a challenging review of current problems of
agricultural policy.

During the post-war period developed industrial countries, including the UK, have consistently pursued policies to support farm incomes. This has involved the use of a variety of product market intervention measures. Since all of these measures, as indicated in the next section, involve establishing floor prices in excess of free market prices, producer prices have been largely determined by administrative actions rather than by market forces. Hence pursuit of income support objectives has automatically brought about a degree of price and income stabilisation. The fourth objective mentioned above, the heavy taxation of agriculture, is clearly inconsistent with income support policies and is not therefore an element of agricultural policy in industrialised nations. The income support objective also conflicts with that of orderly resource adjustment, but because of the inevitability and importance of agricultural adjustment, various measures to encourage rational adjustment are present in the policy packages of the UK, Western Europe, North America and Japan. These include retirement grants for elderly farmers, retraining grants for agricultural workers, small farm amalgamation schemes, and subsidies on certain inputs. The effectiveness of these measures is, however, greatly restricted by the effect of income support policies which artificially raise all farm incomes, including those of the least efficient, thus diluting the pressures for adjustment at the margin.

As previously indicated, the priorities of the poorer nations are different, and the one policy which is virtually ruled out is that of general income support, although selective producer price support for key crops is frequently undertaken. The other three major objectives are capable of being operated simultaneously. In countries such as those in Africa, where crop taxation has been pursued through state established monopsonies (Marketing Boards), a price stabilising element has been introduced through the expedient of setting producer prices which do not yield any tax revenues in the very worst years; indeed in such years a subsidy may be paid. However, the major aim of policy in developing countries has been the pursuit of rapid agricultural adjustment and improved efficiency. Great emphasis in poorer nations is devoted to encouraging the use of new inputs and the adoption of new technology to increase yields and reduce production costs.

Policy measures include the financing of fertiliser factories and irrigation schemes and the establishment of agricultural research and training centres and free advisory services to farmers.

Analysis of the Operation of Major Policy Instruments

From the preceding discussion it will have become apparent that there are three major classes of agricultural policy instruments: product market intervention measures; factor market intervention measures; and institutional reform. Attention in this section will focus on analysis of the operation of the most important amongst the first two sets of measures, using the procedures of elementary supply and demand analysis. The virtue of this approach is that it readily uncovers important issues about the choice of policy instruments, and it has shed much light on such controversies as the UK's replacement of Deficiency Payment Schemes by the European Community's Common Agricultural Policy (CAP)[7] as the means of farm income support. We will therefore start the analysis with a consideration of the major product market intervention measures.

Product Market Intervention Policies

Deficiency Payments. The essence of the Deficiency Payment Schemes, as operated by the UK in the post-1930 period, is that at an Annual Review the government decides upon *minimum average prices* which farmers should receive for their produce in the following year. These guaranteed prices have almost invariably been established at levels in excess of those at which imports were expected to be available. They have therefore been designed to increase farmers' incomes above levels which would occur in the absence of the policy, and have required continuous government subsidies in the form of deficiency payments equal to the difference between guaranteed prices and market prices.

The effects of such a policy are indicated by figure 1. If we

[7]See for example Josling (1970) and (1972).

Figure 1.

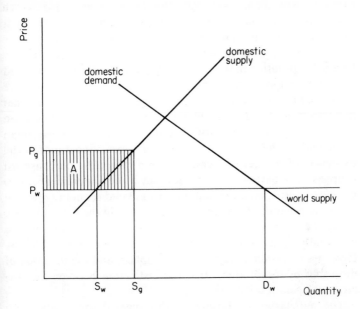

assume that there is an infinitely elastic supply of a particular commodity on the world market at price P_w, the establishment of a guaranteed price of P_g would result in domestic supply increasing by an amount $S_g - S_w$. Because domestic supply can only be sold at P_w in competition with imported supplies, the additional domestic production has the effect of reducing imports by the same amount, but leaves unchanged the price paid and quantity consumed by households at P_w and D_w respectively. The shaded area A represents a transfer payment (subsidy) from taxpayers via the Exchequer to domestic producers.

Note that it would be possible to employ deficiency payment schemes in such a way that they play a strong price stabilisation role, but a much weaker income support role than they have in recent British experience. This could be accomplished by setting guaranteed prices in line with expected average world market prices, so that deficiency payments would not be required in years of average or above average price.

Intervention buying and buffer stock schemes. These are formally equivalent, although the terms have come to be associated with different objectives for which the basic instrument can be used. The term intervention buying is associated with the intervention agencies under the CAP and with the Commodity Credit Corporation in the USA − organisations which have acted largely to support farm prices and incomes, and which are subsidised in their operations. Buffer stock schemes on the other hand are considered in the literature as 'pure' price stabilisation instruments which are self-financed in the long run (Bateman 1965, Duloy 1966). The essence of both types of operation is the existence of an agency which is empowered to purchase all supplies of a particular commodity at a pre-announced (*floor*) price. It is clear, on reflection, that in a closed economy produce will only generally be offered to the agency in the event of there being an excess of domestic supply over demand at the intervention price. It is from the frequency of intervention buying, the types of produce to which it is applied, and the methods of disposing of the produce, that the distinction between the two types of operation has arisen.

The purchasing operations of this type of organisation are depicted in figure 2, in which a hypothetical agency is empowered to purchase any amount of a commodity at a floor price P_i. The agency thus creates a perfectly elastic demand curve at P_i, so that the total demand curve facing farmers becomes the sum of the normal domestic demand curve and the agency's demand curve; this is shown as the curve XYZ. At the the intervention price the agency can expect to be offered the quantity $D_i − D_d$. It will be appreciated that, if intervention prices are fixed so that intervention purchases are made in the majority of years, both domestic demand and imports will be less over time than they otherwise would be, while domestic supply and exports will be greater. In figure 2 an export (stored) surplus of $D_i − D_d$ is seen to be created, domestic demand is reduced by $D_m − D_d$, and domestic supply increased by $D_i − D_m$. In comparison with the free market pricing situation, farmers' net incomes improve by the amounts in the shaded areas B + C + D. It will similarly be appreciated that continuous intervention involves a cost to consumers who have to pay the higher price P_i instead of the equilibrium price P_m; in figure

Figure 2.

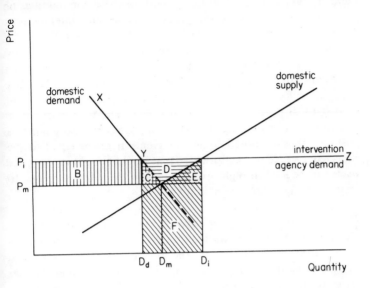

2 consumers are shown as losing consumer surplus B + C . This also creates a liability to the Exchequer, since the costs C + D + E + F of purchasing produce into intervention may not be fully recoverable from later sales of the stored commodity.

In practice intervention agencies do not operate in closed economies, and for intervention prices to exceed market prices in an open economy implies that the intervention price exceeds the world market price. In this situation it may be necessary to restrain traders from importing grain at world prices in order to sell it to the intervention agency at the higher price P_i. Under the CAP this is achieved by imposing variable import levies (see below) with threshold prices set above P_i.

The more serious problem of intervention agencies concerns the disposal of the purchased produce. One alternative as practised by the US during the 1950's and 1960's is to allocate surpluses as food aid to developing countries. Another alternative is for the agency to sell off the produce at the low prevailing world price, thus incurring trading losses. In the case of perishable commodities this solution is inevitable as the EEC has recently discovered with its 'butter and beef mountains'. The EEC has been forced to subsidise the disposal of large quantities of both of these commodities at prices well below those at which they were taken into intervention. Trading losses of this type are also inevitable with non-perishable commodities when income support policies are pursued by persistently setting intervention prices above world prices. This situation arose with wheat in the European Community of the Six in the late 1960's, when grain export subsidies (restitutions) were needed to dispose of intervention stocks. The theoretical price stabilising buffer stock agency is not supposed to get caught in this position. It is supposed to set intervention prices equal to the expected average market price, so that stocks bought in low price years can be sold in high price years with the price gain used to finance storage and administrative costs.

Taxes and Subsidies on Agricultural Trade. Where countries are involved in international agricultural trade the imposition of taxes or payment of subsidies on the traded produce provides a straightforward means of causing domestic and international prices to diverge. Such divergence may be created in pursuit of income support and/or price stabilisation objectives.

Two major instruments of this type are employed under the CAP, with which British policy may be fully integrated by 1978. One of these instruments is the imposition of import levies, which operate to raise domestic prices above international levels for commodities of which the country would be a net importer at the international price. The second is the granting of export subsidies, employed by the USA as well as the CAP, which achieves basically the same outcome as import levies or tariffs, but for commodities of which the country is a net exporter at the protected domestic price.

Under CAP import levy schemes, as shown in figure 3, a threshold price is fixed[8] below which no imported produce is allowed to enter the country.[9] This threshold price P_t is enforced by charging levies to importers, the amount of the levy being varied depending upon the desired level of price support. Because

[8]The threshold price is linked to a domestic 'target' price for the product concerned.

Figure 3.

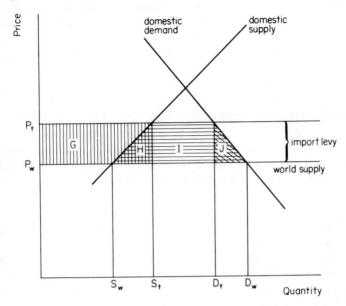

importers cannot afford to charge consumers less than P_t for their product, this becomes the domestic market price in net importing situations. As with the guaranteed price and intervention buying policies, pushing the price above P_w increases domestic supply and thereby reduces import demand by a similar amount. There are, however, a number of effects which import levy policies share with intervention buying and export subsidy policies, but not with guaranteed prices for producers. These are that consumers are forced to pay P_t rather than the lower free market price P_w, which results in a cut-back in demand from D_w to D_t and an equivalent further reduction in imports. It also causes a reduction in consumer surplus, represented by shaded areas $G + H + I + J$ in figure 3. It is because of these various effects that import levy and

---

[9]With this method the levy varies inversely with movements in the world price level, and is known as a variable levy. More common in international trade are constant absolute or proportionate value tariffs or levies. The basic analysis in figure 3 is applicable to all types of tariffs or levies.

intervention buying schemes for supporting agricultural prices are considered more damaging to the interests of domestic consumers and overseas producers than guaranteed price policies through deficiency payments. To domestic producers the choice of policy is not so important, as under each they can obtain the same net income transfer, shown for the import levy scheme as shaded areas $G + H$ in figure 3. The one group who in abstract clearly benefit from import levy or tariff schemes are taxpayers, for as shown in figure 3 the government receives revenues equal to shaded area I for the levy on imports $D_t - S_t$. This is not so for the British taxpayer under the CAP, however, since 90% of all revenues from food imports into the UK are transferred to the Agricultural Fund of the EEC and not retained by the British Exchequer.

Export subsidy schemes have almost identical effects to import levies, except from the point of view of the taxpayer, who has, as shown in figure 4, to bear a subsidy cost represented by the shaded areas $L+M+N$. The effect of paying this subsidy is that exporters continue to export home-produced output until the domestic price rises to the level of the world price plus unit subsidy. Thus as with import levies, domestic prices are forced upwards, stimulating additional output (with a consequent increase in net farm incomes of $K+L+M$), domestic demand is reduced and the volume of exports increased. Hence domestic consumers again suffer higher prices with a loss of consumer surplus (shown as shaded areas $K+L$), and foreign producers are made to face additional (subsidised) competition in international markets.

Crop Taxation Policies   This type of policy is of particular interest as a classic illustration of the exercise of monopsony power. The usual pattern, as found mainly in developing countries, is for a statutory organisation to be established to which all farmers have to sell their produce. For simplicity let us call such monopsonies Marketing Boards (although in practice not all so-called Marketing Boards have such power). Monopsony Marketing Boards can then employ their power to raise tax revenues for government by paying farmers lower prices than are received by the Boards. This type of policy has been extensively pursued by African Marketing Boards in relation primarily to export crops (Helleiner 1966, Bauer 1971); because of the ease with

Figure 4.

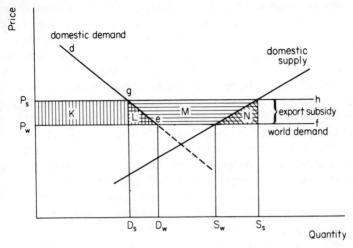

which Boards can be circumvented in the marketing of food crops consumed domestically, monopsony power is difficult (and perhaps undesirable) to enforce for domestic food crops.

Marketing Boards which are sole purchasers of farm produce are also found in Britain in the form of the Milk and Hops Marketing Boards. These organisations, however, use their monopsony position at the farm-gate to establish monopoly power at the wholesale level, which they exploit via discriminatory pricing in different markets (for example the liquid and manufacturing milk markets) to raise producer revenues. The essential characteristic of these Boards is that they use their monopsony powers to exploit monopoly power at a higher stage in the market.

Factor Market Intervention Policies

Input Subsidies. As previously indicated, input subsidisation is a widespread agricultural support measure and is also employed in the form of direct grants and concessionary taxation allowances on capital investments. It is commonly applied to inorganic fertilizer. Unlike intervention in product markets which requires a scheme for each commodity, the subsidisation of, say, fertilizer reduces the production costs of all products which rely directly or indirectly upon fertilizer. It thus makes more sense to analyse the effects of such a policy using the aggregate agricultural supply and demand functions, rather than those for individual commodities.

The main effect of an input subsidy is to shift outwards the agricultural supply curve, that is lower the marginal cost of production curve. If, however, the agricultural land area is fixed, each additional increase in output will require successively larger applications of fertilizer and non-land inputs per acre, with the consequence that the subsidy per unit of output rises with the level of output. This is represented in figure 5 by a non-parallel shift of the supply curve. As can be seen, the effect of the subsidy is to increase domestic supply from S_o to S_s and to reduce imports by the same amount. In the open economy depicted, the subsidy has no effect on consumers since the aggregate product price is unchanged at P_w. Producers too, however, gain to the extent of an addition to net incomes equivalent to the shaded area S, and this is at the expense of taxpayers who have to bear a subsidy cost of S+R.

This static analysis of the benefits of the input subsidisation policy perhaps does it less than justice. One of the characteristic outcomes of subsidising the inputs of the new technology is that it induces a permanent change in technology, and a shift in the supply function which is not eliminated by terminating the subsidy. Product price support policies are not usually considered to exhibit this property; cessation of price support being assumed to cause supply to fall back to near its pre-support position.[10]

Acreage Diversion. This unusual, but well-known, policy was instituted in the USA after intervention buying schemes to support farm prices during the early 1950's had resulted in the accumulation of large surpluses of grain and cotton which were costly to store. Moreover the grain stocks had continued to grow

---

[10] In other words supply curves are usually assumed to be reversible. This, however, may be an unjustified product of static theory. If an increase in price induces investment to support additional output, the supply curve will shift to a new position, and any subsequent fall in price will not cause a reversal along the original curve.

Figure 5.

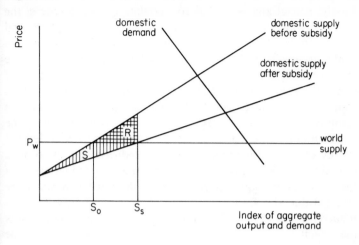

despite large-scale exports at subsidised prices. To combat the increasing public costs associated with the disposal or continuous holding of such stocks, the novel policy was introduced of paying farmers a subsidy for diverting some of their land to 'non-productive' use. Effectively this caused the agricultural supply curve to shift to the left, causing a reduction in the excess of domestic production over commercial demand at the intervention price, and hence reducing the amount of produce offered to the Commodity Credit Corporation. Broadly speaking the policy can be considered to have been neutral from the standpoint of domestic consumers, taxpayers and producers; obviously so in the case of consumers. For producers the diversionary payments compensated for the loss of net income from the sale of produce. From the taxpayers' point of view the costs of handling excess stocks were exchanged for the costs of the diversion subsidy.[11]

General Remarks

A few words are called for on the limitations of the partial,

[11]Perhaps this exchange was not entirely equal. James (1971, p.244) suggests that the early acreage reserve scheme was astronomically expensive.

comparative static supply-demand analysis employed above. Firstly, partial analysis tends to overstate the magnitude of the effects of policy, especially when applied to single agricultural commodities which are both produced and consumed in competition with close substitutes. To illustrate this with a simple example, consider the case of an increase in the guaranteed price of wheat. This, as shown in figure 1, will cause increased domestic supply and increased net farm income. But to the extent that the resources to produce the extra wheat are drawn away from the production of other commodities such as barley or potatoes, the supply of these other products will be reduced, and in an open economy this will cause some decline in net farm income from these sources. For agricultural market systems it can in general be asserted that the 'feedback' effects of the system are such as to reduce the effects of policy upon output, prices and trade below the magnitudes suggested by partial analysis of single commodities.

The other major qualification concerns the static property of the analytical method. Throughout it has been emphasised that agriculture is undergoing a continuous process of adjustment through time. This involves continuously changing farm structure, methods and prices. Clearly, full comprehension of the implications of policy towards this adjustment requires analysis in which inter-temporal change is allowed for. It will have to be left to readers to explore methods of handling this problem of time.

One other problem, which may not have been adequately emphasised so far, is the conflict between price and income stability. Stabilising prices in the face of large year-to-year fluctuations will actually destabilise incomes. In normal conditions, years of low yield and supply would be high price years and *vice versa*. If, therefore, prices are fixed and prevented from *counteracting* changes in supply, incomes will be forced lower in low output years and higher in years of high output. The ability of price stabilising policies to produce long-run agricultural supply stability must, however, be questioned, but the answer needs more complex analysis than is possible here.

Mention was made initially of institutional reform as being the third major arm of agricultural policy. Problems associated with this type of policy are at the interface of economics with the other social sciences, and are not susceptible to the sort of formal analysis applied above to market intervention policies. The effects of market intervention policies do, however, depend upon the type of institutions existing. Pricing policies are clearly only fully effective where well-functioning markets exist. Where efficient markets do not exist, chiefly in underdeveloped countries, policy action is often required to correct this by the setting up of state marketing organisations, small-farmers credit schemes and by the building of physical infra-structure. The thorniest questions of institutional change surround the question of land reform. Some authors argue that in developing countries the potential effects of land reform upon agricultural output and rural welfare exceed those of any alternative policies[12], but the great political problems associated with redistributing land make this as much a political as an economic issue.

Future Directions in Agricultural Policy

The agricultural policies implemented in developed economies over the last three decades have largely been directed at supporting farmers' incomes above the level that would be achieved through the free working of the domestic market in agricultural products. In most cases this results in higher prices facing the consumer — potentially a politically sensitive issue, but one which has not been too noticeable during an era when world food prices were generally low.[13] In addition, these policies can be seen to have directed resources into expanding domestic food production at the expense of cheaper imported supplies.

Inevitably, interference in the process of market price formation results in some net loss of aggregate welfare (as conventionally measured in economic analysis), with different policies having different net social costs. However there are now growing

[12]This is strongly argued by Myrdal (1970, pp.117-124) and also by Griffin (1974, Chapter 8).
[13]Strong arguments were made in favour of the former British 'deficiency payment' scheme as being more consistent with a cheap food policy, and one which was perhaps more socially equitable in that the support costs fell on the taxpayer rather than the consumer.

indications that we may be at something of a turning point in the whole outlook on national agricultural policy, and that in future the richer nations will place progressively less emphasis on domestic farm income support, but concentrate more on the rational restructuring of agriculture. There are several factors conspiring to make this change probable.

Firstly, an increasing volume of evidence is accumulating which suggests that the income support measures that have been most commonly used have been less than fully effective in achieving what would seem to be their prime objective — i.e. protecting the most vulnerable sections of the farming community from the full force of rapid economic changes. Since the total income support received is directly proportional to the level of output, the benefits of the policies are distributed in such a way that the smaller, poorer and less competitive farmers receive proportionately less than the larger, more prosperous and efficient farmers.[14] Consequently the policies appear to be inefficient in supporting those in greatest need, and would seem to operate in direct contradiction to their avowed aims.

In addition to this problem of the inequitable manner in which the income transfers to the agricultural sector are distributed amongst the recipients, there is a very real question as to whether the income transferred actually remains in the farmers' hands. It has been argued that much of the benefit has passed on to those who supply the essential (and increasingly non-agricultural) inputs into agricultural production — and certainly the observed growth in the demand for fertilizers, machinery and other capital resources has been underpinned by agricultural support measures that have been operating over the last 25 years. In particular, it is argued that the prices and rents of agricultural land would have been considerably lower in the absence of agricultural support policies. In other words, the benefits have been capitalized into land values and have to a large extent accrued to agricultural landlords, rather than to the typical tenant farmer. If this is so, of course, it calls into question whether there was any necessity to support agricultural incomes in the first place; for if the recipient

[14]See for example Josling *et al.* (1972).

farmers merely bid up resource prices with these payments, perhaps a fundamental need to augment their disposable income did not really exist.

Furthermore, there would seem to be an essential paradox involved in a policy which, although framed in terms of a recognition that the secular economic pressures on agriculture imply a need for continuing structural adjustment in the sector, then acts to nullify these pressures and impede the progressive transformation of agricultural production. Seen in this light, measures to support low farm incomes seem to be a classic examples of treating the symptoms of the disease rather than its cause.

It is a growing realization of factors such as these that has led to a re-appraisal of the income support policies characteristic of the post-war era. Two more recent and notable events of world-wide significance have added further weight to the questioning of domestic policies which artificially raise food prices. The first is the quadrupling of oil prices and the associated re-alignment of energy costs, which suggests that the costs of food production — especially in the technologically advanced agricultures where production techniques consume high levels of energy inputs through fertilizers, machinery etc. — will necessarily rise dramatically adding greatly to the resource cost of expanded domestic food supplies. Secondly, the acceleration of general price inflation in all Western countries since 1970 has increasingly caused governments to focus special attention on food prices in their attempts to curb inflation. In the United Kingdom, this was revealed in the introduction in 1974 of consumer subsidies on bread and milk with the express objective of holding down retail prices. In a similar vein in 1973/74, the EEC introduced grain export *taxes* in an attempt to hold the domestic grain price below international levels.

The ability of these governments to adjust their policy stance on farm income support has been assisted by the growth in the political power of consumers and some corresponding decline in that of the farm lobby. This latter has always been held to have disproportionate power as a result of the smaller electoral districts found in rural areas, and of the powerful agricultural institutions developed in days when the agricultural population was a larger proportion of the total and national food supplies were a more critical political consideration. It is significant, for instance, that the industrial countries all possess separate Ministries of Agriculture — but not of other industries. It is, however, clear that the political support for agriculture has in some sense weakened, a view supported by the increasing resistance within the EEC to meeting the demands of farmers for higher prices. Paradoxically, this has coincided with a period in which the real need for government support is greater than ever before for certain sections of the agricultural industry — particularly livestock producers.

Possibly the most important factor facilitating the change in policy emphasis has been the run-down in world, and particularly North American, stocks of grain. The large stocks of grain held in the 1950's and 1960's in the USA and Canada provided a buffer against year-to-year variations in grain supplies and they consequently helped stabilise the prices of grain and grain-consuming livestock. The large Asian demand for imported grain following the poor harvests of 1965 and 1966, the emergence of Russia and China as periodic major grain importers, plus the effects of the American acreage diversion programme, have all served to whittle away the large grain stocks held by the world's two main grain exporters. This changed situation has induced a sharp rise in the market price of grain and livestock product prices, and has reduced the pressure by American farmers for more protection. It also encouraged President Nixon to announce that "We must reduce the farmer's dependence on government payments through increased returns from sales of farm products at home and abroad" (Bonnen 1973). It is doubtful if this trend in policy in the USA and Europe will be reversed, even if, as is equally doubtful, the agricultural surpluses of these countries re-emerge in the future at their levels of the last two decades.

References

Bateman, D. L., Buffer Stocks and Producers' Incomes, *Journal of Agricultural Economics*, December 1965.

Bauer, P.T., *Dissent on Development*, Weidenfeld & Nicolson 1971.

Bonnen, James T., Implications for Agricultural Policy, *American Journal of Agricultural Economics*, August 1973.

Duloy, J. H., More on Buffer Stocks and Producers' Incomes, *Journal of Agricultural Economics*, September 1966.

Griffin, K., *The Political Economy of Agrarian Change*, Macmillan 1974.

Helleiner, G. K., *Peasant Agriculture, Government and Economic Growth in Nigeria*, Irwin 1966.

James, P. G., *Agricultural Policy in Wealthy Nations*, Angus & Robertson 1971.

Johnson, D. G., *World Agriculture in Disarray*, Fontana 1973.

Josling, T. E., *Agriculture and Britain's Policy Dilemma*, Thames Essay No. 2, Trade Policy Research Centre 1970.

Josling, T. E. *et al.*, *Burdens and Benefits of Farm Support Policies*, Agricultural Trade Paper No. 1, Trade Policy Research Centre 1972.

Lipsey, R. G., *An Introduction to Positive Economics* (3rd edn), Weidenfeld & Nicolson 1971.

Myrdal, Gunnar, *Challenge to World Poverty*, Allen Lane 1970.

Agriculture Acts 1947 and 1957: Annual Review and Determination of Guarantees, Cmnd 3558, HMSO 1968.

5. The economics of energy policy

CHARLES K ROWLEY
Professor of Economics,
University of Newcastle upon Tyne

Introduction

The prophets of doom are always with us, especially in the Judeo-Christian segments of the Planet Earth, in which the concept of the apocalypse has enjoyed a widespread, lengthy and an influential tradition. At the present time, when scientists substantially have replaced the theologians in the field of prophecy, when "the clatter of the computer has replaced the wind whistling through the rocks at Delphi", and when more credence is attached to statements emanating from the Club of Rome than from the Vatican, it is only to be expected that those who prophecy doom from the musty pages of the Ancient Texts will be less influential than those who present their message as the outcome of scientific investigation. Thus it is that *The Limits to Growth* has now replaced the last book of the *New Testament* as the revelation of impending calamity and terror; alas! without any accompanying prophecy that destruction is to prepare for and herald the beginning of a new era. Thus it is that rapidly depleting sources of energy, rather than the advance of moral and religious turpitude, is seen to be about to pitch our civilisation into a new Dark Age from which there is to be no return. To those in Britain, especially, who have shivered through successive winters of an energy crisis and who have seen a government toppled by militants in control of energy supplies, the message of the Club of Rome is uncomfortably convincing. For once, however, the economists — alien to the tradition of the dismal science — are able to offer sustenance to those who find doom unacceptable and who look for man-devised solutions to the apocalyptic threat.

Theories of the economic apocalypse in practice fall into two main categories, which may be labelled exogenous and endogenous. The exogenous theory, which is reflected in the viewpoint of the Club of Rome, is based upon the truism that no economic system can grow without limit if it necessarily makes use of resources (of energy) that are limited in quantity. No one can seriously dispute the fact that, if a constant numerator is divided by a growing denominator, the quotient must decrease. What is centrally at issue is the velocity path by which the ultimate finite limit is approached. The apocalyptic viewpoint stresses the exponential characteristic of resource depletion, with the limit approached at accelerating speed and with little warning. In such circumstances a major economic crisis, if not doom itself, is almost inevitable. A less extreme viewpoint urges that the exogenous constraint upon growth will act like any other fixed factor of production, in that growth will begin to encounter diminishing returns at a relatively early stage, that the limit will be approached gradually by a path whose second derivative is negative, and that there will be ample time to moderate any impending crisis. A yet more optimistic viewpoint, in favour with many economists, suggests that as growth proceeds against the energy resource constraint, price signals will activate adjustment mechanisms, which include a more economical utilisation of energy, the development and application of new technologies to permit use of poorer quality resources and the substitution of more abundant resources for scarcer ones. Economists have long-since rejected the notion — associated with Malthus — of an absolute quantity of resources in favour of that — associated with Ricardo — of resources of unlimited quantity but diminishing quality, whilst recognising the role of technology in offsetting the tendency towards diminishing returns. In my view, this less pessimistic scenario is applicable to the present so-called energy crisis.

The endogenous theory of economic apocalypse is quite different. It is based upon the expectation that internal and institutional difficulties of some sort will impede the processes of economic adjustment to the energy depletion situation and that a crisis which in principle is avoidable will be precipitated. In this sense, doom is viewed as the likely outcome of the inability of mankind to control a scarcity problem via the usual media of private markets and of public intervention. With this viewpoint I have a modicum of sympathy, for reasons to be outlined subsequently in this chapter, though I do not consider doom to be a highly probable outcome of predictable imperfections in private and in public markets.

Some Orders of Magnitude

The world has an accumulated capital stock of energy resources mainly, though not exclusively, in the form of fossil fuels and of uranium; and a flow of additional energy resources mainly, though not exclusively, from the sun. In neither case are these resources easily measured. Conceptually, the problem of measurement is centred upon the definition of energy resources. For resources which cannot be categorised as energy inputs at the present time may be so categorised in the future as a consequence of technological change. For this reason, those materials-balances approaches to the energy problem which emphasise a fixed availability of energy resources are likely to prove misleading, especially over the long run. Empirically, the principal problem of measuring known energy resources is that such resources cannot be treated as a physical constant. To estimate the resources likely to be covered, it is necessary to predict the future time-path both of costs of recovery and of energy price. For the availability of resource inputs essentially is an economic issue — a fact which often is ignored by scientists of the doomsday school. At best, therefore, estimates of available energy resources must be conditional upon detailed market assumptions. Inevitably, there will be wide error bars on any specific measure of the world's energy supplies, whether conditional or unconditional in nature.

The principal fossil fuels currently utilised as an energy resource are coal, natural gas and oil (including shale and tar sands). Some estimates of remaining recoverable reserves, due to Colin Robinson, are outlined in table 1. The estimates in this table are

Table 1. *Estimates of remaining recoverable reserves of fossil fuels*

	Million million metric tons of coal or coal equivalent
Coal	4.0 to 7.0
Oil (including tar sands and shale)	0.6 to 0.8
Natural gas	0.4 to 0.6
	5.0 to 8.4

Source: Robinson (1974)

clearly subject to wide error bars, though they are derived from the more authoritative sources. They are also almost certainly conservative, in that they are based upon recovery rates (50% for coal and 30% for oil) which were valid before the recent increases in energy prices. In any event, both the lower and the upper estimates are large compared with present *levels* of world energy consumption, representing respectively about 700 and 1,200 years' supply assuming no energy resources other than fossil fuels to be available. Of course, if energy consumption is assumed to rise, say by the 5% per annum which has been typical in recent years — and such a rate of increase cannot be entirely discounted even in the wake of relative price adjustments — the reserves as estimated would be depleted much more rapidly, indeed by the middle of the 21st century.

In reality, of course, the fossil fuels are supplemented as an energy resource by uranium, which is the principal fuel input for nuclear fission power. Estimated reserves of uranium are likely to be especially inaccurate, both because comprehensive exploration has not yet taken place and because known reserves are likely to be understated for political reasons. Furthermore, the energy content of a given quantity of uranium varies enormously according to the type of reactor employed, with uranium used in breeder reactors offering about 70 times as much energy as the equivalent uranium used in light water reactors. It is estimated that a total of some 4 million metric tons of uranium is available from land-based sources, at prices up to $30 per lb, with a further 40 million metric tons available from the sea, taking no account at all of reserves in the Communist sector. In breeder reactors, the land-based reserves alone are equivalent to the upper limit estimates for coal in table 1 as an energy resource.

A number of other energy resources make small additional contributions to world energy supplies, most notably such non-depletable inputs as hydro, geothermal, tidal, wind, and solar power. Of these resources, it is unlikely that any other than solar power will make major *additional* contributions to world energy consumption in the foreseeable future. The immense potential for solar energy awaits technical progress, but constitutes the single most likely solution to the energy depletion problem in the very long term. In the interim, the possibility remains of obtaining energy from atomic fusion — using hydrogen bomb type reactions — and the resources most likely to be used in such a process, namely deuterium and lithium, appear to be available in large quantities in the sea. Even the more conservative scientists expect that fusion will be technically possible within fifty years, whilst the optimists predict its introduction by the turn of the century. In the event that resource depletion meanwhile culminated in a startling rise in the price of energy, no doubt the fusion process would be expedited.

The long-term rate of world energy consumption is no less difficult to forecast than is the rate of available supplies. Naive models, it is true, simply express energy consumption as a linear function of real income and proceed on the basis of exponential extrapolations of world output to the crisis conclusion. But, however well such models may reflect past experience, it cannot be expected that they will predict effectively a future situation in which the increasing scarcity of energy resources results in sharp increases in energy prices and also is reflected by a negative feedback upon the rate of growth of world real output. Clearly, more sophisticated models are required of aggregate energy demand which incorporate, at the minimum, some estimates of the price as well as the income elasticity of demand for energy and which attempt to pick up the negative feedback implications of resource depletion upon the rate of world economic growth.

At the present time, econometric evidence on the price elasticity of demand for energy, even at the disaggregated level of the nation state, is not available. In its absence, all estimates of long-term energy consumption are little better than crystal-gazing prophecies. Certainly, those doomsters who implicitly assume a zero price-elasticity of demand in their forecasts are not deserving of great confidence, as even the present world reactions of rising energy prices should indicate. If rising prices do temper the long-term rate of growth of energy consumption, as elementary economics would suggest, the exogenous apocalypse must be deferred, providing further breathing-space for technical progress. We may attach high probability to the proposition that energy-based economic doom does not await us, just around the corner. Moreover, we may reasonably assume that doom itself is a figment of the apocalyptic imagination.

The Optimal Rate of Depletion of Finite Energy Resources

Let us explore, nevertheless, the pessimistic position in which energy resources indeed are finite and in which technical progress does not offer any prospect of salvation. Can we say anything at all about the optimal rate of depletion of such energy resources? Clearly, this is a normative question, concerning what should be done, and, as such, any solution that is suggested must be based upon a set of value assumptions which will determine, not least, the relative importance to be attached to the present and to the future generations. Suppose, therefore, that some discount factor is selected as a basis for weighting the present in terms of the future and that this is embodied, as an explicit value judgement, in a social welfare function. Suppose further that some relevant constraints are chosen to represent a few important traits of reality. Important insights may then be derived into what is implied in optimising the depletion rate of the energy resource in terms of such a social welfare function. A simple illustration, avoiding the complex mathematics of the optimal control approach which is central to such a model, will indicate what is involved.

Let us denote the given stock of energy resources by C and let us suppose that consumption of that stock will proceed at rate c_t, which may vary over time. The population lives at full strength until the stock is exhausted, at which time, T, life ceases.

Figure 1.

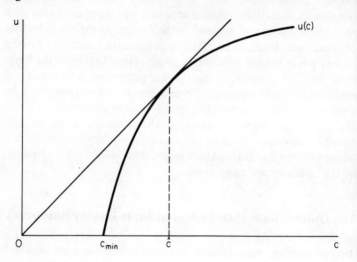

Technology is assumed to be constant over the relevant time-period.

The social welfare function to be maximised will take the form

$$U = \int_o^T e^{-pt} c_t \, dt$$

and the feasibility constraints will be

$$\int_o^T c_t \, dt = C, \quad c_t \geqslant c_{min} \text{ for } O \leqslant t \leqslant T, \ c_{min} > O$$

where

    C = total stock of the energy resource
    c_{min} = minimum consumption flow required for survival
    T = period of survival

Here C and c_{min} are given positive numbers. The survival period T is bounded by

$$O < T \leqslant \overline{T} = C / c_{min}$$

but T is a decision variable.

Now let us suppose the life at the survival minimum has no utility and that the utility function $u(c)$ has the shape depicted in figure 1. If future utility is not discounted, as is the case in figure 1,

Figure 2.

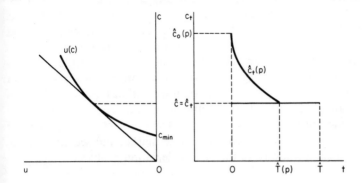

the optimal constant path proceeds at the rate c_t corresponding to the point of tangency of $u(c)$ with a ray out of the origin. It can also be proved that this path is also optimal among all feasible paths, constant or not. If future utility *is* discounted at a positive rate p, as in our social welfare function, it can be shown that the new optimal path $\hat{c}_t(p)$ will never fall below the value that is constantly optimal for $p = 0$. As figure 2 illustrates, however, the optimal path starts at a rate $\hat{c}_o(p)$ and follows a descending curve such that the rate $\hat{c}_t(p) = \hat{c}$ is reached at that time $T = \hat{T}(p)$ at which the available stock C is exhausted. As is evident from figure 2, and as is intuitively obvious, a positive discount rate shortens the survival period, with those nearer to the present consuming ever more energy resources than those who are further away. In an ideal market solution, this would be reflected in monotonically increasing prices for the resource in question through time. There is no need to emphasise the inter-generational conflict inherent in the initial choice of discount rate to be incorporated into the social welfare function.

In practice, of course, there are many problems in applying such an optimal control approach to the so-called energy problem. First, the utility function, so easily drawn in figures 1 and 2, is highly elusive in the real world and, indeed, cannot be derived at all without making interpersonal comparisons of utility of a kind that modern welfare economics shuns. Second, the likelihood of agreement on the discount rate is remote indeed. Third, technical progress cannot be ruled out in the case of energy resources. Fourth, the resources may indeed be finite, but the precise stock is itself dependent upon the divergence between energy prices and energy recovery costs. Fifth, the world economy is segmented into nation states and any global analysis of optimal depletion rates must be disturbed by national rivalry, international rivalry and suspicion. Finally, even if the analysis itself was spot-on, it is by no means evident that the institutional machinery exists to translate its messages into practical policy. The problem will be illustrated with reference firstly to the private market and secondly to the political 'solutions' to the energy depletion problem.

The Private Market Solution

Although a range of alternative mechanisms exists for achieving a Paretian optimum (henceforth an efficient solution), by far the most widely discussed in the welfare economics literature is the mechanism of universal perfect competition. For, on certain restrictive assumptions — most notably that production sets and preference orderings are convex, and that markets exist for all goods, services and contingencies — perfect competition will provide an efficient solution, with prices an appropriate indicator of social scarcity, given the preferences of society. In equilibrium there will be no way of improving the lot of one consumer without worsening the lot of another, and thus the Paretian value judgement will be satisfied. This, in essence, is the basis for allowing market determination of energy resource prices in the private market solution. Unfortunately there are several ways in which such a system can run into difficulties. In this section the more important problems will be evaluated and an attempt will be made to assess their implications for efficiency on the (unrealistic) assumption that world energy markets are capitalistic and unfettered by political interventions.

The Impossibility of Perfect Competition

It is self-evident that the assumptions upon which perfect

competition rests not only do not, but indeed cannot, exist within modern complex industrial economies. Perfect knowledge does not and cannot exist, even concerning the present. Firms and factor inputs are not, and cannot realistically be made to be, price-takers in all markets. Products and factors are not, and can not realistically be made to be, homogeneous, even within closely drawn classifications. Scale economies do not always peter out at output rates which are insignificant from the total market viewpoint. Entry into all markets is not, and can not reasonably be rendered, free. In such circumstances, those who advocate perfect competition as a solution to the economic problem demonstrate only their ignorance of real world conditions. At most, perfect competition is relevant only as a polar model, useful in that it provides an insight into real world divergences which pose problems (in the efficiency sense of Pareto) for economies which give free rein to market forces. Yet, it must be recognised that any other competitive solution, even the tangency solution of the Chamberlin monopolistic competition model, gives rise to efficiency losses, with prices diverging from marginal cost. Furthermore, even if perfect competition was attainable in the energy resource market, its absence in other markets might well imply inefficiency in the energy market itself, given the interdependence of all markets in the modern economy. It is not possible to predict at this level of discourse whether the impossibility of perfect competition would result in excessive or in sub-optimal rates of utilization of energy resources.

Externalities

If a socially efficient solution is to be achieved, it is crucially important that all the costs and benefits of a particular activity should be internalised to the decision makers. For this to occur, there must be markets for all contingencies. This implies that there must be futures markets for the various energy resources say for the year 2000, and that there must be insurance markets for various technological contingencies, such as, for example, the possibility that fusion processes fail economically. Without such markets, an efficient solution cannot be guaranteed.

In practice, however, a full set of futures and insurance markets is not available in energy resource markets. Even long-term contracts are rare and — where they do exist — are susceptible to political interference. What are the likely consequences of such externalities in the energy resource markets? Firstly, the absence of futures markets may result in myopic decision taking. Suppose, for example, that investors in energy resources pursue a short-term speculative policy, purchasing titles to resources with an eye to capital gains rather than the ongoing process of resource supply. It can be shown that market equilibrium in such circumstances will occur when investors expect the short-period capital gain on the asset to be equal to the risk-corrected interest rate. There is no unique solution to this condition which, in the short run, is compatible even with a path of zero royalties. In the absence of futures markets, it cannot be assumed that the short-term pricing outcomes from such a process will optimise the long-run rate of depletion of finite energy resources. Furthermore, the very nature of the myopic equilibrium, with its emphasis upon short-run speculation, is such as to lend instability to the energy resource markets, perhaps culminating in severe cycling of energy prices, with disruptive implications for the world economy.

In the absence of insurance arrangements designed to internalise the risk that technical progress may not supplement energy resources in the future, and given the natural tendency of the present generation to under-regard the preferences of the future generations, it must be expected that the overall impact of externalities in capitalistic energy markets will be that of inducing an excessive current rate of depletion. Whether or not this implies a case for political intervention cannot be assessed without first taking a realistic view of the imperfections to be anticipated in a world economy composed of nation states organised with varying degrees of representative government (see next section).

Supply Monopolies

Energy resources are especially susceptible to supply monopolisation, in that they tend to be located in a limited number of geographical centres which facilitate centralised control. Moreover, existing monopolists are protected against new entry competition by the high costs of exploration for, and development of, new reserves. Oil and natural gas are particularly suitable to long-term supply monopolisation in markets which are not regulated by a vigorous anti-trust policy. What are the policy implications of such monopoly, be it in the form of a single enterprise or of a cartel? Here, the answer can be more precise.

In the absence of externalities, a profit-maximising monopolist would supply energy resources at a sub-optimal rate, with prices exceeding marginal costs in the equilibrium solution. In the case of the single-firm monopolist, such a situation might well survive into the medium term, whilst potential competitors marshalled the necessary resources and engaged in time-consuming developments of newly-discovered reserves. In the case of a cartel, however, internal pressures would erode the monopoly position, as individual suppliers attempted to benefit by secret price cutting beneath the agreed level. The cartel would be especially susceptible to chiselling of this kind where separate suppliers were actually drawing off energy supplies from a common pool, as happens occasionally, for example, in the oil industry. But, in general, cartels tend to instability, with the inference that a long-term cartel monopoly is not to be anticipated.

Given the pervasive nature of externalities in the energy resource markets, and the associated prediction that depletion will occur at too fast a rate, there is a sense in which an effective supply monopoly might be viewed as socially beneficial. For, insofar as the restrictions thereby imposed on the rate of depletion counteracted the effect of externalities, an optimal rate of depletion might fortuitously emerge. On the other hand, the monopoly itself might result in economic welfare losses as a consequence perhaps of technical inefficiency in production, and might well constitute a threat to political freedoms. Moreover, the redistributive consequences of monopoly behaviour might well prove unacceptable in many parts of the world economy. For all these reasons the supply monopoly solution is hardly likely to prove the most acceptable method of regulating the energy market and we must now turn our attention to alternative forms of intervention.

Political Solutions

Let us suppose that the externality effects predominate in the
world energy market and that the rate of resource depletion is
excessively high. A situation of market failure exists and some
form of political intervention might be deemed acceptable. Such a
situation is outlined in figure 3, where BC represents the marginal
net benefits to the producers from supplying energy resources and
OA represents the marginal cost to society (future as well as
present) from the depleted energy reserves. In the absence of
political intervention the market solution would be at C, where BC
intersects the horizontal axis, and costs reflected in the triangle
OAC would be imposed upon society. The optimal rate of
depletion is at E, defined by the equation between marginal costs
and benefits; the problem is how to get there. In this case, private
bargaining, in which the energy suppliers are bribed to move to E
by those who otherwise would suffer, is out of the question, since
future generations cannot bargain. Two possibilities remain:
either governments should tax energy resources so as to lower the
net benefit curve of the suppliers to FE, implying that the rate E
would be freely adopted; or they should regulate directly the
supply of energy resources, perhaps via public ownership, so as to
ensure that rate E is adopted. Neither solution is as simple as it
sounds even on the assumption that a world government is
motivated to attain an efficient solution. For the information
depicted in figure 3 is not easily obtained, as was emphasised
previously. Without knowledge of the optimal rate of depletion,
governments are unable to intervene effectively; indeed, they are
unable even to decide whether or not intervention is justified.
Furthermore, even where information concerning the optimality
conditions can be obtained in return for search expenditures, it is
by no means always the case that it should be obtained. A careful
balance is required between the costs and benefits of search
behaviour to ensure that the information is worth collecting.

Even in the abstract world of unified energy policy, therefore,
there are many obstacles to the political solution to a market
failure problem which themselves, in a comparative institutions
analysis, may imply that the market system should be free from
intervention, despite its own inefficiencies. In reality, more

Figure 3.

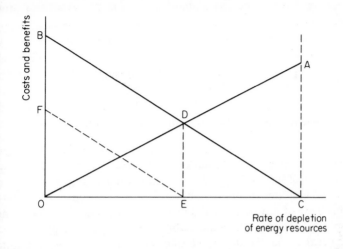

fundamental problems circumscribe the political solution, namely the existence of nation states and the restrictions of representative government. To these problems we must now turn.

The Existence of Nation States

There is no unified world energy policy at the present time, nor is there any prospect that such a policy will emerge in the foreseeable future. Instead, the separate nation states are scrambling in pursuit of energy autarky, sub-optimising by reference to the preferences of their own citizens (in countries where citizen preferences are not treated with contempt by authoritarian dictatorships). There is little chance, in such a situation, that the implications of the global energy situation will gain more than fleeting lip-service. For national policy invariably is in the interests of self-betterment, without consideration of international repercussions, and the more pressing the energy situation becomes, the more rivalrous are the nation states in the protection of their own positions. One consequence of such nationalism is that many of the economic benefits of free international trade (following comparative advantage theory) are lost as the system becomes throttled by trade regulations. This implies an inefficient high-cost solution, given the structure of energy demand and the relative costs and availabilities of energy resources and transportation.

Nirvana is an elusive phantom, and the world of nation states is here to stay. But even the process of nationalistic sub-optimisation is obstructed by the inevitable distortions of the political market place.

The Restrictions of Representative Government

So far the political solution to the energy problem has proceeded on the supposition that national governments are the impartial servants of the public good — a notion which is deeply embedded in the economic theory of public policy. It is now time to moderate this view of government and to analyse the forces at work in the political process, which inevitably impinge upon energy policy in the real world. To do so, we shall work with a simple, but quite powerful, model of the political process in two-party systems based upon the majority vote principle. Clearly, such an analysis is inapplicable to the fascist and socialist dictatorships, where energy policy will evolve independently of citizen preferences; but it is highly relevant for democracies.

Let us then apply the self-interest axiom to politicians, just as we apply it to households and to firms in conventional economic theory, and assume that each politician has a utility function defined for a probability of re-election variable as well as for such variables as pecuniary gain, personal power, and idealism etc. The governing coalition is assumed to maximise some such aggregated utility function subject to a political survival constraint, which involves it in retaining the favours of a decisive set of the electorate. The opposition party is similarly motivated. The government thus is viewed as a party competing with one other party for control over the governing apparatus and the election process is viewed as one in which policies are swapped for votes. If the government is to survive politically, it must adopt a vote-maximising position on the main policy issues, though it is shielded to a limited extent from voter preferences by the length of the election period and by its ability to full-line force its policy package. This provides some leeway for the non-re-election arguments in the group utility function. It also provides an opportunity for the bureaucrats to distort policy making by presenting false information to the government, as a means of satisfying their own ambitions to increase their influence.

Let us now suppose that voter preferences are clearly defined and firmly held on the energy issue, with a decisive cluster of voters favouring an excessively high rate of energy depletion, as a consequence of myopia and of self-centred negligence concerning the preferences of future generations. In such circumstances, our model of representative government predicts that both political parties will be pressed into adopting the policy approved by the decisive voter-set, implying a political consensus on energy policy, and that the government will act decisively to implement that policy position. Suppose, alternatively, that voter preferences on energy policy turn out to be ambiguous, with voters torn between the desire to live well in the present on the one hand and the pressure-group activities of the conservation lobby on the other. In such circumstances, the political parties will tread warily on energy policy, fearful of a major net loss of votes, and the bureaucrats will step in with a package of regulatory devices, which may or may not improve energy policy but which certainly will accentuate their own power and prestige. Departments of Energy will mushroom and major policy interventions will be recommended as a means of safeguarding their longer-term influence upon the public market place. In both situations, evidently, imperfections in the political market place distort the policy decisions. Whether or not imperfections such as these are likely to outweigh the imperfections of the market solution is an open question, in which instinct and judgement as well as political philosophy must determine the reader's own conclusions. In either case, the endogenous theory of economic apocalypse cannot be entirely discounted.

Britain and the Energy 'Crisis'

At the present time, Britain is commonly viewed as being in the throes of a serious energy crisis, precipitated by the cartel activities of OPEC oil-producing countries and by the militancy of the

National Union of Mineworkers. The pessimists argue indeed that the 'crisis' is so severe as to jeopardise living standards in the British economy over the longer term, and that British citizens must now adjust to life in a zero-growth economy. Such a view does not stand up to close scrutiny for an economy which itself is relatively rich in fossil fuels and which possesses advanced nuclear technology. Rather is the British energy problem the outcome of political interventions in the domestic energy market of a particularly damaging nature. Let us review recent political initiatives within the framework of the supply monopoly situation.

Supply Monopolies and the Security of Energy Supplies

The two principal supply monopolists whose recent behaviour has brought the energy issue to the forefront of British policy discussion are the Organisation of Petroleum Exporting Countries (OPEC) and the National Union of Mineworkers. We shall argue that the latter is by far the greater long-term threat to the well-being of the British economy.

OPEC was formed by oil exporters in 1960 and now controls 50% of world oil output, 66% of world proved oil reserves and over 90% of world crude oil exports. It comprises 11 nation states spanning several continents, and it has only shown itself to be capable of effective monopoly pressures since 1970, with prices rising from around $3 per barrel in mid 1973 to some $11·65 per barrel in January 1974, and with an effective boycott of major oil consumers during the Middle East War in October 1973. Perhaps the most pertinent measure of the stability of a cartel is provided by the Herfindahl Index[1] — a highly sensitive index of relative concentration with an upper limit of 1 in the case of single firm monopoly and a lower limit of 0 in the case of perfect competition. If we apply this measure to the OPEC exports of crude oil in 1972 (thereby taking the most favourable measure of OPEC market power) the Herfindahl value is only 0·118. Few economists would predict that such a deconcentrated cartel would survive for long as an effective monopolist, especially in a market characterised by a range of competitive substitutes which are capable of significant

[1] $H = \sum_{1}^{n} s_i^2$, where s_i is the market share of the i'th firm.

market penetration in the medium term. Indeed, if the recent OPEC price increases are effective in drawing the attention of national governments to the long-term depletion problem of fossil fuels, the cartel may have provided an important benefit to the future generations, albeit at the price of severe adjustment costs at the present time. It is predictable that by 1980 OPEC power will have been disrupted by internal dissension and by external substitutes for OPEC oil resources. Britain, especially, will then have a specific interest in high oil prices as a significant exporter of oil in the world economy.

The National Union of Mineworkers is a more serious menace to the medium-term well-being of the British economy, specifically within the context of continuity of energy resource supplies. Two very serious disputes, in 1971-72 and in 1973-74, caused far more damage to the British economy than resulted from the October 1973 oil boycott and there is now an annual threat of strike activity if the National Coal Board fails to accede to ever-spiralling wage-rate claims. The National Union of Mineworkers itself, despite internal dissension of a political nature, has shown itself to be a decisive and unified monopoly bargainer, prepared to infringe the rule of law in pursuit of its objectives. There is no sign at the present time of any split within the union that could conceivably result in a return to the more responsible negotiating policy of the 1960's. Any move by the British government further to subsidise coal to the detriment of oil will reduce the probability of energy resource continuity within the British economy.

The Institutional Defects

For the most part, the institutional defects arise as a consequence of political intervention by the British government in the energy market. The supply of coal, gas and electricity in Britain has been entrusted to public enterprises which, throughout their existence, have been subjected to government intervention as both major parties have reacted to short-term political pressures. Price controls exercised in the name of macroeconomic stabilisation policy have consistently distorted the pattern of energy consumption in Britain, for the most part involving coal subsidies as a means of limiting the market penetration of oil. In support of such a policy the Central Electricity Generating Board (CEGB) has been allowed little commercial freedom in its choice of energy inputs, with the consequence that electricity supply is now very vulnerable to the miners' militancy. Fuel oil has been heavily taxed in the past as a further means of restricting the market for oil. Substantial net welfare losses remain from such distortions, even taking account of balance of payments considerations. The policy of subsidising coal, even to the extent of shielding the National Coal Board from the repercussions of inflationary wage settlements conceded under the duress of disruptive strikes, undoubtedly has created the militancy now evident within the National Union of Mineworkers. Only by stripping coal of its subsidies and by requiring the National Coal Board, on the threat of liquidation, to meet its full financial obligations whilst simultaneously releasing fuel oil from its now minor tax impediments, and allowing the CEGB full commercial discretion, will collective bargaining within the coal industry be returned to pre-1971 conditions.

Further problems arise in connection with contract arrangements for gas and oil supplies located in the North Sea. The present pricing restrictions on North Sea gas are severely distorting the British energy market and threaten to result in excess demand for gas, resolvable only by some form of rationing, as energy users attempt to switch from high-cost oil and coal to low-cost natural gas. Given the constraints on the rate of supply of natural gas, the appropriate policy is to allow prices to rise for market clearance purposes, thereby avoiding wasteful and ineffective attempts by consumers to avoid the implications of the rising scarcity of energy resources. The problem with North Sea oil at the present time arises as a consequence of the political decision by the Labour government to take an active part in the mining activities. Inevitably, this has raised the risks perceived by potential mining companies, thereby delaying the process of making oil available and, probably, raising the costs of such an exercise. For overseas companies are naturally wary of involving themselves in government-controlled ventures, especially when the profit-sharing proposals of the government discriminate against those who are to commit private capital to a hazardous venture.

A Policy Proposal

The British energy market currently is distorted by a welter of often inconsistent · regulatory interventions, which have been introduced sporadically in response to short-term political considerations. In my view, there are net welfare gains to be reaped from dismantling the regulations, providing full commercial freedom for all energy suppliers to respond in profit-conscious fashion to the changing dictates of the energy market, and for maintaining fair competition between the separate energy suppliers. This does not imply a complete withdrawal of government from the energy scene. Insofar as externalities impede the market process — and arguably some weight must be given to the respective pollutant implications of the separate fuels in balancing the structure of supply — tax-subsidy interventions have a legitimate role to play. Insofar as major balance of payments deficits threaten the short-term viability of the economy, petroleum taxes must be countenanced as a means of discouraging household consumption. Insofar as those who would consume energy now take inadequate account of the plight of future generations, one cannot deny the right, though one can doubt the willingness, of national governments to take the longer view. Clearly, the legitimate area of government activity is significant.

However, if any credence is given at all to the economic theory of representative government, one should not place too much faith in the politicians. Few people recognise as clearly as they might that to urge the transference of private decision making on energy matters to the public sector is to pledge faith in the good sense and far sighted vision of the decisive electors and in the altruism of the bureaucratic machinery.

References and Further Reading

Adelman, M. A., Politics, Economics, and World Oil, *American Economic Review*, May 1974.

Beckerman, W., *Economists, Scientists and Environmental Catastrophe*, Oxford Economic Papers, November 1972.

Bradley, P. G., Increasing Scarcity: The Case of Energy Resources, *American Economic Review*, May 1973.

Cordon, W. M., and Oppenheimer, P., *Basic Implications of the Rise in Oil Prices*, Moorgate and Wall Street, Autumn 1974.

Downs, A., *An Economic Theory of Democracy*, Harper and Row 1957.

Gordon, Scott, Today's Apocalypses and Yesterday's, *American Economic Review*, May 1973.

Koopmans, T. C., Ways of Looking at Future Economic Growth, Resource and Energy Use, in Makrakis, M.A. (ed), *Energy*, MIT Press 1974.

Meadows, D. H., *et al.*, *The Limits to Growth*, Earth Island 1972.

Nordhaus, W. D., Markets and Appropriable Resources, in Makrakis, M.A. (ed), *Energy*, MIT Press 1974.

Nordhaus, W. D., Energy in the Economic Report, *American Economic Review*, September 1974.

Posner, M. V., *Fuel Policy: A Study in Applied Economics*, Macmillan 1973.

Posner, M. V., Energy at the Centre of the Stage, *The Three Banks Review*, December 1974.

Robinson, C., *A Policy for Fuel?* Occasional Paper 31, Institute of Economic Affairs 1969.

Robinson, C., *The Energy 'Crisis' and British Coal*, Hobart Paper 59, Institute of Economic Affairs 1974.

Rowley, C. K., Pollution and Public Policy in Culyer, A.J. (ed), *Economic Issues and Social Policies*, Martin Robertson 1974.

Energy for the Future, Institute of Fuel 1973.

6. The economics of educational policy

ADRIAN ZIDERMAN
Senior Lecturer in Economics,
Queen Mary College, University of London

The Education Industry

The economics of the nationalised industries was the subject of an earlier chapter; yet *education*, in fact, is our largest nationalised industry. Looked at as an industry, the educational sector is vast indeed. Although we do not have readily available measures of the outputs of the industry, total public expenditure on education (in its wider sense, including spending on libraries and the arts) rises by some 5% a year in real terms and now exceeds £4,000m annually.

Relating total educational expenditure to GNP provides a broad measure of its relative importance — but a rough and ready yardstick only, because educational expenditure includes such items as transfer payments which are not part of GNP. With this caveat in mind, educational expenditure in 1972 was some 6.5% of GNP, compared with only 3% 25 years earlier. Taking a recent year, 1972/3 for example, current expenditure on nursery, primary and secondary schooling by central and local government was £1,866m, with capital expenditure on schools adding a further £429m. The universities spent £485m including £89m in capital grants; further education and teacher training accounted, respectively, for expenditures of £408m (including £74m on capital account) and £160m (£11m). A further indication of the sheer size of the education sector is its total employment of over 1.6 million;

second only to retail distribution, it has the largest labour force of any industry (Annual Census of Employment, June 1973), and includes a half million of the nation's most qualified workers. This compares with total employment in other major industries of some half million workers in motor vehicle manufacture, nearly 400,000 in agriculture and 315,000 in coal mining. However, the most interesting economic issues in educational policy stem not from the magnitude of the industry but, as we have already hinted, from the fact that it is predominantly operated by the state and, in common with most nationalised industries, its services provided below cost (but in this case virtually free).

The role of the state is dominant at all levels of educational provision, particularly so in the schools. As shown in table 1, over 90% of schools in England and Wales, accounting for 94% of all pupils, are maintained by the local educational authorities (LEA's). The vast majority of these schools are virtually nationalised institutions run directly by the LEA's and financed out of central and local government funds. Although those maintained schools that are voluntary controlled or aided do have a slight margin of autonomy and, in the case of aided schools, meet a very small part of their expenditure out of their own resources (most of which can be reimbursed by the DES), these schools too are essentially state-run. The direct grant schools officially described as schools whose governing bodies are 'assisted' by grants from the DES, in fact obtain three-quarters of their income from government funds. The private sector therefore accounts for less than 8% of schools and, because of smaller average class size, only 4.6% of all pupils. Moreover, the size of the private school sector has been falling over time, both in absolute and relative terms; ten years ago over 6% of all pupils were in the independent sector. A similar picture emerges from an examination of the official statistics relating to other parts of the education system, whether technical college, teacher training college or polytechnic. Although the 45 British university institutions are, in a formal sense, private institutions, some 85% of their income comes from public provision via the Universities Grants Committee which exerts a powerful influence on the scope of their activities.

Education provision in Britain, then, is dominated by the state; and it is also highly subsidised. No fees are charged at the local

Table 1. *Distribution of schools and pupils between private and state education in England and Wales 1972*

	Schools		Pupils	
	(No.)	*(%)*	*(No.)*	*(%)*
Schools maintained by local education authorities	30,288	91·3	8,568,401	94·0
Direct grant schools	304	0·9	128,730	1·4
Independent schools	2,604	7·8	422,309	4·6
	33,196	100·0	9,119,440	100·0

Source: Department of Education and Science, *Statistics of Education 1972,* Volume 1, HMSO 1973

education authority schools, of course, except for a small part of the cost of school meals and milk; even at the 175 direct grant grammar schools, fees account for less than a quarter of total expenditure. Only 5% of further education college expenditure is met from fees; at teacher training colleges maintained by the LEA's and by voluntary bodies, fees account respectively for only 1.8% and 3.7%. Finally, whilst 7% of university expenditure in 1970/71 was covered formally by fees, in fact the bulk of this fee income was paid directly by LEA's rather than by the student consumers themselves, or their parents.

Why State Provision?

We may well ask: why is the provision of education made in this way in Britain? Does it stem simply from the interplay of historical factors, with the pattern once set, maintained — even strengthened — mainly by institutional inertia? Or, as was briefly suggested in Chapter 1, does education constitute such a clear case of market failure that the present well-established system of state

Figure 1.

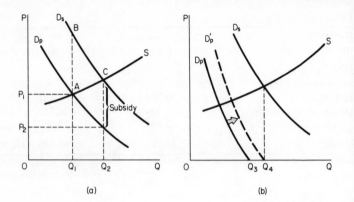

(a)   (b)

intervention in education remains as necessary now as in its formative years? Put another way, why do we not rely upon the interplay of market forces, in the form of the private educational choices of parents and students as consumers, and of the profit-maximising activities of privately-run schools and colleges, co-ordinated by the price mechanism, to ensure the provision of a socially optimal amount of schooling? Could education not be produced by private enterprise and purchased by consumers on the free market? In short, does the state have to educate?

To help answer these questions, consider an education system contrastingly different from that existing at the present time. Assume that schools, colleges and so on are operated by the private sector rather than the state, on profit-maximising lines; parents (or students) purchase amounts of education according to their preferences, at non-subsidised prices on the free market.

This hypothetical situation is illustrated in figure 1a, which shows, at varying prices, the supply and demand of schooling, here assumed to be a homogeneous good. The supply curve S is the long-run marginal cost curve of educational services and assumed to be upward sloping. The demand curve D_p represents the quantities of education that would be purchased, other factors being equal, at various levels of tuition fees. The amount of education provided in such a free market would be Q_1 at price P_1.

Is this situation socially (i.e. Pareto) optimal? This would be so, as with most goods provided by private markets, if the marginal valuations of the benefits of the good by the consumers (as measured by demand curve D_p) were coincident with the benefits at the margin to society as a whole, and if the marginal costs incurred by private producers equal marginal social costs. Whilst we may assume that the latter condition does hold, there are good reasons for believing that the private demand for education substantially understates the value of education derived by society as a whole. Hence too little education is demanded (and so provided). Although the proposition that the private market would under-provide education can be supported by a wide range of arguments, most of which can be traced back to the writings of the major classical economists, West (1965), in one of the most thought-provoking books written on education in recent years, subsumes these arguments under two main headings. Essentially, it is argued on two counts, namely the externality effects of education and the alleged incompetence or ignorance of parents, that a strong case can be made for state intervention in education (but not, as we shall see, for direct state *provision* of education). We now discuss these arguments in turn.

Externalities

Education is widely believed to provide benefits to society over and above the benefits enjoyed by the direct recipients, the 'educatees'. These positive externality, or spillover, effects are both multiple and far-ranging. They include *inter alia* raising the earnings of certain complementary factors of production (e.g. less educated workers working alongside the educated), the creation and dissemination of new knowledge through research and invention, a more flexible labour force, and so on. They may also lead to such intangible benefits — which Blaug (1972) prefers to call 'atmospheric effects' — as a more enlightened, literate and cultural society. However, one should not overstate the extent of these beneficial spillovers. For example, it is often asserted that they include a reduction in crime and greater political stability. Yet the evidence supporting this view is not only contradictory but, if anything, suggests that the externality effects may frequently be negative.

Be that as it may, we can accept the view that, on balance, these spillovers are likely to be both positive and substantial.[1] Since the educatees' consumer satisfaction derived from marginal purchases of education does not include or take account of these spillover benefits, the educational system will under-provide; resources flowing into education will be too few and societal welfare will fall short of the Pareto optimal level.

These conclusions may be presented more formally. Returning to figure 1a, we may conceive of a societal demand curve D_s which includes both private consumers' valuations of benefits (measured by curve D_p) and the spillover benefits, over and above these, that accrue to society generally (as measured by the vertical distance between D_p and D_s). If only the benefits of the direct purchasers of education are considered, then the free market equilibrium level of educational provision will be Q_1, at which quantity the direct benefit of education, measured in terms of willingness to pay, are equal to costs at the margin. However, at Q_1 the amount of education provided by the free market is too small, because no account has been taken of the externality benefits: marginal social benefits of education exceed marginal private benefits, which in turn are equal to marginal private (and social) costs. Marginal benefits to society as a whole exceed marginal social costs by the vertical distance AB. The correct level of educational provision is at that quantity Q_2 where society's valuation of education corresponds to the costs (i.e. the equilibrium point C). Here there is no divergence between the social benefits of education (measured along D_s) and the social-private costs (measured along S).

However, at Q_2 the private valuation by the purchasers of education is only P_2, considerably below the costs. Fortunately, state intervention can bring about an optimal situation by providing a subsidy to the education producing firms, as shown in the diagram, so that education is made available to purchasers at the low tuition fee P_2; at this price quantity Q_2 will be purchased. The cost of the education subsidy may be legitimately met out of general taxation, on the grounds that society as a whole does

---

[1]See Peacock and Wiseman (1964) and West (1965) for a dissenting view.

benefit (via its spillover effects) from the extra education provided.

A situation could well arise in which education must be made available at zero (or even negative) tuition fees, in order to secure a socially optimal level of provision. This possibility is illustrated in figure 1b: curves D_p, D_s and S have the same interpretation as before. The socially optimal level of output (where curves D_s and S intersect) is now at Q_4. However, even with zero fees and taxpayers meeting the full costs of education, no education will be purchased in excess of Q_3 (at which point D_p touches the quantity axis). In this case, the state may induce individuals to purchase extra education up to the socially optimal level Q_4, by the offer of monetary bribes (in the guise of student maintenance grants?), thus effectively raising the private demand curve for education to D_p'.

Summarising the argument so far: market failure, in the form of externalities associated with the private demand for education, does make out a case for state intervention, but only through state *finance* of education. Nothing in the externality argument warrants either state *provision* or *compulsory consumption* of education, two of the most characteristic features of Britain's school system.

Parental Incompetence

There is, however, a second and more forceful argument popularly advanced in support of state intervention in education (though at the school level, rather than in further or higher education). The argument runs along the following lines: in privately functioning markets for education, some parents — particularly the less well-off — will demand too little education in the sense that they are generally unaware of the benefits to be derived from education or, if they are so aware, are so irresponsible or negligent that they prefer to 'mis-spend' their income on goods (from which they enjoy more immediate benefits) rather than spending on the education of their children. Alternatively, poor parents may lack the means to purchase sufficient amounts of education in the free market. In these cases, since some consumers would purchase less education than the state (i.e. the majority) thinks they require, state intervention is necessary to correct the 'inadequacies' of parental choice. In other words, education is seen as a *merit want*, a class of goods defined by Musgrave (1959) as those "considered so meritorious that their satisfaction is provided through the public budget, over and above what is provided for through the market and paid for by private buyers".[2] Here we have deliberate state interference with consumer sovereignty, justified on the grounds that the basic assumptions on which it rests — market knowledge and rational appraisal — do not hold. The state intervenes to ensure that at least a certain minimum amount of education is consumed by all.

Whilst both parental incompetence and externalities, in the absence of state intervention, result in too low a level of total market demand for education, the sense in which demand is inadequate differs in the two cases, with consequent differences in their policy implications. In the externalities case, the state subsidises education in an attempt to secure a socially-adequate *total* level of educational provision; the fact that some individuals, with high demand elasticities for education, will purchase considerably more education whilst others may not respond positively at all, is not relevant to the issue. In the parental incompetence case, however, state intervention is focused primarily on those particular consumers (perhaps a minority) who would otherwise purchase inadequate amounts of education, rather than on the adequacy of total market demand for education *per se*. In this case, educational subsidies may produce a satisfactory *total* quantity of educational provision but its distribution may well be sub-optimal, since some individuals are not thereby induced to increase their purchases of education to a level generally regarded as necessary for their personal well-being (or that of their children). Therefore, compulsory education, up to a certain minimal quantity, is required; since this may place a heavy financial burden on some families (particularly the poor), compulsory education may have to be subsidised, offered free or even with maintenance grants to offset family earnings forgone during the period of study.

[2]Alternatively, certain merit wants may be generally regarded as having such undesirable effects on the direct consumers, that their provision and consumption may be discouraged through taxation or prohibitions; drugs and alcohol are cases in point.

Yet all this is a far cry from general state provision of education. Indeed, it has to be conceded that publicly provided education cannot be justified on purely economic grounds; rather it is in non-economic terms that the issue is usually argued. Advocates of state education in the past have usually rested their case predominantly on the two extra economic considerations of equality of opportunity and social cohesion which, according to Blaug (1972), "have become literally everyone's argument for publicly provided education".

Social Cohesion

The relevance of the social cohesion argument, which sees in the uniform, universal provision of education by the state a powerful tool for creating and promoting social cohesion through common values and national unity, differs both over time and geographically. It carries more force in less homogeneous societies, such as in the USA with its large immigrant and racial minorities or in poor countries that are rent by linguistic and tribal divisions, than in Great Britain at the present time. Even given the view that provision by the state is the most effective form through which education can contribute to the achievement of these social goals, these are likely to be secured only at the cost of a school system that is highly uniform in structure and affords limited scope for the exercise of parental discretion over the type of education (particularly in relation to their ethnic background or religious adherence) that their children should receive. Indeed, in more highly developed societies such as ours, one sees perverse effects: not only is the conflict between social uniformity and freedom of the individual likely to become more marked, but the educational system itself, in stressing social conformity and accepted ideas, may produce the very opposite of the result intended in the form of student protest, alienation and opting out.

Equality of Opportunity

Turning now to the equality of education opportunity argument, we come to the very centre of contemporary debate on educational policy. For many, egalitarianism in education is seen as a powerful force for the achievement of a more just and equitable society, through its contribution to greater social mobility, the "breaking of any connection between the distribution of education and the distribution of personal income" (Blaug) and the erosion of class divisions and privilege. Yet the equality of education concept can be given a variety of interpretations, each leading to different policy outcomes; in particular, equality of education may concern equality of *access* to education, equality of educational *treatment* or equality of ultimate educational *performance*.

Such diverse policies as compulsory schooling up to a certain age, tax allowances for children receiving full-time education and maintenance allowances for students in higher education, can be seen partially as attempts (usually less than successful) to make education, at the various levels, more equally accessible to all social-class groups.[3] The 1944 Education Act which made free secondary schooling universally available was heralded as a major step in this direction, since the equality of opportunity in education was then seen as something relating primarily to secondary education. Yet subsequent research has shown that in many areas working class representation in the grammar schools was smaller than previously (when a quota of places had been available for children from poor families). The methods of selection to the grammar schools militated against working class children, whose physical and cultural backgrounds are not conducive to successful performance in such seemingly objective tests of ability as the 11-plus examinations. The growing evidence — in Douglas (1966) and others — that educational selection inevitably involves some social-class bias (and an enormous waste of talent), underpins the massive shift in recent years towards comprehensive schooling, replacing separate grammar and secondary modern schools. Comprehensive schooling fits in well with what Husen (1972) has called the 'liberal' conception of

---

[3] However, even nominally free and readily accessible education does not provide equality of educational opportunity beyond the minimum school leaving age, because of the inability of many working class homes to forgo the wages that their children contribute to family income; the high drop-out rate of poorer children from full time schooling between the ages of 16-18 stems largely from the dearth of student maintenance support for this age group.

equality of educational opportunity: equality of educational treatment whereby all children regardless of social class have the opportunity to be educated up to (but not exceeding) a level commensurate with their ability. This objective of uniformity of educational provision, in which education is available not in accordance with parental willingness to pay but rather in relation to capacity to learn, underlies Labour Party policy for the merging of the partially autonomous direct grant grammar schools into the state comprehensive system as well as, ultimately, the abolition of the independent sector (the 'public' schools) which, it is argued, exhibits a pronounced class-based ethos and inculcates socially divisive values.

The private purchase of extra education, outside the state system, would be disallowed, since education is to be provided on purely meritocratic grounds. In sum, the case for state provision of education here rests on the view that this is the most secure method of ensuring a socially acceptable degree of uniformity of the standard and type of education provided at each level of schooling, with the ultimate aim of achieving a more just, open society.

Yet the underlying premise of the 'liberal' policy approach to educational equality has been called very much into question by recent sociological research into enrolment rates and educational achievement in relation to social class. This has shown that the massive expansion of educational provision in recent years, involving the increased formal accessibility to free secondary and higher education of all children of a given age, has not succeeded in changing the social structure of the post compulsory school age enrolment, to any marked extent. Further, at all levels of schooling, children from poorer homes going to the same or similar schools as the better off, did less well: education not only seems to fail to offset the disadvantages of deprived home backgrounds but may even reinforce, rather than diminish, existing social inequalities.

Two contrasting policy conclusions may be drawn from this accumulating sociological research. Firstly, those who adopt what Husen (1972) calls the 'radical' approach to educational equality, would see here strong arguments for extending even further the state's role in educational provision. They argue that the 'liberal' goal of providing education according to each individual's capacity or aptitude (rather than his socio-economic background) is unhelpful because the criteria used for identifying aptitudes, or 'intelligence', are themselves correlated with social background. Hence society must adopt special methods to compensate for the deficiencies of the environment in which children grow up and which account largely for their unequal educational performance; this would take the form of a national policy of 'positive discrimination' in education in favour of the underprivileged. This approach was first given official recognition in 1967 in the Plowden Report on primary schools, which led to the designation of education priority areas (EPA's), i.e. neighbourhoods where children were most severely handicapped in their educational performance by their environment. Special provision of extra educational resources was made for schools in EPA's. The recent expansion of nursery education is to be seen as an attempt to compensate, at an even earlier age, for the disadvantages of home backgrounds. Basically, this approach calls not for equality of educational treatment (i.e. equal schools) "but equally effective schools, whose influences will overcome the differences in the starting point of children from different social groups" (Coleman 1966), so that each child "is equipped at the end of school to compete on an equal basis with others, whatever his social origins." Whether or not the widely adopted policy of positive educational discrimination can, in fact, succeed in adequately compensating for the inequalities arising from differences in parental background in the pre-schooling years is a hotly debated issue.

A counter-reaction, however, comes from those adopting a so-called 'conservative' approach to educational policy (Husen), typified, for example, in the views held by the authors of the recent Educational Black Papers (Cox and Dyson 1969 and 1970). They see some vindication of their opposition towards current egalitarianism in educational policy, in the doubts raised about its efficacy by the recent sociological research referred to earlier. Fundamentally, their opposition towards a more uniform, increasingly state-run educational system is ideological. The grammar schools and the independent sector should be preserved and private markets in education protected, even extended, with the aim of encouraging educational variety, elitism, a more economically efficient schooling system and, above all, broader scope for the exercise of parental choice over the type and amount of education that their children should receive (Wiseman 1959, Peacock and Wiseman 1964). The advocates of this approach are untroubled by the implied concomitant reversal of trends towards greater educational equality, the over-enthusiastic pursuit of which, they argue, has brought about a marked decline in educational standards.

The widely canvassed proposal for *educational vouchers* is associated with those who adopt this generally 'conservative' approach to educational policy. The voucher idea is not new and variants of the scheme have been propounded on a number of occasions this century, not always with the same objectives in view.[4] The revival of the educational voucher proposal in Britain in recent years has come largely from economists basically interested in widening the extent of educational choice open to parents. Although differing in detail, the essential characteristic of the various schemes is the cessation of the direct state financial support of schools; instead all parents of school-age children would receive a non-transferable voucher (or coupon) of a certain value which would be used to pay for education in any school of their choice, provided only that it meets the general standards set by the state. It is usually envisaged that vouchers would have a monetary value equal to the average costs of schooling; state and private schools would co-exist, the former providing education at the price (and cost) of the nominal value of the voucher, whilst private schools would be free to provide a more expensive education, the difference being paid as a fee by parents who wished to send their children to these higher-cost schools.

Vouchers could be made into a more flexible instrument of social policy in a number of ways; they could be made subject to a means test with their value falling as parental income rose. Alternatively, vouchers of the same nominal value could be issued

---

[4]In 1926, for example, a restricted voucher scheme was put forward by Cardinal Bourne aimed at giving additional aid to Roman Catholic elementary schools; see Robinson (1968).

to all parents but, as with family allowances, be subject to income tax; in addition, vouchers issued to parents with school children over minimum school leaving age could be supplemented by cash grants, in relation to parental income, to help offset family income forgone.

The advocates of the voucher proposal see many advantages of its implementation: competition between educational suppliers would lead to a more efficient school system; a greater variety of educational institutions would develop, in response to the diversity of parents' interests, values and beliefs; more resources, it is asserted, would be brought into education; above all, parents would be able to enjoy a real choice (rather than being faced by a virtual state monopoly) and thereby basic educational decisions would no longer be made by civil servants but by parents themselves. Against the voucher proposal, it is argued that the scheme would be cumbersome and costly to administer; that it would not necessarily bring extra resources into education, and yet if it did so, these would be spent on better-off children; the state schools offering a basic minimum provision only, would gradually decline into a type of second-class institution, basically catering for poor and problem children, in disadvantaged neighbourhoods; it would thus be divisive, exacerbate social tensions and above all reverse the trend towards greater equality of educational provision. Fundamentally, the debate over educational vouchers is one of political and ideological objectives and centres on the basic policy conflict of parental free-choice versus educational equality. On the resolution of this conflict economic theory, as such, has little to offer.

Educational Planning and Efficiency

Whatever balance is finally struck between private and state provision of education, we now turn to a more immediate policy issue. Given the state dominance in education expenditures in Britain, how socially optimal are expenditures on education at the various levels? The problem essentially arises from the absence of freely functioning private markets and decentralised decision making in education by consumers and suppliers; there is no mechanism whereby consumer valuations of extra amounts of education can be signalled to the producers nor, in turn, are producers constrained by consumer sovereignty to supply amounts and types of education that are socially desirable. How then does the state decide on the amount and type of education at the various levels and how optimal is the resultant educational mix?

Until recently, there has been very little serious planning of education in Britain. If anything, the major attempts at educational planning over the last two decades have taken the form of a series of major reports by specially designated external committees (usually named after their chairman), on various areas of education; these include Crowther on 15-18 year olds, Newsom on secondary modern children, Robbins on higher education, Plowden on the primary schools and, last and least, James on teacher training. Only in the past few years have more serious planning attempts been made by the DES and the role of the external committee has waned.

The dominating factors in planning educational provision are demographic; demographic trends determine the school population size up to age 16; estimates of its rate of voluntary staying-on beyond the school-leaving age applied to population trends give forecasts of the number of school children above 16. The number of students in teacher training is based on future teacher requirements, as forecast from the estimated size of the future school population and desired pupil-teacher ratio norms. For higher education the DES has adopted similar mechanical procedures, which follow rather rigidly the methodology of the Robbins Report. Basing the number of student places on the 'social demand' for higher education, the forecasts proceed in a number of stages: estimates, mainly based on past trends, are obtained in turn of the school population by age; of the number of school leavers; of the output of 'qualified school leavers' (in terms of 'A' level attainment). Assumptions are then made about the proportion of qualified school leavers that will apply for admission to courses of higher education and about the proportion of these that should be provided with places. The famous 'guiding principle' of the Robbins Committee that "all young persons qualified by ability and attainment to pursue a full-time course in higher education should have the opportunity to do so" (Report, p.49) was in practice replaced by the convention that the proportion of qualified school leavers going on to higher education should be no lower than it was in 1961, the time at which the forecasts were being made, though some improvement in the proportion was envisaged over time.

In passing, it should be noted that these 'social demand' forecasts are not very useful from the economist's viewpoint, and meeting them does not imply that the level of educational provision is socially optimal. Implicit in the social demand estimate is a very strong *ceteris paribus* assumption; yet the future demand for education by students depends on a large number of factors. These include: the price of the education (in terms of gross earnings forgone during study *minus* maintenance grants and vacation earnings); the stream of higher future earnings resulting from this education, as perceived by the students, which in turn is related to the level of market demand for the particular skill; any psychic benefits derived from the education process itself (or psychic costs, in terms of loss of leisure time, examination 'nerves' or general student anxiety and stress), and so on. The problem is not only that some of the factors, very much subject to change over time, cannot be taken as given; but further, being themselves much influenced by government decision (student maintenance grants are a case in point), they should not be considered as exogenous variables in the context of educational policy making.

Total educational expenditure at each level depends not only on the numbers of pupil (and student) places, but also on the costs of educational provision per pupil, which have been rising sharply in real terms over recent decades. These rising unit costs over time have been differentially interpreted, as evidence either of a steadily rising quality of the education provided or of declining productivity of educational institutions. In a series of pioneering studies (summarised in Blaug 1972), Blaug and Woodhall have used this unit cost information to calculate productivity trends in secondary and higher education in Britain. Trends in real terms of total weighted educational inputs (including student time of those over minimum school leaving age) and various measures of output (corrected for changes in educational quality) were examined to calculate total factor productivity trends; these were shown to have declined steadily over time. For example, in the study of secondary school productivity over the period 1950-63, Woodhall and Blaug show annual average productivity falls of between $4\frac{1}{2}$ and 1% depending on the particular measures of input and output used. These results, taken at their face value, imply a decline in efficiency, and wasteful expenditures, in education; however, one is inhibited from drawing such a firm conclusion because the attempt to correct educational output measures for quality changes is not entirely convincing. On the other hand, there are no grounds for adopting the opposing viewpoint taken by so many educational administrators, who seem to welcome almost any increase in educational inputs on the grounds that an improvement in the quality of education must necessarily, almost automatically, follow.

Whatever the implications of rising unit costs of education in terms of the efficiency of educational institutions, the question concerning the breakdown of *total* educational expenditures, to which we have already referred, remains as yet unanswered: how optimally are these total educational expenditures spread between the various levels and types of education? One device that is broadly favoured by economists for probing this issue (but whose use is strongly opposed by a minority of economists, nor generally accepted either by educationalists or educational administrators) is that of the rate of return on educational investment. This arises out of the recent interest in the concept of human capital and its application to policy issues of planning the provision of education. Since expenditures on education raise the productivity and earning power of the individual and thence the levels of output available to society, questions concerning the profitability of these investments in human capital become relevant. Rates of return on educational investment (i.e. cost-benefit analysis applied to education) may then provide guidelines to governments on how appropriate current expenditures are on different levels and types of education.

Educational cost-benefit analysis involves the systematic comparison of the resource costs to the community of educational provision with the resulting increase in resource benefits to society as a whole. The investment costs are measured by the monetary value of goods and services that must be withdrawn from other uses to make possible the educational provision. Although, in fact, externality benefits should be included in the measure of the resource benefits, in practice the benefits measure is confined to the increase in national production resulting from the educational expenditures and (on the basis of marginal productivity theory) as reflected in the earnings differentials of those individuals benefitting from this extra education.

Educational Rates of Return for Britain

In the past, work on estimating the rate of return on educational investment in Britain has been seriously impeded by the lack of necessary data: nationally representative earnings information cross-classified by age, sex and education. This omission was repaired by the educational questions included in the 1966 Census and a subsequent earnings sample survey of the educationally qualified, on which basis the author, together with researchers at the DES, has computed educational rates of return. The procedures and assumptions used are discussed in Morris and Ziderman (1971), which presented a range of alternative results, based on varying assumptions. One set of these results — which the authors regard as the most realistic — are given in table 2.[5]

The outstanding features of the table are the low rates of return on postgraduate qualifications (the high resource costs of which are not sufficiently offset by extra earnings) and the very high rates of return on the Higher National Certificate (both alone or supplemented by extra qualifications to gain membership of the major technical professional institutions). What implications do these results carry for questions concerning the adequacy of educational investment at various levels in Britain? Using as a rough standard for comparison the 10% test discount set by the Treasury for appraising the public sector investment projects, it appears that the British education system is turning out the wrong

[5]These results relate to educational rates of return accruing to society as a whole; these should not be confused with somewhat similar calculations relating to the individual students themselves (private rates of return). For some recent estimates see Ziderman (1973B).

Table 2. *Alternative estimates of rates of return to society on male educational investment in England and Wales 1966/67*

Full-time courses:	Per cent+
'A' levels (from 'no qualification')	9.0
First degree (from 'A' levels)	12.5
Masters degree (from first degree)	3.0
Doctorate (from first degree)	2.5
Part-time technical courses:	
ONC (from 'no qualification')	9.0
HNC (from ONC)	21.5
HNC/PQ* (from HNC)	18.0

Source: Ziderman (1973A)

+rounded to the nearest 0.5 per cent.
*HNC with additional qualification, giving membership of professional institutions.

mix of educationally qualified persons (or at least was in the late 1960's). Societal investments in education for the GCE 'A' level, the Ordinary National Certificate and first degrees seem to have been at roughly the right order of magnitude. However, whilst postgraduate education is not very profitable, part-time technical education at the higher level is extremely so, indicating that a relative expansion of the latter and a relative decline of the former would result in a more efficient use of resources within the educational sector. The validity of this conclusion, however, would depend on the weight to be given to the (unestimated) externality effects of education, at each level.

Yet the failure to include a measure of the externality effects of education, in the results given in table 2, may not be as serious a problem for policy purposes as some of the critics of educational rates of return suggest. In principle, educational rates of return are useful, in a policy context, in two regards: as a means of achieving an overall balance *between* the educational sector and the rest of the economy and as a guide for resource allocation *within* the educational sector itself. In practice, however (and second-best problems apart), the inherent difficulties involved in measuring spillovers in both education and the other sectors would effectively preclude the use of educational rates of return in the first role. In any case, however, the well established practice in Britain is for the overall allocation of resources between the private and public sector and between the broad divisions of the public sector — defence, education, roads and so on — to be settled not by reference to rates of return but by the political-cum-administrative processes of government. In fact, resource allocation within the public sector may best be seen as one of capital rationing (in which the capital rations are negotiated), and each public sector branch is then faced with the task of optimally allocating its resources within a budget constraint. This, however, is precisely the second possible role for educational rates of return, noted above: that of making the best use of available resources engaged in the educational sector.

If this is our focus, we need be less concerned with precise estimates of social rates of return (including spillovers) at each educational level than with their broad rankings. In this case, our inability to measure educational externalities need not trouble us; all we need to consider is their relative importance at the margin, for different educational levels. If external effects of education are roughly proportional to the direct measured benefits (or even broadly equal for each level of education), then no problems of misallocation will arise, since the rankings of educational investments would remain unchanged whether or not spillovers had been included. There is, however, the possibility that externalities may exert a disproportionately large effect at certain levels and types of education. Relatively fewer spillover effects may be expected from part-time technical qualifications (e.g. HNC) than from full-time, more academic ones and, for example, the wider benefits to society from education that take the form of general increases in knowledge, may be more significant for doctorates than for lower-level degree qualifications. If this were so, it would imply, unfortunately, a ranking of the spillovers by level of education (in descending order: postgraduate degree, first degree, HNC) the opposite of that shown in table 2, based on the direct costs and benefits of education. Yet the issue is not whether spillovers differ systematically or otherwise by level and type of education, but whether they are generally sizeable enough to change the relative order of magnitude of the results shown in table 2, if included. Is it *likely*, for example, that the inclusion of externalities would raise the doctorate rates of return towards those of the first degree? When it is recalled that we are concerned not with the *total* value of spillovers for each level of education but only with the *additional* spillover benefits attached to changes in education at the margin, then we may feel that the results shown in table 2 may not be too far off the mark after all.

References

Blaug, M., *An Introduction to the Economics of Education*, Penguin 1972.

Coleman, J. S., Equal Schools or Equal Students?, *The Public Interest*, Summer 1966.

Cox, C. B., and Dyson, A. E., *Fight for Education: A Black Paper*, London 1969.

Cox, C. B., and Dyson, A. E., *Black Paper Two: The Crisis in Education*, London 1970.

Douglas, J. W. B., *The Home and the School*, Macgibbon & Kee 1966.

Husen, T., *Social Background and Educational Career*, OECD 1972.

Morris, V., and Ziderman, A., The Economic Return on Investment in Higher Education in England and Wales, *Economic Trends*, May 1971.

Musgrave, R. A., *The Theory of Public Finance*, McGraw-Hill 1959.

Peacock, A. T., and Wiseman, J., *Education for Democrats*, Institute of Economic Affairs 1964.

Robinson, G., The Voucher System of Education Finance and Independent Education, *Social and Economic Administration*, January 1968.

West, E. G., *Education and the State*, Institute of Economic Affairs 1965.

Ziderman, A., Rates of Return on Investment in Education: Recent Results for Britain, *Journal of Human Resources*, Winter 1973 (A).

Ziderman, A., *Does it Pay to Take a Degree?* Oxford Economic Papers, July 1973 (B).

Suggestions for Further Reading

In addition to references indicated in the chapter, a fuller discussion of all the issues raised is given *inter alia* in the standard work on the Economics of Education:

Blaug (1972).

A shorter, general introduction to the subject, is provided by:

Sheehan, J., *The Economics of Education*, George Allen & Unwin 1973.

7. The economics of health

A J CULYER
Assistant Director,
Institute of Social and Economic Research, University of York

In Britain, formal medical care is mainly provided by the state[1] and decisions are taken by politicians, professional administrators and members of the medical professions. In many ways there is a lack of explicit consideration of the economic issues underlying these decisions, yet the problem of efficient allocation of life-saving and life-enhancing resources subject to a severe budget constraint falls plainly within the economic field. Much of the disquiet that exists about the National Health Service, both amongst those who work in it and those who are its reluctant customers, stems from a failure to face up to these issues: the doctors always want more resources but resolutely resist the invasion of 'clinical freedom' required to ensure that resources are put to the best use; the administrators find themselves in a relatively weak position because of the difficulty of quantitative comparison between frequently (but not invariably) obvious costs with usually elusive benefits.

This chapter emphasises the problem of choice within the NHS. It is divided into four sections. In the first the general nature of health care technology and the supply of health care is examined in a historical context. In the second, we discuss the principal

---

[1]But much also takes place outside the National Health Service. Besides the small private medical market there is much amateur diagnosis and treatment. About 30% of drug spending is outside the NHS.

features of the National Health and the demand for health care. Section three examines investment decisions in the NHS. The final section draws some conclusions and indicates further aspects of health economics not discussed in the chapter.

Health Care Technology

For the greater part of man's history, the relatively crude information provided by population and mortality data is sufficient to chart the story of the social impact of medicine. The remarkable fact appears to be that only after the 20th century was well into its majority is it possible to produce any evidence that the clinical procedures of medicine had any substantial impact on health.

Causes of death were first registered in Britain in 1838 and there is little doubt that the principal factor contributing to population increase since and before that time was a decline in mortality rates due to a reduction in the number of deaths from communicable diseases. Since mortality was falling and life expectancy rising before the causes of death were properly understood, the reduction cannot be attributed to medical science. But could it be attributed to medicine? Knowledge of smallpox was an exception to the relative ignorance prevailing in the 18th and 19th centuries and, since smallpox accounted for about 30% of all deaths, inoculation against it in the 18th century has been held by economic historians to be the principal explanation for the dramatic population rise after 1700. Although the increase was relatively small from 1700 to 1750, after the middle of the 18th century, population rose rapidly and steadily right through to the end of the 19th century. From 1750 to 1850 the best estimates indicate that population increased threefold.

Despite the plausibility of this thesis, it is unlikely that smallpox inoculation, even had it been done with the most effective of modern vaccines, could really have had such an impact. A more important cause of the fall in the mortality rate and the rise in population was the improvement in general living standards over the period. Better nutrition can enable people the better to withstand disease — especially TB, rickets and other then prevalent chronic diseases, which also accounted for a large proportion of all deaths. There can be no doubt that nutrition improved enormously at this time, partly because of greatly increased agricultural productivity and also — despite its squalor — because of increasing urbanisation as the industrial revolution got under way; for agricultural life was far from Arcadian. The sanitary reforms of the 19th century had an undisputed impact on mortality. Adequate drainage, refuse disposal away from publicly frequented places and the improvement of water supplies began to be generally introduced half way through the century. The decline in mortality from intestinal infections such as cholera is alone an adequate indicator of their effectiveness.

Until this century, then, it would appear that, apart from any spontaneous declines in the virulence of disease that may have occurred, the chief agents improving the health of the British people were improved nutrition and hygienic measures. The activities of the medics, whether the humble apothecary or the Fellows of the hugely prestigious Royal College of Physicians,[2] were relatively insignificant.

During the 20th century entirely new developments in medical technology and, especially, in pharmacology made it possible for the first time for medical intervention to have a marked and indisputable impact on the natural history of disease. The principal causes of death today are cancers, heart disease, cerebrovascular disease, pneumonia and bronchitis; all of which strike at older persons. Mortality rarely occurs before the age of 45 and is even then unlikely to be caused by infection or contagion from another diseased person. Such a death is more likely to have been caused by a road accident. There has also been a remarkable reduction in the severity of spells of morbidity. Effective

[2]As late as 1834 membership of the College (established in 1518) could be obtained (provided you were an Oxbridge graduate and, of course, Church of England) for 50 guineas and by passing three twenty-minute examinations. Sir David Barry, in 1834, remarked that the exams could be passed by a man "who is a good classical scholar but knows nothing of chemistry, nothing of medical jurisprudence, nothing of surgery, little or nothing of anatomy, nothing of the diseases of women in child-bed, and nothing of delivering them". The College of Surgeons (far from 'Royal' at the time) was a mean affair and the social status of surgeons was low — and probably deservedly so. (See Abel-Smith 1964.)

treatments now exist for pernicious anaemia, high blood pressure, juvenile diabetes, rheumatic disease, allergies and respiratory diseases, and mental illness. Simple surgical repair work on hernias, haemorrhoids, prolapsed wombs, etc., is now a matter of routine with only minor risks attached. The wonders of modern surgery have become effectively applicable only in the last two decades with the development of anaesthesiology, which has made long and complicated operations on the vital organs both safer for the patient and easier for the surgeon.

The great killers of previous centuries — the infectious diseases — are, with the possible exception of influenza, almost entirely vanquished. The great decline in mortality from pneumonia began only, however, in the 1940's, as did death rates from diphtheria and TB. Today, the diseases from which men die in Britain are chronic and their onset insidious. The major impact of the pharmaceutical revolution on bacterial infections and spirochaetal diseases such as syphilis (stemming mainly from the antibiotics) and on virus diseases (mainly preventive rather than curative) is possibly over. Once again the biggest contributors to further reductions in morbidity are probably environmental. But while once it was an environment of poverty that killed, today it is an environment of wealth. Traffic accidents, smoking, obesity and the emotional stress of urban living are among the principal causes of mortality and morbidity.[3]

This, then, appears to have been the broad pattern. Until the 1930's the chief causes of improvements in health were improvements in the environment. From the 1930's to the 1950's the chief contributors to better health were drugs and new surgical techniques. In the 1960's the revolution in psychotropic drugs took place and really effective treatment of mental illness became possible for the first time. The same period saw the introduction of really effective drugs against high blood pressure. Today, the major sources of further improvement appear once more to be

[3]The implication here that the costs of effecting a given improvement in health by improving environmental arrangements (e.g. by reducing speed limits, curbing tobacco consumption) are lower than the costs of medical intervention does *not* imply that such restraints are justified in social or economic terms. The value of the better health may be much less than either set of costs.

environmental. The wheel has come full circle.[4]

Diagnosis and treatment are, today, highly technical procedures. But the mystique and prestige of modern medical science can serve to give a false picture of its precision. It is now increasingly difficult to distinguish unambiguously between a healthy and a diseased state using technological measurements. For haemoglobin levels, blood pressure, blood sugar levels, and several other testable indicators, a decision has to be taken as to how far above or below average a measure must read before action is warranted. Observer error exists, notably in the reading of X-ray photographs, but also in the measurement of blood pressure. Even among the most experienced hospital doctors, diagnoses can vary quite markedly. Table 1 compares the diagnoses made by consultants in a major hospital with the final diagnosis reached, usually after surgery had taken place. For one common condition, appendicitis, only 75 of the 85 cases were correctly diagnosed by the most experienced men in the hospital. Overall, they were 80% correct in their diagnoses.

Appropriate treatment is likewise far from being as easy and unambiguous to identify as may be popularly thought. There is generally a choice of treatment. In an appendix to the Sainsbury Committee's report on the pharmaceutical industry it was reported that 455 general practitioners prescribed over 30 different prescriptions for each of five common illnesses. Only 8 out of a total of 2,275 prescriptions were found to be unacceptably toxic or ineffectual, but the cost variation was substantial. For painful osteo-arthritis, for example, 11% of GP's recommended Indocid at a prescription cost of 180 old pence, while 10% recommended Aspirin at a cost of 2d.

Hospital practices can also vary widely. For example, despite strong evidence that bed rest is unimportant in the treatment of

---

[4]Though the drug industry is still, fortunately, introducing ever improved and finer psychopharmacological products — with fewer bad side-effects and quicker action. The next decade is likely to see more effective treatment for schizophrenia. If major breakthroughs occur in chemotherapy for viral infections or chemotherapy and/or immunotherapy for cancer, then the judgement reached above, about the relative productivity of environmental adjustments compared with clinical procedures in improving health, would have to be modified.

Table 1. *Diagnoses made by senior clinicians in charge of case: 304 patients with acute abdominal pain (Leeds 1971)*

Final diagnosis	Senior clinical diagnosis								Total
	1	2	3	4	5	6	7	8	
1. Appendicitis	75	1	6	—	—	—	—	3	85
2. Diverticular disease	—	2	—	1	—	—	—	1	4
3. Perforated duodenal ulcer	1	—	5	—	—	—	—	1	7
4. Non specific pain	27	—	1	117	2	—	1	1	149
5. Cholecystitis	—	—	—	—	20	1	3	2	26
6. Small bowel obstruction	—	—	—	—	—	17	—	—	17
7. Pancreatitis	—	1	1	—	1	—	5	—	8
8. Other	3	1	—	1	—	1	—	2	8
Total	106	5	13	119	23	19	9	10	304

Source: F.T. de Dombal *et al., British Medical Journal,* 1 April 1972.

pulmonary tuberculosis, the mean length of stay in hospital is falling only slowly and is very variable from specialist to specialist. (In one case nearly 20% of male patients were discharged in under a month and all within 3 months. In another 10% were discharged in under a month and over 20% were still in hospital after a year.)

Hospitalisation is, of course, extremely costly. Some costly treatments in hospital may actually do patients harm. There is evidence that surgery for small-celled cancer of the bronchus reduces life expectancy compared with radiotherapy without surgery. Intensive care in hospital coronary care units has the effect, it appears, of reducing life expectancy for coronary patients compared with bed rest at home. When death approaches a relatively young patient, dramatic and costly interventions may be undertaken, of little or no therapeutic value in terms of improving the prognosis, whose major value seems to be to provide evidence that 'all possible is being done'.

The effects of several standard treatments on the normal course of disease is unknown or in dispute. Tonsillectomy, for example, is the commonest cause for the admission of children to hospital and the operation has a positive (if small) mortality. Yet there is evidence to suggest that the best medical treatment may be superior, or not inferior, to surgery. Certainly, admissions for tonsillectomy vary enormously per head of population from region to region in Britain (from 234 per 100,000 population in Sheffield to 410 in Oxford in 1971, of which 81% of the cases were aged 14 or less). The treatment of mature diabetes is in doubt, as compared with diabetes in the young for whom insulin appears effective. Modern psychiatry is replete with therapies whose theoretical foundations are in dispute and whose effectiveness remains very largely untested in any systematic way.

Finally, modern therapies have introduced new considerations into the choice of technique: detection of abnormalities in foetuses still in the womb raises the question of abortion as a probably increasingly common surgical operation done on clinical grounds; and contraception, spare-part surgery (including blood transfusion), euthanasia in an increasingly ageing population, all these raise major ethical problems of choice for patients, doctors and society.

This preliminary excursion into medical technology today and since 1700 has not been inflicted on the reader with the intention of belittling the great achievements of medical science and the chemical industry. Rather, the intention has been to disabuse the reader of many commonly held fallacies about the nature of medical 'productive processes'. Rarely does any person have an unambiguously identifiable 'need' for any specific course of medical action. Medical inputs are widely substitutable. Increased real spending on known clinical techniques is unlikely, these days, to have a substantial pay-off in terms of improved health.

At the same time the NHS is very big business, employing around 900,000 people and spending over £3,000 millions a year. For most of its services the patients pay nothing at all, or are heavily subsidised. Hospitals, which spend two thirds of the total, enjoy, even under the new organisation of the NHS, substantial autonomy within the system of accountability to District Management Teams, to Area Health Authorities, to Regional Health Authorities and, ultimately, to the Department of Health and Social Security. Devolution of decision making has always been a feature of the NHS since its inception in 1948 and, within a hospital's budget, substantial discretion exists as regards methods of treatment, intensiveness of treatment (such as length of hospital inpatient stay), selection of patients (and length of waiting list, waiting time) and so on. The medical profession in Britain, as elsewhere, has jealously and successfully guarded its freedom against the threats of encroachment by the state. Whether the disadvantages of some restrictions upon clinical freedom would outweigh the advantages seems, on the face of it, to be far from obvious.

The Demand for Health

One of the basic beliefs of the founding fathers of the NHS was that the provision of medical care free of charge would enable the 'backlog' of sickness to be worked off. With the removal of the price barrier, the health service bill would, after an initial period, tend to decline as a healthy nation became yet healthier. Instead, the utilisation of health services has, on almost every indicator, increased continuously since the Second World War. Table 2 indicates some of the principal dimensions over this period.

How could they all have been so wrong? The major error lay in supposing that there was a fixed stock of sickness in society which, once the 'needs' were treated, would eventually lead to a reduction in the incidence and prevalence of sickness. Rather, as we have seen, the clinical distinction between a 'sick' and a 'well' person is sometimes rather an arbitrary one. There is also doubt about what 'needs' to be done in some cases. As Shaw spitefully wrote in the Preface to *The Doctor's Dilemma* (Shaw 1906) "the distinction between a quack doctor and a qualified one is mainly that only the qualified one is authorised to sign death certificates, for which both sorts seem to have about equal occasion"! Since Shaw's day, and especially since the Second World War, both the definition and the scope for treatment have changed a great deal. Despite the difficult choices that exist, there can be no doubt that there is more *effectively treatable* disease today than in Shaw's time. But the language of 'need' is as misleading today as it was then.

Second, there was an error about what determines people's behaviour in going to the doctor. Just as clinical distinctions between sickness and health are sometimes ambiguous, neither do people behave as though there were a clear-cut division between them. In fact, feeling unwell is a perfectly normal thing. A recent survey in London revealed that 95% of those interviewed had some

Table 2. *Some key statistics of the NHS.*

	(a) NHS expenditure[1] (£m) (UK)		(b) (a) as % national income (UK)		(c) Hospital expenditure (£m) (UK)		(d) (c) as % (a) (UK)		(e) Hospital waiting lists per 1,000 population (England and Wales)	(f) Working days lost through sickness (millions) (Great Britain)
1950	477		4.4		262		54.9		12.1	—
1951	500		4.2		280		65.0		11.5	—
1952	523		4.1		293		56.0		11.4	—
1953	548		4.0		303		55.3		11.9	—
1954	567		3.9		320		56.4		10.7	280.64
1955	607		3.9		348		57.3		10.2	276.77
1956	662		3.9		381		57.6		9.6	275.28
1957	721		4.0		411		57.0		9.8	262.42
1958	764		4.1		443		58.0		9.8	292.38
1959	828		4.2		475		57.4		10.5	282.49
1960	902		4.3		509		56.4		10.2	274.93
1961	981		4.4		557		56.8		10.3	278.95
1962	1025		4.4		605		59.0		10.0	280.00
1963	1092		4.4		656		60.1		10.1	288.86
1964	1186		4.5		718		60.5		10.5	286.95
1965	1308		4.6		791		60.5		10.8	299.24
1966	1434		4.9		873		60.9		11.2	311.47
1967	1594		5.1		954		59.9		11.1	301.13
1968	1741		5.2		1045		60.0		11.0	327.58
1969	1886	1823[2]	5.3	5.1	1154	1150	61.2	63.1	11.5	329.39
1970		2083		5.4		1337		64.2	11.4	342.07
1971		2369		5.5		1552		65.5	10.8	314.13
1972		2732		5.7		1803		66.0	10.2[3]	—

[1]Includes fees paid by NHS patients.
[2]From 1969, some local authority services were transferred from NHS to Social Services.
[3]England only.

symptoms of ill-health during the preceding two weeks. But only 20% had consulted a doctor; the rest either ignored their symptoms or treated them themselves. The patient normally makes the first and all-important general judgement about seeing a doctor, and here economic, social and cultural factors, as well as clinical ones, come into play. Some demand reassurance. Job

Table 3. *The clinical iceberg: England and Wales 1962.*

		No. of recognised sufferers ('000)	Estimated total no. of cases ('000)	Cases in which no treatment was being sought ('000)
Hypertension	males 45+	170	620	450
	females 45+	500	2720	2220
Urinary infections	females 15+	420	830	410
Glaucoma	aged 45+	60	340	280
Epilepsy		160	280	120
Rheumatoid arthritis	aged 15+	230	520	290
Psychiatric disorders	males 15+	560	1200	640
	females 15+	1290	2120	830
Diabetis mellitus		290	600	310
Bronchitis	males 45-64	500	980	480
	females 45-64	390	500	110

Source: J. M. Last, *Lancet*, 1963 and Office of Health Economics, *New Frontiers in Health*, OHE, London 1964.

satisfaction is an important determinant of 'sickness' absence from work.

On purely clinical criteria, there is a vast potential yet for new demands on the health service. An early attempt to identify the magnitude of the so-called 'iceberg of sickness' found in the late 1930's that over 90% of more than 3,000 people examined had some identifiable sickness, but only 26% were aware of being sick and only 8% had been receiving medical attention. Far from this 'backlog' disappearing, table 3 shows the results of a similar study in 1962, fourteen years after the inception of the NHS.

Social class, income, education, the price of health care, all are known to affect the demand for health care by the patient. It is tempting to treat the demand for health services in an *ad hoc* fashion by just listing the factors that seem to be relevant. And yet

Table 4. *Age-specific male death rates per 100,000 population in England and Wales, 1951 and 1961.*

	Social class 1		Social class 5	
Age group	1951	1961	1951	1961
25-34	162	76	214	179
35-44	230	165	386	381
45-54	756	528	1027	1010
55-64	2347	1765	2567	2716
65-69	4839	4004	4868	5142
70-74	7614	6278	7631	8390

Source: D. Butler and D. Stokes, *Political Change in Britain: Forces Shaping Electoral Choice,* 1969, footnote 1, p.265.

this is not good enough. For one thing, the 'facts' are not always as clear cut as one might wish. For example, the age-adjusted mortality rate seems to be negatively correlated with income within the USA and the UK (see table 4), yet the death rate is higher in the rich USA (946 per 100,000 population in 1960) than in the relatively poorer England and Wales (927) or Netherlands (766). Why should this be? Why should ill-health and age be positively correlated and ill-health and education be negatively correlated?

As it happens, there is no need for *ad hoc* theorising about these phenomena. There is a general theory to account for them, a theory based on the proposition that individuals to a large extent *choose* the state of their health: a theory based on the familiar propositions of general demand theory in economics. Note that a theory that will account for these phenomena cannot be merely a theory of the demand for health care. It must be a theory of the demand for *health itself.* It may seem obvious that a fall in an individual's health status will (*ceteris paribus*) increase demand for health care, but why has his health status changed? If we cannot predict this, then we cannot predict the demand for health care; nor can we predict what the future trends of mortality and morbidity will be.

The demand for good health is the demand for an investment good — one that yields services over a period of time. The services yielded by a person's 'stock' of health are basically two: the direct 'utility' of feeling well and the indirect benefits derived from the increased amount of healthy time available for productive use both in work and non-work activities. At any point of time, an individual 'owns' a particular stock of health which is subject to depreciation as time passes and which, if depreciation goes far enough, falls low enough to result in death. Like other capital stocks, the stock of health can usually be increased by investment. The investment production function for any individual can be regarded as dependent upon the amount of time he puts into improving the stock. Key variables involved here are diet, exercise, housing, consumption habits and environmental factors such as public health provision and education — health education naturally affecting the efficiency with which other inputs in the production function are combined. Finally, an important input is, of course, consumption of medical care.

Since many of these variables are under the control of the individual, he may be regarded as *choosing* his preferred stock of health, or rate of investment, subject to constraints which are principally the amount of time available to him and the value of his time in work (i.e. his wage).

Some of the implications of this approach to the demand for health are relatively straightforward implications of the law of demand. If, beyond a certain age, the rate of depreciation of the capital stock is positively correlated with age, the cost of health capital rises as age increases and a lower stock will, *ceteris paribus*, be chosen as optimal: as a person becomes older, he will become less healthy. Rising wages influence both the cost of health (via the cost of time in the production function) and the demand for health (via the value placed upon future healthy days). If X is the proportion of the cost of investment accounted for by time, then a 1% rise in the wage would increase marginal cost of investment by X per cent and the proportional (net) increase in the return on one unit of health capital (marginal efficiency of capital) would be $1-X$, assuming no change in the cost of capital. So long as time is not the only input in the production of health ($X \neq 1$), the net effect is an increase in the demand for health, *ceteris paribus*. Richer persons (earned incomes only), according to this analysis, would also be healthier if other factors are held constant. Mortality and real wage rates should be inversely related. If consumption goods that are harmful to health, such as tobacco, alcohol and motor cars, have high income elasticities, it may also be the case that health and *income* are inversely related: implying a positive relation between mortality and income. Thus, in cross-section analysis comparing different countries, it is not inconsistent with theory to find that mortality and income may be positively correlated, while at the same time rising earnings in one country are associated with reduced mortality.

If education improves the efficiency of health production, it reduces the amount of inputs required to produce a given amount of investment and thus increases the marginal efficiency of health investment, causing the demand for health to shift to the right. To the extent that education also increases the productivity of working time, the effect on the demand for health would be intensified. Note that increases in the demand for health need not always be associated with increases in the demand for health care services. For example, improved education raises the productivity of inputs in the health production function *other than* medical care and can thus induce some substitution *away from* medical care consumption[5].

The data in table 4 are broadly consistent with the educational and earnings implications of the theory of the demand for health. The disturbing rise in mortality for older men in social class 5 during the late 1960's could be due to a changing composition of that class, with those having a higher demand for health moving into higher social class categories. It may have been due to adverse changes in the environment of older poorer men, for example, to a declining real wage for this section of population at this time, or to increased discrimination against this social class of older men by the health services.

Some empirical results for the USA that are consistent with the analysis are shown in table 5. The signs of the relationship between mortality rates and income and education are particularly striking.

---

[5]Decreases in the demand for health can also cause increases in the demand for care. For example, self-poisonings, which are showing a disturbing upward trend for all ages and sexes, are increasingly using up hospital resources.

Table 5. *Percent changes in US age-specific mortality rates resulting from a ten per cent change in several variables.*

	Variables (10% change in):			Per capita health expenditure
	Income	Education	Cigarette consumption	
% change in mortality	+2.0	-2.2	+1.0	-0.65

Source: R. Auster *et al.*, The production of health, an exploratory study, in V. Fuchs (ed), *Essays in the Economics of Health and Medical Care*, NBER, Columbia University Press 1972, Table 8.3, p.145.

More speculatively, we might conceive the demand for health as being complementary to other dimensions of the 'good life'. It has been widely noted that *age-adjusted* mortality rates are much higher for widowed and divorced men than for single men. It is surely not implausible to suppose that this is because they lack some other dimensions of life that make good health valuable. Some evidence in support of the hypothesis is that death rates for the widowed and divorced men are much higher from suicide, motor car accidents, cirrhosis of the liver and lung cancer, where 'choice' is more possible, than from vascular lesions, diabetes or cancer of the digestive organs, where it is less possible or, at least, where the relationship between life-style and health status is somewhat obscure. Married persons, generally, have better health and live longer. In addition to the demand effect discussed above, there may also be a 'production effect' here — good health is possibly produced more efficiently in a marriage or with cohabitation (persons with a natural propensity to ill-health may also be discriminated against in the marriage/cohabitation market).

It is thus clear that both the demand for health and the demand for health care services depend upon a complexity of factors, only one of which is, of course, the monetary price of purchasing inputs (including the price of medical care). The hopes of the founding fathers of the NHS to abolish sickness were, with hindsight, extremely naive. The contemporary approach to NHS economics is less concerned with such broad declarations of good intentions and more with specific aspects concerned with efficiency and equity. In the remainder of this chapter we focus on efficiency problems. Two in particular will be discussed: the measurement of outcomes in the health service, and cost-effectiveness and cost-benefit analysis of specific therapeutic processes.

Cost-Benefit Analysis and Health Service Policy

Outcome Measurement

Health Service planning is in practice largely dependent upon a multitude of political, administrative and professional pressure groups and other influences. It is often conceptualised in terms of the institutional features of the system and the language in which they are rationalised, such as norms of provision and finance, and the health 'needs' of the population. It is a major task to separate out value judgements from purely positive analysis; to identify clear objectives, treatment modes (technologies), outcomes, costs (whether financial or social) and priorities (valuations of outcomes relative to the cost of the technologies for effecting them). There is a general, and perhaps understandable, reluctance by the public at large, patients and the medical profession to recognise the real economic issues, though things have fortunately begun to change of late.

An explicitly rational system of resource allocation in the health field, as in any other, would ideally be based upon knowledge of (a) the technology (the means of attaining ends), (b) the values placed on those ends and (c) the costs of attaining them. Again ideally, the latter two dimensions would be measured in units comparable with those (again ideally) used in other resource-using areas, from private consumption to public investment in, say, education. In practice, however, as we have seen, technologies are sometimes uncertainly successful and many are in dispute. Certainly practice varies widely. Outcomes are barely known. The hospital statistics characteristically measure inputs, throughputs and utilisation rates only. Valuation is held in profound suspicion. Costs tend to be identified with public expenditures, with rather little thought being given to the wider concept of *social* cost, familiar to economists, and of key importance in the health field which is highly labour-intensive and where wages and salaries are administratively fixed or the outcome of bilateral bargaining, and where patients' time, and often that of friends and relations, is a significant input in many therapeutic processes. A consistent treatment of the dating of costs and benefits and their reduction to comparable units, by a technique such as discounting, is generally very poorly understood. There has been and, one suspects, still is a widespread resistance, particularly in the medical profession, to techniques that explicitly expose the key issues and question publicly the traditional theoretical assumptions that life and good health are priceless (i.e. either of infinite value or inherently incapable of being reasonably valued); that doctors are the only conceivable arbiters of what needs to be done; and that clinical freedom is in the best interests of both society in general and patients in particular.

The absence of a really satisfactory measure of outcome is the most fundamental difficulty facing national planners. Ideally, this would measure individuals' states of health — and changes in their states of health — in response to at least some of the multiplicity of variables which affects them. At one level, some people are seeking an aggregate measure of more subtlety than the current morbidity and mortality data — a social indicator of health — which might ultimately be placed among similar indicators in other social areas to qualify and complement the conventional, but narrowly economic, measures of the progress of human societies (such as national income). While such an indicator may be of interest in calling attention to broad 'problem areas', it is unlikely to be of great value in planning health, or any other, services. On the other hand, a satisfactory and reliable indicator at the micro level could be of inestimable value in decisions concerning the deployment of specific sums of money (will X thousand pounds spent here yield a greater increase in 'health' than the X thousand spent there?), in the assessment of the effectiveness of alternative methods of treatment and in the development of a science of prognosis — especially long-term prognoses for patients with chronic conditions (such as elderly persons tend to suffer), for conditions that might produce symptoms only after long periods of time (many industrial diseases are of this type) and for conditions whose cure or amelioration needs to be monitored over long periods (such as head injury victims). Many of these areas are, of course, those where measurement is very complicated and, at least in the first instance, multi-dimensional. (Geriatric cases, for example, are complex because they are multi-symptomatic and because sickness and disability in the old tends to interfere with the entire life-style in a drastic way and over long periods of time.)

Any such index of health (or ill-health) will normally be derived from a set of 'characteristics' measuring (i.e. assigning numbers to) particular dimensions of a condition that are considered (by whom? Surely not doctors alone) to be relevant. Pain, both physical and emotional, mobility, sensory perception, emotional stability, ability to care for oneself, are some illustrative dimensions that would probably figure in anyone's list of potentially relevant characteristics. A number of studies have proved the feasibility and reliability of such measurement, provided that each dimension is not measured too finely (e.g. Wager 1972).

The next stage is to combine the characteristics into a single indicator. This involves value judgements about which levels of which characteristics are regarded as equally good or bad. It also involves value judgements that identify how much worse (or better) one combination of characteristics is than another. Thus, if the dimensions are such that 'more' means 'worse health state' (e.g. pain, disability, mental confusion), it becomes possible to locate those combinations regarded as equally bad in an 'indifference surface' with higher planes corresponding to lower health states. The basic economic model of individual choice, with its familiar indifference curves, provides the guidelines for evolving a consistent methodology of the health indicator and has the advantages of distinguishing those elements in its construction that involve social value judgements and those that are technical or scientific. The final index will be a variable measured in pure numbers — any set of numbers will do, provided that they are linearly related.[6] The final tasks then become to assign values to

[6] Thus, if X is one vector of such numbers and Y is another, they should be related by the linear equation $X = a + b\,Y$, where a and b are any constants. This differs from the usual indifference curve analysis. (How?)

the index (monetarily expressed ones would be the most convenient but should not be confused with market prices), to define production functions relating inputs of medical and other resources to the output index, and to compare the social costs of the inputs with the social value of the output. Alternatively, if the problem is of establishing the most cost-effective means of achieving an objective, defined in terms of the output indicator, *that has been predetermined*, the difficult step of placing values on the indicator becomes unnecessary.

Cost-Benefit and Cost-Effectiveness

The basis of cost-benefit analysis is to compare the full costs and full benefits of a procedure and only to adopt it or continue with it if the latter exceed the former *and* if no alternative procedure would achieve the same end with a greater differential of benefit over cost. Cost-effectiveness analysis focusses on alternative procedures by which a pre-selected objective may be fulfilled and seeks to identify the least cost procedure. Cost-effectiveness cannot establish whether or not the objective is worth pursuing — it may be that even for the least costly procedure, the costs exceed the benefits and to this extent cost-effectiveness analysis is more limited than cost-benefit. In this section the analytical techniques are illustrated by reference to two empirical studies in the health field: one of the cost-effectiveness variety; the other a more ambitious cost-benefit study.

In the cost-effectiveness study by Piachaud and Weddell (1972) two alternative procedures for treating varicose veins were examined. Since the medical outcome of each procedure was taken to be the same, the thorny problem of output valuation was avoided. The method of treating varicose veins is to remove them either by injection-compression sclerotherapy in an outpatient clinic or by surgery as an inpatient.

Since injection-compression treatment takes place in special clinics, the costs of an outpatient session were relatively unambiguously identifiable and amounted to £41.50. It was assumed that money outlays measured the relevant dimensions of cost accurately. The average number of patients treated per session was 31 and the average number of attendances per patient was 7.3. The total cost of the procedure per treated patient was thus, on average, £9.77. The estimation of surgical costs was complicated by the substantial amount of resources shared by veins patients with other surgical and medical inpatients (e.g. catering, laundry, administration, nursing). These costs were divided up according to estimates (some of which are at variance with those used in other studies) of the relative intensity of their utilisation by veins patients. The estimated total cost per case (which was probably, if anything, an underestimate) was £44.22. The institutional costs of surgery thus substantially exceeded those of injection-compression.

Two further dimensions of cost were also considered in this study: time off work and patient-time used up in treatment. The average number of days off work due to treatment and convalescence for surgery was 31.3 days compared with 6.4 days for injection-compression treatment. As for patient-time, allowing for post-operative outpatient attendances and travelling time, surgery cost about 100 hours and injection-compression sclerotherapy about 30 hours. Since these results reinforced the institutional cost results, there was no necessity to express them in monetary units: the cost-effective solution is rather unambiguous. Even with substantial reductions in the inpatient length of stay, surgery appears not to be cost-effective. Cost differentials of this magnitude occur with surprising frequency amongst those cost-effectiveness studies that have been undertaken in the health service field and suggest that even though some refinements of analysis were not utilised, the results would not be substantially altered: the conceptual difficulties that may intimidate at the *a priori* stage sometimes vanish in the context of practical application of the basic analytical apparatus.

The existence of the submerged 'clinical iceberg', discussed above, as well as other more general humanistic concerns and technological developments has led to an increasing demand for mass screening of the relevant populations at risk to identify pre-symptomatic disease and to cure patients in the early stages. Cervical smear programmes, amniocentesis with abortion for women carrying mongol foetuses, testing for high blood pressure, are much talked about screening procedures. But perhaps the best known screening programme in Britain was the mass miniature

Table 6. *Maximum average present value of finding a TB case by MMR (£)*

		\multicolumn{3}{c}{Case avoided after:}		
		10 years	20 years	30 years
Assumed annual rate	5%	285	75	26
of decline of new				
cases notified	10%	181	34	7

Source: D. Pole, Mass radiography: a cost/benefit approach, in G. McLachlan, *Problems and Progress in Medical Care 5*, Oxford University Press for NPHT, London 1971.

radiography (MMR) programme for detection of pulmonary tuberculosis — now, of course, being abandoned on a large scale.

At the end of the 1960's, this programme was costing around £1m per annum — not a large sum by comparison with other expenditure categories; but was it money well-spent? The objects of MMR were basically threefold: to identify cases at a stage when they could be 'nipped in the bud', to tackle part of the submerged clinical iceberg, and to prevent the infection of others by those with presymptomatic TB. The cost of finding an active case of pulmonary TB was around £500. The benefits depend upon the probability of secondary infection from primary cases, the time lags involved (time discounting becomes important here), the differential cost of treatment earlier rather than later, and the reduction in output resulting from reducing or eliminating disability, prolonged hospitalisation or death.

Technological developments in pharmacology imply today that drug therapy is almost completely effective, irrespective of the stage of the TB. Disease activity ceases within a few days of the start of treatment. There is little or no cost differential in identifying cases picked up by MMR or symptomatically — and many of those positive cases picked up by MMR would have cured themselves anyway. In recent years there has been an annual rate of decrease in notifications of TB of about 9% per year. The principal potential gain from MMR clearly has to lie in the prevention of secondary cases, if the programme is to be regarded as worthwhile in today's conditions.

Pole (1971), using a 10% discount rate, found the range of potential benefits from finding a case of TB indicated in table 6, assuming that MMR works with maximum effectiveness by completely eliminating the infectious phase of the disease. On the assumptions that are thus most favourable to MMR, the costs are almost twice the benefits. In a social sense, prevention need not be better than cure, and here is a case in which it appears not to be. The decision to abandon mass screening for pulmonary tuberculosis was, it would appear, amply justified.

Conclusions

The health service problems to which economic analysis has been applied are much more numerous than those that we have been able to illustrate here and include, for example, the optimal size of hospitals, the control of waiting lists, investment in medical education and area allocation of resources to achieve equity. In addition there is a substantial literature on the welfare economics of the NHS dealing, among other issues, with the vexed question of the appropriate roles of the market and the government in health care provision. Finally, there are macro descriptive studies dealing with international comparisons, the role of health service expenditure in macro stabilisation policy and so on. For the reader whose appetite has been whetted, the further reading will help to guide him into these and related areas. We have had to be severe in what has not been covered in the present chapter.

One of the fascinations of health economics lies in the twin facts that the organisation of health care systems has been a traditional political battleground, and in the difficulty of overcoming the contemporary awe of doctors and fear of illness sufficiently to clarify issues and get conceptual approaches straight. Yet, clearly, the potential pay-off to improved decision making and clearer thought about organisational forms is enormous. In an age of wealth and expectations unthinkable before the therapeutic revolution, and at a time when we are witnessing an ever-increasing aged population, there are few fields more worthy of thoughtful economic attention; or, given its importance, less thoroughly tilled.

References

Abel-Smith, B., *The Hospitals 1800-1948*, Heinemann 1964.

Auster, R. *et al.*, 'The Production of Health, An Exploratory Study', in V. Fuchs (ed.), *Essays in the Economics of Health and Medical Care*, Columbia University Press 1972.

Butler, D. and Stokes, D., *Political Change in Britain: Forces Shaping Electoral Choice*, Macmillan 1969.

Cochrane, A. L., *Effectiveness and Efficiency, Random Reflections on Health Services*, Nuffield Provincial Hospitals Trust 1972.

de Dombal, F. T. *et al.*, *British Medical Journal*, 1 April 1972.

Last, J. M., *New Frontiers in Health*, Office of Health Economics 1964.

Piachaud, D. and Weddell, J. M., 'The Economics of Treating Varicose Veins', *International Journal of Epidemiology*, vol 1, 1972.

Pole, D., 'Mass Radiography: A Cost-Benefit Approach', in G. McLachlan (ed.), *Problems and Progress in Medical Care 5*, Oxford University Press 1971.

Shaw, G. B., *The Doctor's Dilemma*, Longman 1906.

Wager, R., *Care of the Elderly*, Institute of Municipal Treasurers and Accountants 1972.

Suggestions for Further Reading

Cochrane, A. L., *Effectiveness and Efficiency: Random Reflections on Health Services*, The Nuffield Provincial Hospitals Trust 1972.

Cooper, M. H., The Economics of Need: the Experience of the British NHS, in M. Perlman (ed), *The Economics of Health and Medical Care*, Macmillan 1974.

Cooper, M. H., and Culyer, A. J., Equality in the NHS, in M. M. Hauser (ed), *The Economics of Medical Care*, Allen and Unwin 1972.

Cooper, M. H., and Culyer, A. J., *Health Economics*, Penguin Books 1973.

Culyer, A. J., On the Relative Efficiency of the NHS, *Kyklos*, vol. 25, 1972.

Culyer, A. J., *The Economics of Social Policy*, Martin Robertson 1973.

Culyer, A. J., Lavers, R. J., and Williams, Alan, Social Indicators: Health, *Social Trends*, No. 2, 1971.

Feldstein, M. S., *Economic Analysis for Health Service Efficiency*, North Holland 1967.

Fuchs, V., (ed), *Essays in the Economics of Health and Medical Care*, NBER, Columbia University Press 1972.

Grossman, M., *The Demand for Health: A Theoretical and Empirical Analysis*, NBER, Columbia University Press 1972.

Miller, H., *Medicine and Society*, Oxford University Press 1973.

Piachaud, D., and Weddell, J. M., The Economics of Treating Varicose Veins, *International Journal of Epidemiology*, vol. 1, 1972.

Pole, D., 'Mass Radiography: A Cost-Benefit Approach', in G. McLachlan (ed), *Problems and Progress in Medical Care 5*, Oxford University Press for the Nuffield Provincial Hospitals Trust 1971.

Pole, D., The Economics of Mass Radiography, in M. M. Hauser (ed), *The Economics of Medical Care*, Allen and Unwin 1972.

Wager, R., *Care of the Elderly*, Institute of Municipal Treasurers and Accountants 1972.

Williams, Alan, The Cost-Benefit Approach, *British Medical Bulletin*, vol. 30, 1974.

Wiseman, J., Cost-Benefit Analysis and Health Service Policy, in A. T. Peacock and D. J. Robertson (eds), *Public Expenditure: Appraisal and Control*, Oliver and Boyd 1963.

8. Income inequality in the UK

A J HARRISON*
Lecturer in Economics,
University of Strathclyde

The extent of inequality in the distribution of personal incomes has for many years been of concern to successive governments, and in consequence has been a crucial consideration of economic policy. For example many advocates of faster economic growth have used as their justification the 'painless' redistribution of income which growth makes possible, contrasting this with the limited opportunities for reducing inequality in a stagnant economy. Similarly successive post-war governments' acceptance of full employment as an important objective of government policy has had obvious implications for the distribution of income.

Possibly the clearest indication of the continuing desire among governments to achieve greater equality, however, occurred in 1974 when the Royal Commission on the Distribution of Income and Wealth was appointed and asked to investigate, among other things, trends in the degree of income inequality. This was preceded by a debate on the same subject which had been continuing for many years, and which was not conducted with a very high regard for objectivity. Too often normative judgements on the question of whether the extent of inequality was acceptable seemed to influence the prior question of how unequal the

*The author wishes to acknowledge the helpful comments of Professors A. B. Atkinson and A. A. Tait.

distribution was. In this chapter we therefore intend to present the reader with the evidence on the latter question, leaving him to draw his own conclusions.

The chapter is divided into three parts. We begin by examining the pre-tax distribution of incomes to determine the trend in income inequality over the post-war period. Next we turn to an investigation of the difference between pre- and post-tax distributions, and in particular we ask whether the various changes which have been made in income tax legislation have made it a more important instrument of equalisation. We conclude with an analysis of some of the policies which have been proposed with the purpose of further redistribution of personal income.

The Distribution of Pre-tax Incomes

In spite of a number of articles in the past 10 years suggesting that the apparent post-war trend towards more equality in the distribution of pre-tax incomes has either slowed considerably or even stopped completely, the view that the trend is continuing unabated is still heard. Probably the most important example of this is the interpretation placed on the official data by the Inland Revenue, and in this section we examine the validity of this interpretation.

Since the war the Inland Revenue has carried out a series of quinquennial sample surveys of personal incomes starting in 1949-50, supplementing these with a further series of smaller annual surveys from 1962-3. These surveys form the basis of the Blue Book distributions of personal income[1] (publication of which has now ceased), and they have also been used by the Inland Revenue to discern trends in inequality. The report of the results of the 1969-70 survey (Inland Revenue 1972) includes a brief 'Historical Review' examining the size distribution of personal incomes

---

[1]These were produced by supplementing the Inland Revenue survey data to adjust for some of the more obvious deficiencies. A precise account of the adjustments is given by Stark (1972, pp.16-19), but perhaps the most important for our purpose was the addition of transfer payments.

derived from earlier surveys and assessing the changes which have
taken place in the twenty years up to 1970. The review concludes
that "the broad picture of the last twenty years is of a tendency for
variations between incomes to diminish" and suggests that two
major influences working in this direction have been "changes in
the composition of income before tax and the operation of the tax
system itself". In other words they believe both that the
distribution of pre-tax incomes has become more equal and that
taxation has reinforced this equalising trend. We will investigate
the latter possibility in the next section which deals with the
influence of taxation, and concentrate our attention here on the
basis for the former claim. Before this, however, we must consider
the adequacy for our purposes of the basic data, which in this case
are taken from the information supplied on income tax returns.

Before the publication of Richard Titmuss's book questioning
the validity of conclusions about inequality based on Inland
Revenue survey data (Titmuss 1962), acceptance of the trend
towards equality implied by the statistics had been total. Titmuss's
contribution changed this air of complacency to such an extent
that, since his book appeared, no discussion of the extent of
income inequality has been complete without at the very least a
mention of the points Titmuss raised.

Of the problems associated with the use of Inland Revenue
survey data, we consider two here. Firstly it is important to note
that an income tax return does not require declaration of many
items which would nevertheless constitute income as defined by
the economist.[2] Capital gains and losses and fringe benefits are
perhaps the most important of these, although there are many
others of less importance. Consequently any analysis which
ignores these will give a false impression of the extent of inequality
if, as seems likely, they are not distributed in proportion to
recorded incomes.

The second deficiency results from the Inland Revenue's
recording of income units rather than individuals; this may give

[2]"No concept of income can be really equitable that stops short of the
comprehensive definition . . . 'net accretion of economic power between two points
of time'." (Royal Commission on the Taxation of Profits and Income 1955.)

rise to an apparent trend towards equality which is entirely spurious. Thus a married couple will typically appear in the statistics as one unit with their incomes aggregated, which approximates neither to a per capita basis nor to a genuine household basis. Quite apart from the practical relevance of a distribution of income among income units at a point of time, we are faced with the possibility that over time the composition of units might be changing, perhaps because of earlier marriages, with an accompanying effect on the distribution of income. However this observed change will not be the result of underlying changes in the per capita distribution, so that trends deduced from official statistics could be purely reflections of social change.[3]

We now investigate the validity of the Inland Revenue's conclusion of a continuing reduction in inequality. One method of measuring changes in the inequality of income distribution is to compare the share of total personal income going to different groups of income units, counting from the richest to the poorest over time. This procedure has its problems, in particular the question of whether we believe it is more important for certain groups in society to improve their position than it is for others. To consider a simple example: imagine that we are comparing two distributions, in one of which both the top and bottom groups of income recipients have a greater share of total income than their counterparts in the other distribution. Is this distribution less equal than the other because of the higher share of the group at the top, or more equal because of the higher share of the group at the bottom? The only way to resolve this question is by resorting to a specific weighting of individuals' utilities via a social welfare function, which requires of course that we introduce value judgements.

One recent contribution which adopted the procedure proposed here is by R. J. Nicholson who based his work (Nicholson 1967) on

---

[3]A further consideration which must be recognised is the problem of the relevant time period for an analysis of income distribution. The evidence presented here implies a 'snapshot' picture of the distribution at a point in time, but there are strong arguments in favour of considering lifetime income instead. Clearly we would expect this in general to reveal a reduced degree of inequality (Atkinson 1975).

Table 1. *Percentage distribution of incomes before tax (Blue Book estimates)*

Group of income recipients	1949 %	1957 %	1959 %	1960 %	1961 %	1962 %	1963 %	1964 %	1967 %
Top 1%	11.2	8.2	8.4	8.5	8.1	8.1	7.9	8.1	7.4
2% - 5%	12.6	10.9	11.5	11.4	11.1	11.1	11.2	11.4	11.0
6% - 10%	9.4	9.0	9.5	9.8	9.7	9.7	9.6	9.5	9.6
11% - 40%	34.9	37.6	38.4	38.5	37.6	38.6	39.0	39.1	38.9
41% - 70%	19.2	23.1	22.5	22.1	23.5	22.6	22.6	22.3	22.8
Bottom 30%	12.7	11.3	9.7	9.8	10.0	9.8	9.7	9.6	10.3

Source: 1949-63 (Nicholson 1967, p.14); 1964-67 (Walsh 1972, p.224).

comprehensive data on the size distribution of incomes which appeared in the annual Blue Books for the years 1949 to 1967.[4] Table 1 shows the findings of Nicholson supplemented by those of Walsh (Walsh 1972), which may be viewed in conjunction with the percentage shares of income derived from Inland Revenue survey data[5] for the years 1949-50 to 1970-71, shown in table 2. It must be stressed that the two series are in no sense comparable, for it is clearly possible for a particular adjustment radically to change its influence on the distribution over time. However the clear impression to emerge is the striking similarity between the trend in this table's results and the trend in table 1. Thus we propose the tentative suggestion that some indication of the likely trend from 1967 onwards in table 1 is supplied by that actually indicated in table 2.[6] If we accept this we are now in a position to analyse the period 1949 to 1970 as a whole, which in fact divides conveniently into two distinct sub-periods.

The greatest degree of change took place between 1949 and 1957, when the top income recipients and in particular the top 5%

[4] See footnote [1].

[5] The 1970-71 survey (Inland Revenue 1973) contains a complete list of all the surveys and where they are to be found on p.131.

[6] With one important exception: the share of the bottom 30%. This in fact illustrates the importance of our remarks above regarding direct comparisons of the two tables. The share of the bottom 30% declines noticeably in table 1 but not at all in table 2, stressing the effect of transfer payments and, in particular, the increased number of pensioners over the period.

Table 2. *Percentage distribution of incomes before tax (Inland Revenue survey estimates)*

Group of income recipients	1949-50 %	1954-5 %	1959-60 %	1964-5 %	1967-8 %	1969-70 %	1970-71 %
Top 1%	10.6	8.8	7.9	7.7	7.0	6.8	6.3
2% - 5%	12.5	11.0	10.8	10.6	10.4	10.3	10.3
6% - 10%	9.1	8.5	8.7	8.7	8.8	8.7	8.8
11% - 40%	32.5	35.3	35.5	35.9	36.5	36.8	37.2
41% - 70%	21.3	23.1	23.7	23.8	24.2	24.2	23.9
Bottom 30%	13.9	13.5	13.4	13.5	13.2	13.2	13.5

Source: calculated by the author.

saw their share fall quite sharply. On the other hand, the bottom 30% also experienced some decline in their share, so that the "redistribution was from the extremes to the middle ranges" (Nicholson 1967, p.14). For reasons already stated we should therefore be cautious about labelling this change as clearly in favour of greater equality.

Turning to the trend for subsequent years, we find our dilemma is somewhat resolved, although not perhaps to the satisfaction of those who feel greater equality is desirable. This is because there has been no significant change in the pre-tax distribution between 1957 and 1970. In table 1 the percentage shares are remarkably constant from 1957 to 1967, while in table 2 the trend from 1967-8 to 1970-1 is similarly static. Thus Nicholson's prediction in 1967 that greater equality seems unlikely has been borne out by events. Furthermore this analysis is substantially at variance with the views expressed by the Inland Revenue on the subject.

The Inland Revenue's conclusion of a continuing reduction in inequality is based exclusively on one table in the 'Historical Review' which contains values of an inequality index, the Pareto coefficient, for each of the survey years. The value of this coefficient serves as an indication of the dispersion of incomes within a distribution, a higher value implying a reduction in dispersion;[7] and for the period 1949-50 to 1969-70 the coefficient is estimated to have increased from 1.95 (1949-50) to 2.32 (1959-60) and to 2.55 (1969-70), suggesting an unchecked trend towards a more equal distribution. The major objection to the validity of this conclusion is that the Pareto coefficient has rather limited applicability, since it assumes that the mathematical expression which describes the income distribution is of a certain type. In fact this restriction is quite severe, since the assumed expression is only satisfactory for that part of the distribution relating to higher incomes. In consequence, the published coefficients are calculated for incomes above £550 per annum in 1949-50 and £1,350 per annum in 1969-70, and all units receiving incomes below these levels are effectively ignored. An idea of the implications of this deficiency for such an analysis can be obtained from a consideration of the proportion of income units below the cut-off points in the relevant years: in 1949-50 16% of the income units were below £550 and in 1969-70 40% were below £1,350. As the reader will appreciate, this rather reduces the value of the conclusions drawn and it is therefore clear that our approach, which makes fuller use of the available data, is preferable.

Even with an alternative approach, however, our conclusions are still based on rather shaky foundations, in that the most comprehensive estimates of the distribution of income are no longer produced. It is indeed a sad commentary that in an area of such social and economic importance this is the case. In one important respect they are nevertheless of use, for they demonstrate beyond doubt that the conclusion of the Inland Revenue is not one which a fuller investigation of the data can support. Next we examine whether the same is true when taxation enters the picture.

The Distribution of Post-tax Incomes

It is a widely-held notion that the system of income taxation in the United Kingdom is a very important redistributive factor and, as we have noted above, the Inland Revenue has also argued that this particular effect has intensified in the period since 1949. To

[7]In graphical terms the Pareto coefficient is the absolute value of the slope of the relationship between the logarithm of the number of people with incomes greater than a given income and the logarithm of that income, where the relationship is linear.

examine whether this is in fact the case, we use the same techniques adopted in the previous section to study before-tax incomes. Clearly much of what we have already said of the dangers involved in the interpretation of the evidence still applies, and in particular the basis for any comparison of relative inequality either before and after tax, or at different points in time, must be clearly stated. In at least one important respect, however, our task is perhaps easier. Insofar as the data we use are the same as those used in the previous section, we do obtain a clear picture of the extent of redistribution of recorded incomes caused by taxation, since we are comparing pre-tax incomes with incomes net of the tax levied on them. Thus if the system of taxation is strongly progressive, this will be highlighted by the comparison and distinct changes in percentage shares will be observed. Alternatively little change will suggest that taxation is less important for redistribution than is sometimes claimed. A more difficult consideration is whether the tax base satisfies the requirements of equity — in other words whether income as defined for tax purposes approximates to the comprehensive definition of income — and, of course, the greater the extent of avoidance allowed by a system of taxation, the less efficient it will be overall as a vehicle for egalitarian measures. Perhaps the best example of this is supplied by estate duty, which appears highly progressive but affords many opportunities for avoidance so that it has become widely acknowledged as a 'voluntary' tax.

We begin our analysis by once again making use of Nicholson's and Walsh's work in this area, which examined the percentage shares of after-tax income implied by the Blue Book distribution (Nicholson 1967, Walsh 1972). In table 3 we reproduce the findings of these studies, while table 4 shows the post-tax percentage shares implied by the Inland Revenue surveys. These must of course be compared with tables 1 and 2 respectively, to assess both the extent of the redistributive effect and whether or not this effect has intensified.[8] Let us consider each of these

---

[8] Again our use of Inland Revenue survey data to indicate the trend for the most recent years is only valid if it is accepted that the trend for earlier years is sufficiently close to that in table 3.

Table 3. *Percentage distribution of incomes after tax (Blue Book estimates)*

Group of income recipients	1949 %	1957 %	1959 %	1960 %	1961 %	1962 %	1963 %	1964 %	1967 %
Top 1%	6.4	5.0	5.2	5.1	5.5	5.5	5.2	5.4	4.9
2% - 5%	11.3	9.9	10.6	10.5	10.5	10.7	10.5	10.3	10.1
6% - 10%	9.4	9.1	9.4	9.4	9.1	9.4	9.5	9.4	9.4
11% - 40%	37.0	38.5	39.8	39.8	38.9	39.2	39.5	40.3	39.6
41% - 70%	21.3	24.0	23.7	23.5	24.3	23.6	23.5	23.8	24.3
Bottom 30%	14.6	13.4	11.2	11.7	11.9	11.7	11.8	10.8	11.7

Source: as table 1.

questions in turn.

As we would expect, there is no doubt that the imposition of taxes has caused a redistribution of incomes of an equalising nature. In 1949, for example, the shares of the groups at or above the top 5% fell, while the groups below the top 10% have clearly increased their percentage shares, with the greatest proportionate increase going to the bottom 30% of income recipients. Furthermore, this picture is repeated for all the years analysed. It is also of importance to note that these changes are of a type which enable us to state categorically that the distribution of post-tax incomes is more equal than that for pre-tax incomes in all years. This is because any social welfare function of implied weightings of the welfare of different groups will rank the post-tax distributions as preferable to their equivalent pre-tax distributions.

Turning to the second question of whether or not taxes have increased their redistributive effect, the task is a slightly more difficult one. This is because any movement towards greater pre-tax equality will by itself reduce the influence of a tax system with progressively higher rates, the proportion of incomes subject to the higher rates falling over time. Consequently, although the fall in the share of the top 1% as a result of taxation in 1949 is, for example, clearly greater in both absolute and proportionate terms than that in 1957, this may only be attributable to the higher pre-tax share of the top 1% in 1949. After 1957 this problem becomes less acute since, as we have earlier noted, the percentage

Table 4. *Percentage distribution of incomes after tax (Inland Revenue survey estimates)*

Group of income recipients	1949-50 %	1954-5 %	1959-60 %	1964-5 %	1967-8 %	1969-70 %	1970-71 %
Top 1%	5.8	4.8	4.9	5.0	4.6	4.4	4.2
2% - 5%	10.9	9.8	9.7	9.5	9.4	9.3	9.3
6% - 10%	9.0	8.6	8.6	8.5	8.5	8.5	8.6
11% - 40%	34.6	37.2	37.1	37.2	37.8	37.7	38.0
41% - 70%	23.8	23.7	25.2	24.9	25.3	25.5	25.1
Bottom 30%	15.9	15.9	14.5	14.8	14.5	14.6	15.0

Source: as table 2.

distribution of pre-tax incomes is fairly constant.

In tables 5 and 6 we present the post-tax shares from tables 3 and 4 as percentages of their equivalent pre-tax shares for a representative sample of the years covered. Thus we see that in our example above, comparing the top 1% in 1949 and 1957, taxation reduced the shares to 57% and 61% respectively of their pre-tax levels, although whether this change is attributable to the levelling of incomes or to the reduced effect of taxation we are not able to say without further evidence on the nature of the tax system in the two years in question. From 1957 onwards, however, there is a slight but nevertheless identifiable trend. From 1957 to 1964 the pre-tax share of the top 1% remained approximately constant, although this same group actually increased its share of post-tax incomes; so that expressed as a percentage of its pre-tax equivalent, we observe a further increase which is undeniably associated with a diminution in the influence of taxation. This picture continues throughout the distribution so that the bottom 30% are only raised by 13% in 1964 compared with 19% in 1957. We are therefore forced to agree with Nicholson that in this period "tax changes underline the ending of the movement towards equality since their effect is to improve the relative position of the top income groups" (Nicholson 1967, p.17). Finally, this seems to change once again when we look at the more recent years 1964 to 1970. In these years, there is a marked constancy in the effect of taxation brought out by the similarity between both the final two columns of table 5 and the final three columns of table 6.

Table 5. *The effects of taxation: post-tax shares as a percentage of pre-tax shares (Blue Book)*

Group of income recipients	1949 %	1957 %	1959 %	1964 %	1967 %
Top 1%	57.2	61.0	61.9	66.7	66.2
2% - 5%	89.7	90.8	92.2	90.4	91.8
6% - 10%	100.0	101.1	99.0	99.0	97.9
11% - 40%	106.0	102.4	103.7	103.1	101.8
41% - 70%	110.9	103.9	105.3	106.7	106.6
Bottom 30%	115.0	118.6	115.5	112.5	113.6

Source: calculated from tables 1 and 3.

For example the post-tax share of the top 1% represented 65% of the pre-tax share in 1964-5, 66% in 1967-8 and 67% in 1970-1. Similarly the bottom 30% saw their position improved by 10%, 11% and 11% respectively, while groups in between remained likewise unchanged. This seems to suggest that after 1964 the effect of taxation began to reassert itself as an agent of redistribution, after a period of at least seven years during which its power was somewhat reduced.

Thus we are now in a position to summarise our findings on the extent of the reduction in inequality attributable to the income tax system and the changing strength of this influence.[9] There seem to be three basic sub-periods. First, from 1949 to 1957 there occurred an apparent change in the distribution of pre-tax incomes, which may have been responsible for the observed reduction in the effect of taxation; at the limit, when all incomes are equally distributed, the ability of taxes to cause greater equality is clearly completely

[9] It is important to remember when considering the evidence we have presented that the Inland Revenue surveys give only a limited indication of the extent of redistribution induced by government policy. Besides the obvious deductions they ignore, such as national insurance contributions, and the obvious additions such as transfer payments (which are included in the Blue Book estimates), no consideration is given to the effects of taxes other than income tax and surtax. Estimates are prepared by the Central Statistical Office of the full effect of government budgetary policy, based on Family Expenditure Survey data; but for reasons already noted (see footnote [1]) these data, and work based on them, are not considered here.

Table 6. *The effects of taxation: post-tax shares as a percentage of pre-tax shares (Inland Revenue)*

Group of income recipients	1949-50 %	1954-5 %	1959-60 %	1964-5 %	1967-8 %	1969-70 %	1970-1 %
Top 1%	54.7	54.6	62.0	64.9	65.7	64.7	66.7
2% - 5%	87.2	89.1	89.8	89.6	90.4	90.3	90.3
6% - 10%	98.9	101.2	98.9	97.7	96.6	97.7	97.7
11% - 40%	106.5	105.4	104.5	103.6	103.6	102.5	102.2
41% - 70%	111.7	102.6	106.3	104.6	104.6	105.4	105.0
Bottom 30%	114.4	117.8	108.2	109.6	109.9	110.6	111.1

Source: calculated from tables 2 and 4.

extinguished. From 1957 to 1964, the second sub-period, there was a relative relaxation in the intensity of the tax system, so that those receiving higher incomes and comprising the top groups in the distribution were able to maintain their share of post-tax income, in spite of small reductions in their pre-tax shares. Finally, from 1964 to 1970 the situation again changed, so that the relaxation ceased but was not reversed. Consequently in this last period the effect of taxation remained unchanged, suggesting that the legislative alterations in the tax system were broadly in line with the rising level of money incomes. We therefore observe a degree of inequality in 1970 which some will consider acceptable and others excessive. In the belief that this latter group form a sizeable section of public opinion, we now examine policy proposals to achieve a further redistribution of income.

Policies for Redistribution

Any government which feels there is a need to encourage a more equal distribution of income[10] is faced with essentially two alternatives to achieve its objective. It can attempt to influence the distribution of pre-tax incomes, by inducing employers to favour those on low incomes when awarding pay increases for example.

[10]In October 1974 the newly-elected Labour government made this an explicit aim of policy, as an integral part of the 'social contract'.

On the other hand it might prefer to operate via the tax system, structuring the level of rates and exemptions to incorporate greater progressivity and hence a more equal distribution of post-tax incomes. Indeed these approaches are by no means mutually exclusive and both may be combined in an effort to attain the stated objective. Since the war successive governments have tended to adopt the latter method when they have considered it necessary to pursue greater equality, although as we have noted there was a period prior to the publication of Richard Titmuss's book when they may have been falsely complacent about such a need. In this section we briefly discuss the advantages and disadvantages of each of these approaches in turn, using as examples both schemes which have been introduced by different governments and others which remain as mere policy suggestions.

Although successive governments have attempted to influence the level of wages through incomes policies, these policies have been directed at limiting the rate of increase of wages rather than bringing about long-term changes in relative income levels. Despite the prominence in most formal statements on incomes policies of some commitment to improve the relative position of the low paid, experience of the operation of incomes policies indicates few concessions to this objective. One exception was the Conservative government's introduction in 1973 of stage II of its incomes policy, which limited group settlements on increased incomes to "one pound per week per person plus 4% of the group's total wage bill in the previous year, excluding overtime" (Trinder 1974, p.23), with a certain amount of latitude allowed for distributing this sum within the group subject only to the constraint that no individual's increase exceeded £250 per annum. Whether or not redistribution of income was the main aim of this policy, there existed within the scheme a clear invitation to employers to favour workers on lower incomes. The maximum increase allowed, expressed as it was as an absolute amount plus a percentage, meant more as a percentage to someone earning twenty pounds per week than to someone earning twice that amount. Also the legislation governing the distribution of the group's increase allowed employers to re-allocate individual increases, which according to the formula were in excess of the upper limit, to other workers lower down the income scale.

One crucial defect of this scheme, judged purely in the context of the likelihood of redistribution, was the fact that the formula by which settlements were to be calculated was only a maximum and not a minimum as well. Hence, if we accept that one reason for the position of the low-paid groups in society is the poor bargaining strength they possess, it is quite possible that this will be reflected by settlements for these groups below this maximum, thereby merely reinforcing their relative position in the distribution of incomes. Putting this possibility aside, it is nevertheless true that high percentage increases on very low incomes mean very low absolute increases and there is some evidence to suggest that this factor·was important in the apparent failure of the incomes policy to achieve substantial redistribution: "information ... does not suggest that the effects were all that large, mainly because people in higher-paid industries usually received larger increases than in the lower-paid, at any rate in absolute terms" (Trinder 1974, p.37). Furthermore, since this analysis was in terms of wage rates, there is a distinct possibility that even this improvement disappears when actual earnings are considered as a result of "wage drift above the formula" (Trinder 1974, p.38).

An alternative method for adjusting the pre-tax distribution of income, as yet unused by any government, is the legal imposition of a national minimum wage.[11] The likely economic effects of a prescribed minimum wage, less than which employers are forbidden to pay, are well documented (Jackson 1972, Hughes 1972) and we therefore dwell only briefly on two in particular here. Both of these, which are not necessarily independent of each other, may diminish the lasting impact of the legislation on the distribution of income. The first is that workers higher up the income scale who see their relative position deteriorating as a result of the increased incomes at the bottom may negotiate increases for themselves in an attempt to reassert their so-called 'differentials'. This will then continue through the entire distribution, accompanied by higher prices either because of the

[11]Although a national minimum wage has never been introduced, there have been attempts to raise incomes in particular industries through Wages Councils, which in fact date back to 1909 (Jackson 1972).

minimum wage itself or as a consequence of the transmission of the effect of the minimum wage in the manner suggested, so that the final outcome could well be exactly as before in terms of relative inequality. This pressure by the better paid to maintain income differentials is a major obstacle to any attempt by government to equalise the pre-tax distribution of income. The second possibility is that the minimum wage will cause widespread unemployment because the industries in which those below the minimum are employed are no longer profitable. In this case the outcome will merely be the substitution of social security and national insurance benefits, themselves typically low, for the 'poverty' wages the workers were previously receiving.

Turning next to the methods a government has at its disposal to adjust the distribution of post-tax incomes, we find that once again there are many possibilities. Of these, a high proportion have appeared (sometimes mistakenly according to some writers) under the title of negative income taxation (NIT) and this therefore seems a logical place to begin our discussion.

According to what is perhaps the fullest account of the merits and demerits of NIT (Barker 1972), four features distinguish such a scheme. These are "an automatic income and needs test; a tax-paying threshold ... ; a rate of negative taxation; and a minimum guaranteed income" (Barker 1972, p.44). Within the context of the current system of income taxation in the United Kingdom for example, the first and second features already exist. All individuals with earnings above a certain minimum level of income are required to make a tax return which contains details of both their income and their needs (at least to the extent that size of family can alone be said to indicate needs). In addition personal and child allowances provide a threshold, although naturally the actual level of the threshold would have to be determined by the precise objectives of the scheme. Thus additional requirements for the implementation of NIT would be the introduction of a rate of negative taxation and a minimum income guarantee, whereby those below the threshold would receive a payment from the Inland Revenue calculated by the multiplication of the rate of taxation by the difference between their actual income and the threshold, subject to the constraint of the minimum guarantee.

Such a scheme has many apparent advantages over alternative

methods of income maintenance, particularly those which require an independent means-test in order to assess eligibility, since it involves an essentially painless means-test via income tax returns. As a result, it is argued, it is able to direct funds precisely where they are needed, avoiding the waste of a system of universal benefits which are distributed to the many who do not need them in order to reach those who do (Lees 1967). However, the scheme is not without its disadvantages and these have tended to cause many who are concerned with the problem of low incomes to prefer alternative solutions (Atkinson 1975, Barker 1972, Meade 1972).

A major disadvantage of NIT is that while it overcomes one deficiency of means-testing — the unwillingness of people to submit to a means-test — it retains others. In particular it is likely to levy very high marginal rates of 'tax' on those it is attempting to help, whether or not it completely replaces the wide range of means-tested benefits. If it does not replace them it will represent one further element of what has come to be called the 'poverty trap', whereby workers on low incomes who receive an increase in pay lose high proportions of that increase in withdrawal or reduction of means-tested benefits. If on the other hand it completely supersedes the existing array of benefits, the rate of negative tax will be so high that it will in itself constitute a 'poverty trap'.

An associated argument used by opponents of NIT relates to the question of the disincentive effect of these high marginal rates of tax. Economic theory has shown fairly conclusively that there is little we can say *a priori* about the likely incentive or disincentive effects of increases in taxation and those attempting to collect evidence on the subject have been forced to admit similar agnosticism. However, there is at least the possibility that a worker will feel no great incentive to increase his gross income (by working longer hours for example) when faced with the prospect of losing a high proportion of the increase in taxation.

The final disadvantage we consider, before discussing a restricted variant of NIT actually in operation, is also concerned with incentives. In this case the question is whether an employer will use the scheme to subsidise low wages, on the assumption that workers will be indifferent between increased incomes and a state-provided supplement. "The spectre which NIT raises is that of

Speenhamland[12] and its supposed dread consequences: a profligate, improvident, demoralised, pauperised labour force" (Barker 1972, p.61). This does seem in the modern context to be rather excessive, although it is of interest to note that when the restricted form of NIT, known as Family Income Supplement (FIS), was introduced in 1970, there were many who made the comparison.

FIS is a scheme for the supplementation of incomes which manages to include all the disadvantages of NIT without any of its attendant advantages. It does not use the income tax system as an automatic means test, relying instead on the willingness of individuals to make application for awards. In consequence it has never attracted more than one-half of those families who were originally thought to be eligible. In addition the award of FIS acts as a passport for many other means-tested benefits, so that its own implicit tax rate of 50% is only one element in a poverty trap with very high marginal rates. Two points must be offered in its defence however. The first is that once awarded the level of payment is unadjusted for one year, thereby partially relieving the worst aspects of the poverty trap: it does not act as a disincentive to a worker in the short run should he be given the opportunity of a higher income. The second is that it was originally intended as a stop-gap for a much fuller scheme, tax credits, which because of the change in government in 1974 will not now be introduced. For this reason we will not consider the proposals in detail here,[13] concentrating instead on the general scheme of which it was an example — the social dividend (SD).[14]

SD has a long history and has recently been revived by Meade, who advocates its introduction in preference to NIT, which he also considers (Meade 1972). The main differences between SD and

[12]A system of income support introduced at the end of the 18th century.

[13]For a sample of conflicting views the reader is referred to (Atkinson 1973, Barr and Roper 1974).

[14]Even on this, opinions appear to differ. One writer has called the tax credit proposals "an integrated negative income tax" (Atkinson 1975), while another describing something akin to tax credits suggests that "the differences between NIT and SD are greater than the similarities" (Barker 1972). In what follows we adopt the latter approach, although we suspect that the problem is mainly one of definition.

NIT according to the definitions adopted here are, first, that a level of payment is guaranteed to all families, varying only according to family size, so that the basic benefit is paid universally rather than on a means-test basis; and second, that the collection of the revenue to pay for the dividends has implications for all tax-payers in a way which is not necessarily true of NIT. This latter difference stems from the fact that, unlike NIT which levies a rate of negative taxation not necessarily the same as the rate of positive taxation on earnings below a given amount, the level of the SD dictates the level of tax rate necessary for all tax-payers, since the gross revenue from taxes equals the amount of total payments — other government expenditure being assumed for the moment to be zero. Thus to quote a particular proposal "if the SD is set at one quarter of average earnings, then the rate of income tax must be set to raise a sum equal to one quarter of total earnings, i.e. at a rate of 25%. This means that every family starts with an SD equal to one quarter of average earnings and then keeps three quarters of its earnings in addition" (Meade 1972, p.305).

The obvious attractions of the scheme tend to diminish, however, when we relax the assumptions on other government expenditure which is clearly non-zero. In fact, referring to the example given above, the composite rate of tax required to finance the SD and all other government activity rose to 53% and even with a modification to the scheme still implied a rate of 43%, which compares rather unfavourably with the current standard rate of income tax of 33%. Thus the epithet 'politically unacceptable' has been applied to SD and this, like many other schemes, remains merely a proposal.

Thus it appears that policies for redistribution designed to affect both the pre- and post-tax distributions are confronted by many obstacles. In the former case we have noted that successive governments have tended in reality to pay only lip-service to redistribution when framing legislation designed to constrain increases in incomes. In addition it is doubtful whether in a mixed economy any substantial redistribution could take place as the result of incomes policies, given the propensity of 'market forces' to reassert themselves when restrictions are lifted. To the extent that this is true, it may also offset the effects of measures aimed at adjusting the post-tax distribution. This, however, requires the further assumption that the individual is primarily concerned with the level of his post-tax income when negotiating increases; and while we would argue that he should be, it is not obviously the case that he is.

Conclusion

What is evident is that the distribution of income over time in Britain has shown a remarkable resilience both to government policy and to economic change. The years since 1957 in particular have displayed a marked constancy in the distribution of income, which is at variance with the Inland Revenue's stated view of a continuing trend towards greater equality. In addition, income taxation has not been an increasingly potent weapon of redistribution, and if anything is relaxing its grip on higher incomes. While the constraints — both social and political as well as economic — upon achieving a major redistribution of income in favour of the less well-off are great, it is not yet clear whether the seeming permanence of a high degree of inequality reflects the immovability of these constraints; or whether it is the result of governments' tacit support for the status quo, which stems from an unwillingness to implement decisive policies in so potentially controversial an area.

References

Atkinson, A. B., *The Tax Credit Scheme and Redistribution of Income*, Institute for Fiscal Studies 1973.

Atkinson, A. B., *The Economics of Inequality*, Oxford University Press 1975.

Barker, D., Negative Income Tax, and Family Income Supplement, in Bull, D. (ed), *Family Poverty* (2nd edn), Duckworth 1972, pp.44-82.

Barr, N., and Roper, J., Tax Credits, *Three Banks Review*, 101, March 1974, pp.24-45.

Hughes, J., Low Pay: A Case for a National Minimum Wage, in Bull, D., (ed), *Family Poverty* (2nd edn), Duckworth 1972, pp.93-104.

Jackson, D., *Poverty*, Macmillan 1972.

Lees, D., Poor Families and Fiscal Reform, *Lloyds Bank Review*, 83, October 1967, pp.1-15.

Meade, J. E., *Poverty in the Welfare State*, Oxford Economic Papers, 24, 1972, pp.289-326.

Nicholson, R. J., The Distribution of Personal Income, *Lloyds Bank Review*, 83, January 1967, pp.11-21.

Stark, T., *The Distribution of Personal Income in the United Kingdom 1949-1963*, Cambridge University Press 1972.

Titmuss, R. M., *Income Distribution and Social Change*, George Allen and Unwin 1962.

Trinder, C., Incomes Policy and the Low-Paid, in Young, M. (ed), *Poverty Report 1974*, Temple Smith 1974, pp.21-39.

Walsh, A. J., Tax Allowances and Fiscal Policy, in Townsend, P.B., and Bosanquet, N. (eds), *Labour and Inequality*, Fabian Society 1972, pp.211-234.

Inland Revenue, *The Survey of Personal Incomes 1969-70*, HMSO 1972.

Inland Revenue, *The Survey of Personal Incomes 1970-71*, HMSO 1973.

Royal Commission on the Taxation of Profits and Income, *Final Report*, Cmnd 9474, HMSO 1955. Memorandum of Dissent signed by Bullcock, W. L., Kaldor, N., and Woodcock, G.

Suggestions for Further Reading

References to further reading on specific topics are indicated in the chapter. For a comprehensive introduction to income inequality see: Atkinson (1975).

Covering the broader area of income distribution and its determination is: Pen, J., *Income Distribution*, Allen Lane 1971.

9. Macroeconomic policy: formulation and implementation

JOHN D HEY
Lecturer in Economics,
University of St Andrews

Introduction

Although nowadays widely accepted, the idea that governments can, and indeed should, assume responsibility for the management of the economy is relatively new. As recently as the 1930's the prevailing official view, throughout the massive unemployment of the Great Depression, was that governments were powerless in restoring full employment. Despite the publication of Keynes's *General Theory* (Keynes 1936), it required the experience of the Second World War to convince many people of the correctness of Keynes's main thesis: that unemployment could be reduced by the stimulation of aggregate demand. Indeed it was as late as 1944 that any UK government had publicly declared that "one of their primary aims and responsibilities [was] the maintenance of a high and stable level of employment" (HMSO 1944, p.3).

The three decades that have elapsed since then have witnessed an increasing involvement of successive governments with the problems of economic management and with the performance of the economy. Naturally, as time has passed, more and more experience of the operation of macroeconomic policies has been accumulated. One of the immediate realisations was that the success of government economic management could not be judged solely on whether or not it had attained the 'high and stable level of employment' objective.

194

Indeed, it was immediately apparent that an over-vigorous pursuit of this objective, by an excessive stimulation of aggregate demand, was likely to create (at least) two further problems: first, the onset of inflation, as supply constraints built up so that excess demand could be dissipated only by price increases; second, balance of payments difficulties, as the pressure of home demand sucked in new imports and simultaneously diverted productive resources from exports to home demand. Thus, in addition to the rate of unemployment, the rate of inflation and the balance of payments came to be regarded as important indicators of the effectiveness of government policy.

It was also realised that the *way* in which aggregate demand was stimulated had important implications — not least of which was the implication for future levels of employment. With a growing population, employment opportunities have continually to be created in order to maintain a constant unemployment rate. Thus policies which increased the growth rate of the economy were clearly to be favoured (of course a high growth rate is desirable for other reasons — not least of which are the possibilities it provides for increasing the welfare of the country). Different ways of achieving the employment objective will also have differing effects on other factors; for example, different policies will have differing implications for the level of interest rates, for the relative importance of public investment *vis-a-vis* private investment, for the 'state' of the stock market and for the distribution of income among individuals.

Successive governments have come to formulate their macroeconomic policies in terms of (and the success of their policies judged by) the achievement of certain *policy objectives.* Clearly different political parties and different individuals may well disagree over what constitutes the relevant set of objectives. Also the set of objectives may well depend on the time period under consideration — what is an objective in the short run may, in the long run, merely be a means to the attainment of some other objective, rather than an end in itself.[1] Despite this multiplicity of

[1]For example, if our ultimate aim is the satisfaction of all human wants, who will care if, in this golden age of 'bliss', we have massive inflation? But we may care if, in the short run, the presence of inflation leads to decreased welfare, either immediately or in the future.

possible objectives and rather surprisingly, in view of the nature of economists and politicians, there is a fair degree of consensus that four objectives may be singled out as being of key importance for short-run macroeconomic policy. These four key objectives concern employment, the rate of inflation, the balance of payments and the rate of growth. Increasingly, Chancellors have come to express their objectives in these areas in quantitative terms. The variables often used for such quantitative expression are, respectively, the rate of unemployment, the annual rate of change of wages (or prices), the current account balance and the annual rate of change of Gross Domestic Product (or some other national income measure). Clearly, the lower the first two the better, and the higher the last two the better (at least in the short run). Figures 1, 2, 3 and 4 of the Statistical Appendix show the movements of these variables during the 20th century. Figure 2 shows clearly the success of post-war policy in keeping unemployment well below the levels observed before the Second World War.

The Instruments of Macroeconomic Policy

The specification of the objectives of macroeconomic policy is clearly only the first step towards its formulation and implementation. Needless to say, in a capitalist society the government cannot control the policy objectives directly, but must control them indirectly through the medium of variables which are directly under government control. Such variables are termed the *instruments* of macroeconomic policy, and include direct and indirect tax rates, the official exchange rate, the 'Bank Rate', the level of government expenditure and so on. Clearly there are relationships between the instruments and the objectives; for example, lowering tax rates will lead to increased aggregate expenditure and hence to reduced unemployment, lowering the exchange rate (devaluing) will lead to an improved current account balance, and raising interest rates will lead to reduced investment and hence a lower growth rate.

In an ideal world, to each and every objective there would

correspond a separate instrument, each instrument would affect one and only one objective, and there would be an exactly-known relationship between each objective and its corresponding instrument. Thus, in this ideal world, there would be four instruments corresponding respectively to the four objectives; and there would be four exactly-known functional relationships specifying precisely the nature of the dependence of each objective upon each instrument. In this ideal world, macroeconomic policy is simple: select the desired values for the objectives; use the functional relationships to determine the required values of the instruments; announce these values in the Budget; sit back and wait for the praise (votes) to flow in.

Unfortunately this is not an ideal world (at least not yet): the conditions described above are not satisfied; macroeconomic policy is not so simple. The first problem is that there is not a one-to-one relationship between instruments and objectives, though the following may be regarded as a rough approximation: demand management (through fiscal policy) could be used to control the level of unemployment; an incomes policy could be used to control inflation; the exchange rate could be used to control the balance of payments; and various methods of stimulating investment could be used to control the growth rate. Even if all these instruments were politically acceptable to the government of the day[2], there would still be problems since each instrument affects more than one objective: for example, as has been noted earlier, the stimulation of aggregate demand not only affects unemployment but also affects the balance of payments and the rate of inflation.

Although we now have a more complicated relationship between instruments and objectives than visualised in our ideal world, the formulation of policy is still relatively straight-forward as long as (i) the functional relationships are known exactly and (ii) the instruments at least equal the number of objectives (in this case four). As Professor Kaldor remarks, this second condition

[2]For a long time Conservative philosophy ruled out the idea of an incomes policy; similarly successive governments, particularly the 1964-67 Labour administration, regarded the official parity of sterling as a kind of virility symbol that could not be tampered with.

means that "in order to secure a stated number of objectives the government needs to operate at least an equal number of policy instruments" (Kaldor 1971, p.3). Only in very rare (and fortunate) circumstances is it possible to attain four objectives with less than four instruments. Despite the self-evident nature of this proposition, it is important to note that British economic policy throughout the 1950's and 1960's was largely conducted with just one instrument — that of demand management — though an incomes policy was added in times of crisis (as was devaluation). This, to a large extent, accounts for the erratic performance of the economy during this period.[3]

Even if the government is prepared to use a sufficient number and variety of instruments, there still remain difficulties in the attainment of policy objectives, for there may be inherent conflicts between the various objectives — conflicts which cannot be removed by any known policy. The most immediate example[4] is that provided by the Phillips curve — named after A. W. Phillips whose article (1958) provided the starting point for many empirical studies. The Phillips curve apparently shows that for many years there was a stable inverse relationship between the rate of inflation and unemployment. Thus if unemployment was high, inflation would be low, and *vice versa*. Although the subject of a considerable amount of current controversy (particularly over its performance in recent years), the implication of the existence of such a relationship is that it may be impossible to have both low levels of unemployment *and* low rates of inflation. If this were so, then governments would be faced with a trade-off problem between inflation and unemployment; they could only have less of one at the expense of more of the other. In such a case, the conflict could only be resolved by political considerations, and different political parties may reach different decisions as to the 'optimal' mix.

Clearly such a conflict adds to the burden of policy makers unless, of course, some policy instrument may be operated to

[3]This period was characterised by alternating expansion and stagnation as balance of payments 'crises' brought to a premature end all attempts at a sustained period of growth. For an excellent commentary on economic policy during this period, see Brittan (1971).

[4]For other examples see Kaldor (1971) and Lipsey (1971, Chapter 50).

remove the conflict. Such considerations led to investigations by Lipsey and Parkin (1970) amongst others, of whether the operation of an incomes policy removed the relationship between inflation and unemployment. Their conclusion was that an incomes policy *changed* the relationship, but did not remove it. If this analysis is correct, it implies that some conflict still remains, but that the range of choice open to the policy maker is widened. However, there is still considerable controversy over the nature and existence of the Phillips curve and the effect of incomes policies upon it. This is one of the many unsolved problems of economics which await further extensive empirical testing before they can be finally settled.

The Relationships Between Objectives and Instruments

The problem, discussed above, of determining the precise nature of the relationship (if any) between variables is, of course, not peculiar to the Phillips curve analysis, and indeed constitutes one of the major problems of formulating and implementing macroeconomic policy. In our previous discussion we have assumed that the relationships between instruments and objectives were exactly known. In practice, however, they are not exactly known and have to be estimated. Although the crucial information lies in the nature of the functional relationships, these are not estimated directly, but an indirect method is employed which allows the use of economic theory as a guide to the validity of the estimated equations.

To illustrate the methods of estimation, consider a very simple closed economy in which there is one policy instrument — the level of government expenditure, and one policy objective — the attainment of full employment income. This example is broadly similar to those used in introductory text books such as Lipsey (1971). Such an economy is usually represented by two equations:

$$C = a + bY \tag{1}$$
$$Y = C + G \tag{2}$$

where (1) is the consumption function and (2) is the equilibrium condition (C is aggregate consumption, G is government expenditure and Y is aggregate income; all investment is assumed to be undertaken by the government). In this simple economy, as is well known, increases in government expenditure G lead to multiplied increases in income Y, the multiplier depending upon the marginal propensity to consume b. Algebraically this can be demonstrated by solving equations (1) and (2) for Y in terms of G by eliminating C. This yields:

$$Y = \frac{a}{1-b} + \frac{1}{1-b}G \qquad (3)$$

Equation (3) shows the relationship between instrument G and objective Y. In order to achieve the desired value for Y, the appropriate value for G can be selected by using equation (3) if $a/(1-b)$ and $1/(1-b)$ are known. Clearly this is possible if a and b are known. Thus the relationship between objective and instrument can be estimated directly from equation (3). However, although the advantage is not very apparent in this particular example, economists prefer to proceed by estimating the relationship between C and Y and then using this knowledge to determine the effect of instrument on objective; this is because the relationship is immediately interpretable in terms of the economic behaviour of a particular group of economic agents (consumers). If, for example, a is estimated to be negative, or b is estimated to be negative or greater than one, immediate warning lights begin to flash — indicating that something looks wrong. In other words, economic theory provides a check on the estimated relationship.

If the model above was a correct description of the economy, then knowledge of a and b would be necessary and sufficient for the successful operation of macroeconomic policy. Unfortunately, this model is too simple to describe real-world economies, though one element is a remarkably good approximation. Consider figure 1, which plots UK aggregate consumption against GDP (both in real terms) for the years 1949 to 1970. The relation between the two can be fairly well approximated by the straight line drawn on the figure. This line has an intercept of £1,022m (i.e. C = £1,022m = a when Y = 0) and a slope of 0.61; this latter, of course, is an estimate of b, the marginal propensity to consume. Visually it appears that

Figure 1. *Annual GDP, Y, plotted against aggregate consumption, C, in UK 1949-70.*

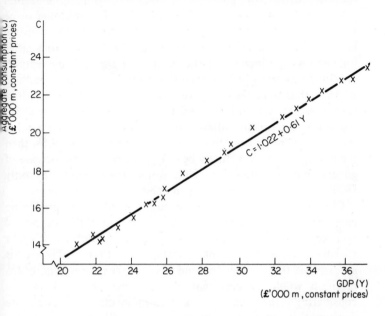

the relationship between consumption and income can be fairly well represented by equation (1) (with $a = £1,022m$ and $b = 0.61$), and indeed it can be shown that 99.4% of the variation in consumption is 'explained' by income. However, for the purpose of operating macroeconomic policy this degree of accuracy is not sufficient: it is not certain that the marginal propensity to consume is exactly 0.61 — in fact, given the information portrayed in figure 1, the most that can be said[5] is that one can be 'reasonably confident' that the marginal propensity to consume lies between 0.58 and 0.64. To place this margin of uncertainty in perspective, suppose that the government knows that, without intervention,

---

[5]This statement is the result of standard statistical techniques; see Hey (1974, p.281-285). The details of the techniques need not detain the reader at this stage. The main point to be grasped is that there is a margin of error in the estimate of the marginal propensity to consume.

income next year will be £1,000m below full employment income; suppose, further, the government takes 0.61 to be the marginal propensity to consume, and thus calculates the multiplier to be $1/(1-b) = 1/(1-0.61) = 1/0.39 = 2.56$. On this basis an increase in government spending of £390m would be required to achieve full employment income. However, if the marginal propensity to consume was actually 0.64, then the multiplier would actually be 2.78 and thus an increase of government spending of £390m would lead to an increase in income of £1,083m; which would be £83m too much, thus causing inflationary pressure. On the other hand, if the marginal propensity to consume was actually only 0.58, then the multiplier would actually be only 2.38 and thus an increase of government spending of £390m would raise income by only £929m; an amount insufficient to achieve full employment.

Clearly, therefore, a more accurate method of predicting consumption is desired. In order to improve the degree of accuracy, economists have investigated the influence of other variables, besides income, on consumption — the rate of interest is an example that springs to mind. Experience has also shown (as intuition would expect) that accuracy may be improved by considering the various sub-components of aggregate consumption separately. For example, separate equations can be estimated for spending on durable goods, and for spending on non-durable goods. Certain factors (such as the existence and stringency of hire purchase controls) are more likely to affect the first category than the second, and *vice versa*. The process of disaggregation can continue virtually indefinitely. However, this process is not without its disadvantageous side effects: every extra variable that is introduced to explain or predict (some component of) consumption must itself be explained or predicted. There is little value, if one wants to predict consumption, in knowing that the rate of interest influences consumption, unless one is also able to predict the rate of interest. Thus, for every explanatory variable introduced, an extra equation must be added, showing how it, in turn, is determined. (This, of course, does not apply to variables directly under government control — such as tax rates, the strength of hire purchase restrictions and so on.)

The economic model given by equations (1) and (2) is over-simplified as a representation of (say) the UK economy, not only because of its over-simplified consumption function, but also because of the other assumptions underlying it. Firstly, not all investment is undertaken by the government — indeed private investment is an important, and volatile, component of total expenditure. Secondly, the UK economy is not closed, so that total expenditure includes exports less imports. Thirdly, but by no means finally, the existence of stocks (of raw materials and fuels, of work in progress, and of finished goods) means that any increase in such stocks constitutes an increase in total expenditure and thus in GDP. Now, in order for the government to be able to assess how its policy measures will affect total income, it will need to know how such policy measures affect each component of aggregate expenditure. It will therefore need to know how each component is determined; that is, not only does it need to know the factors determining consumers' expenditure, but also it needs to know the factors determining private investment, exports, imports, stockbuilding and so on.

For each of these components of aggregate demand, a procedure similar to that discussed for consumers' expenditure may be followed. Taking private investment as an example, the first step may be to investigate whether the accelerator theory (Lipsey 1971, pp.499-501) is valid, by seeing if there is a relationship between investment and the change in income. If there proves to be some relationship, but not a perfect one, then the rate of interest may be tried as an additional explanatory variable. Other variables that economic theory would suggest to be important as explanatory factors might include, for example, the rate of investment allowances, investment grants and the rate of corporation tax. With investment, as with consumption, it may be found that accuracy of explanation is improved by considering the various sub-components of investment separately. Here again, of course, each variable that is used as an explanatory variable must itself, in turn, be explained.

Proceeding in this way, using past data on the UK economy to investigate the relationships between variables, and being guided by economic theory as to the choice of the (hopefully) relevant variables, economists can build up what is termed an *econometric model* of the economy. As is apparent from the above discussion, an econometric model consists of a set of equations, or estimated relationships, each of which is an attempt to discover how a particular economic variable is determined. The number of equations in the model will depend upon the degree of disaggregation and the number of variables introduced as explanatory variables. In any econometric model of a country's economy, a distinction is usually made between two different kinds of variable — exogenous and endogenous. The former refer to variables determined outside the model, that is, those not influenced by the endogenous variables. In the category of exogenous variables would fall variables directly under government control (such as tax rates and tax allowances), variables determined outside the economy (for the UK such variables would include the GNP of the USA and the balance of trade deficit of Australia[6]) and variables whose value is determined outside the period to which the model refers (for example, last year's GDP or last year's consumers' expenditure). Endogenous variables are those determined within the model, that is, those influenced by both exogenous and other endogenous variables. Indeed, it can be seen (as is apparent from any textbook discussion) that the values of the endogenous variables are *simultaneously* determined. For example, the values of the two endogenous variables, income and consumption, depend on each other: consumption depends on income (through the consumption function) and income depends on consumption (since consumption is a large element of income: one man's consumption being another man's income).

The number of equations in an econometric model must be the same as the number of endogenous variables (loosely speaking, this means that to each endogenous variable there must correspond an equation explaining it) so that, given any set of values for the exogenous variables, the model can then be simultaneously solved to yield values for the endogenous variables. Clearly the *size* of an econometric model (the number of

---

[6]Strictly speaking, what happens in the UK may influence the US GNP or the Australian deficit slightly; however this dependence is usually considered so slight as to be ignorable. This example shows that the distinction between exogenous and endogenous variables may not always be clear cut, and may sometimes be more a question of degree than of kind.

endogenous variables it contains) can be indefinitely large, and will depend on the degree of disaggregation and on the explanatory variables introduced. It may at first be thought that the larger the model, the better; but this is not necessarily so. By introducing extra explanatory variables into an equation explaining a particular endogenous variable, the explanation of that variable may be improved *if we know the value of the explanatory variables*; but, since they in turn need to be explained, their introduction may actually make matters worse. To clarify this point, consider the following illustration: suppose an econometrician is trying to decide which of the following two (aggregate) consumption functions is 'best' as far as his econometric model is concerned:

$$C = a + bY \qquad\qquad\qquad\qquad (4)$$
$$C = a + bY - cr \qquad\qquad\qquad (5)$$

(C is aggregate consumption, Y is aggregate income and r is the rate of interest.) Suppose he has collected the relevant data, and has 'fitted' the two functions to the data, thus finding estimates of the coefficients a, b and c. Suppose that he finds that equation (4) explains 99.4% of the variation in consumption while (5) explains 99.9%; that is, the addition of r (the rate of interest) improves[7] the explanation of C. In other words, knowledge of the value of r, and use of equation (5) instead of equation (4), leads to a more precise prediction of the value of C. Now, suppose that r is *not* exogenous; then, if the econometrician uses (5) instead of (4) as the consumption function in his econometric model, he must add an extra equation to his model to explain r. If (as is quite likely) he is unable to explain r with a very high degree of accuracy, then the prediction of C using the expanded model may well be worse than the prediction of C using the smaller model, since the error in predicting r may offset the improved (when r is known) explanatory power of equation (5).

The question of the optimal size of an econometric model is still

---

[7]The discussion here is very heuristic statistically; the purist is referred to any statistical text (e.g. Hey 1974) for a more precise discussion of the relevant technical points.

very much unresolved, though, clearly this depends on the use to
which the model is to be put. If the government is interested solely
in the effects of its policy measures on the four variables
mentioned earlier (unemployment, inflation, balance of payments
and growth), then it may be able to operate with a smaller model
than that needed to assess the impact of its measures in wider
terms. Several models have been constructed for the UK — the
volume by Ash and Smyth (1973) contains brief descriptions of,
and references to, the most important. As most ongoing
econometric models are in a continuous state of flux, with
continuous efforts to improve the performance of the model, it is
difficult to say how large a particular model is even at one point in
time. However, the above-mentioned volume gives rough
indications; for example, the Treasury model (used for giving
advice and forecasts to governments) contained in May 1972
roughly 50 behavioural equations (and a similar number of
identities[8]), while the National Institute model (discussed further
below) contained 10 behavioural equations and 7 identities —
giving a total of 17 endogenous variables. (A model under
construction in 1969 at the Department of Economic Affairs —
now defunct — was considerably more ambitious, consisting of
260 equations, of which 120 were identities.) Probably one of the
best developed and largest models is that of the Brookings
Institute for the US economy, which had over 500 equations (with
plans to extend it to over 1,000) in 1969, though for some purposes
the model was aggregated to 182 equations.

One common feature of all these models is that none of them is
perfect; none of them is able to explain (let alone predict) the
endogenous variables with complete accuracy. This is due partly
to a shortage of data, partly to poor quality data (about which
more will be said shortly), partly to the relative youthfulness of
economics as a science (which means that relatively little
experience has been gained as yet) and partly to the fact that the
models are trying to account for human behaviour which,
whatever economists may like to think, inevitably contains some

---

[8]In the very simple model represented by equations (1) and (2), (1) is a
behavioural equation and (2) is an identity.

random element. Hopefully, with the passage of time, as data and experience accumulate, the accuracy of the econometric models will improve. In the meantime, however, the shortcomings of such models continue to cause problems in the efficient operation of macroeconomic policy.

Forecasting the Future

The government and its civil service advisers maintain a constant watch on the performance of the economy, to see how well the policy objectives are being met, and to see whether any changes are required to the policy instruments. Until fairly recently, any major changes to the instruments were confined to the annual Budget statement (usually in the spring); nowadays, however, 'mini-budgets' and other economic measures announced at other times in the year are becoming more and more frequent due to the realisation that 'managing the economy' is an all-the-year-round job.[9] Before any changes in policy instruments are considered, the past and likely future course of the economy is carefully assessed. The latest statistics on key economic variables are studied closely, not only for the evidence they provide on the performance of the economy in the recent past, but also for the indications they give for the likely future course of the economy. In determining whether any changes in instruments are needed, a key role is played by forecasts of the future economic situation. These forecasts are provided by a variety of methods, both formal and informal,[10] though the formal methods (using econometric models) are becomingly increasingly important.

The first type of forecast that is used in deciding whether any policy changes are needed is a forecast of the movement of the economy over the next eighteen months or so, in the absence of

[9]There is however a growing body of opinion that considers that there is too much short-run 'tinkering' with the economy, and that the economy may perform better if left to its own devices for longer periods. See, for example, Polanyi (1973), whose argument rests on the inaccuracy of short-run forecasting.

[10]See Brittan (1971), particularly Chapter 2.

any such changes. The forecast values of the policy objectives are then compared with the desired values and, if it appears that the divergences are unnecessarily large, consideration is given to possible changes in policy instruments which might reduce the divergences. If some changes are considered necessary, then further forecasts are produced indicating the likely effect of the changes. In order to generate a set of forecasts using an econometric model, forecasts of the exogenous variables must first be provided. Given such forecasts, the model can then be solved to provide forecasts of the endogenous variables. Clearly then, any set of forecasts of endogenous variables is conditional on the forecasts of the exogenous variables, and thus the accuracy of the former depend heavily on the accuracy of the latter. Earlier, three basic types of exogenous variables were described. The first type, namely the policy instruments directly under government control, (should[11]) pose no problem — since the whole point of the forecasting exercise is to determine the effect of changes in these variables. The second type, those determined outside the country (examples given were the US GNP and the Australian deficit), are much more difficult to forecast accurately. Errors in predicting this type of exogenous variable will lead to errors of forecasting and thus to errors of policy. A recent example is provided by the policy decision of the 1970-4 Conservative government in 1973 to introduce threshold agreements into wage bargains; this decision led to considerable problems, since it was based on a hoped-for deceleration in the rate of price inflation of raw materials and fuels which did not materialise in time. The third type of exogenous variable, those determined outside the time period to which the model relates, are in fact determined by prior forecasts produced by the model. For example, suppose that, in a quarterly model, it is found that last quarter's consumers' expenditure is an important determinant of this quarter's consumers' expenditure (due to some kind of habit or persistence effect). Suppose further that quarterly data on consumption (and all the other variables in the model) are available up to and including the final quarter of 1974, and that

---

[11]Curiously enough the Treasury forecasts of public expenditure have been particularly poor; see Ash and Smythe (1973, p.249).

forecasts are required for the six quarters up to the middle of 1976. By using the figure of consumption for the fourth quarter of 1974 (and forecasts of the other exogenous variables), forecasts can be produced for consumption (and other endogenous variables) for the first quarter of 1975. This, in turn, is used to provide a forecast for the second quarter of 1975, and so on. It is important to note, however, that errors can well accumulate, since an error in the forecast of consumption for the first quarter of 1975 will lead to an error in the second quarter's forecast, and so on. This is one of the reasons why forecasts of the more distant future are likely to be less accurate than forecasts of the more immediate future.

In the United Kingdom there are several institutions providing forecasts on a regular basis. However, in no case is it true that total reliance is placed on econometric models. Usually the final forecast is a blend of formal and informal methods, with 'experience' and 'judgement' playing important roles. Through the year the Treasury provides many forecasts to assist government decision making, but the one usually made available to the public is that incorporating any changes in policy announced in the annual Budget statement. The National Institute of Economic and Social Research has been publishing forecasts quarterly since 1959 in its *Economic Review*. These forecasts were initiated to provide an independent check on the Treasury forecasts. The National Institute is particularly open about its forecasting methods and about the quality of its forecasts: a useful introduction to its methods is contained in Surrey's book (1971), while many issues of the *Economic Review* contain articles of special interest on particular topics.

The London Graduate Business School and the London and Cambridge Economic Service also provide regular, if less detailed, forecasts: these are published in the Sunday Times and The Times respectively.

Clearly, if macroeconomic policy is to be based largely on forecasts of the short-term economic situation, it is of paramount importance that such forecasts be accurate. Macroeconomic policy can fail in its purpose for other reasons besides incorrect forecasts, such as totally unexpected shocks to the system (for example, the large oil price rises of the winter of 1973/74 and the miners' strikes of 1972 and 1974), but without a solid base of good forecasts, macroeconomic policy may aggravate the situation rather than improve it. That this is, in fact, what has happened, is the view of several commentators — in particular of Polanyi, whose pamphlet (1973) is devoted to an assessment of the National Institute's forecasts and their effect on government policy.

Certainly no economist would pretend that present day forecasts are accurate or that there was no room for improvement; the crucial question, however, is whether the availability of such forecasts (despite their inaccuracies) provides the policy makers with more and better information than would otherwise be the case. An affirmative answer to this question is the conclusion of the comprehensive study by Ash and Smyth (1973) into the accuracy of various UK forecasters' predictions. Indeed they remark (p.262):

> Our evaluation of UK short-term macroeconomic forecasts gives no support to the view that economic forecasting is a waste of time. With few exceptions, the forecasters' predictions are significantly more accurate than simply extrapolating or averaging past outcomes . . .

However they go on to say:

> Equally, our conclusions do not provide grounds for complacency. In some areas . . . the quality of the forecasts is consistently poor.

As this study shows, the assessment of the accuracy of forecasts is considerably more difficult than might appear. Firstly, most forecasts are based on an assumption of no change in government policy over the forecast period; if this assumption is subsequently falsified, adjustments need to be made to the forecasts before their accuracy can be assessed. Secondly, it is not always clear what forecasts should be assessed against — since published figures often undergo several revisions before being presented in a 'final form'. Thirdly, the accuracy of a set of forecasts may well vary depending on the degree of aggregation, and it may thus be difficult to give an overall measure for the accuracy of the set as a whole. For example, as intuition might lead one to expect, and the Ash and Smyth study confirms, forecasts of a whole year tend to be more accurate than forecasts of individual quarters; similarly, though perhaps more surprisingly, Ash and Smyth find that errors in the forecasts of individual components of GDP tend to offset each other, so that GDP is forecast more accurately than its components.

The accuracy of forecasts can be assessed in various ways: the simplest and most naive is to assess whether the forecasts are correct on average, or whether there is a persistent tendency to over- or under-estimate the variable being predicted. In the crucial case of GDP forecasts, Ash and Smyth observe that "the forecasters tend to under-estimate the average rate of growth of the economy" (1973, p.257). This result is also apparent in the National Institute's study (Kennedy 1969), and indeed provides the basis for Polanyi's argument (1973) that this under-estimation has led to inflationary policy recommendations by the Institute. However, this type of forecasting error (a persistent under- or over-estimation), once identified, can fairly easily be incorporated into the forecasting procedure and then, hopefully, eliminated.

Even if a set of forecasts is correct on *average* (over a period of time), there is still clearly scope for forecasting errors in particular time periods. A comparison of the forecast magnitude of fluctuations with the actual magnitude of fluctuations thus provides a further check on the accuracy of forecasts. Interestingly, Ash and Smyth found that (as with the level) UK forecasters tended to under-estimate the magnitude of the fluctuations, particularly in the more volatile series, notably investment. The implication of this type of forecasting error is that, if the authorities under-estimate the cyclical fluctuations in the economy, their anti-cyclical policy would not remove all the fluctuations but only part of them. However, it may be considered safer to err on the side of under-estimation of fluctuations, since an error in the other direction would actually reverse the cyclical fluctuations (i.e. turn a boom into a slump and *vice versa*).

An even more important test of the accuracy of forecasts is their ability to predict turning points. For example, when monitoring the rate of growth of the economy (as measured, say, by GDP) it is crucial to know when the rate of growth is going to fall (or rise), as this indicates the onset of a 'slump' (or 'boom'). Suppose, for instance, the government is told by its forecasters that the rate of growth of GDP will rise from 3% this year to 4% next year, and that this rate of growth of GDP would cause inflationary pressure because of supply constraints. If the government act on this advice, they would take measures to deflate the economy — that is, reduce aggregate demand — so as to lower the growth rate. Suppose, however, that the forecasters have mis-forecast a turning point, and that (in the absence of government intervention) the rate of growth of GDP next year would in fact be only 2%. In this case, the effect of the deflationary measures makes matters worse by making the downturn in the rate of growth much sharper than would otherwise be the case. Clearly, similar problems arise if the forecasters predict turning points which do not materialise. Thus, if errors in forecasting turning points are at all frequent, then the effect of government policy may well be de-stabilising — making fluctuations in activity worse than they would otherwise have been. The Ash and Smyth study shows that turning-point errors of prediction were unfortunately common among UK forecasters.

Errors of forecasts arise for several reasons, not least of which concern the inadequacies of published data on economic statistics. These inadequacies also create problems for another aspect of macroeconomic policy, namely that of determining the precise state of the economy at any particular time.

Forecasting the Past

Clearly an essential prerequisite for successfully forecasting the future path of the economy is knowledge of where it has been in the past and where it is at the time of the forecast. Unfortunately, since the collection and processing of data take time, there are often lags (sometimes of considerable length) in the publication of data on economic variables. In order to reduce the delay in publication, provisional estimates of key variables are often prepared. By their very nature, these provisional estimates are derived from partial information, and as more information is accumulated they are likely to be revised. Often these revisions are considerable and may continue for several months, if not years. Thus it may be some time before a clear picture emerges of the movement of the economy in the past, and thus 'forecasting the past' constitutes an essential part of formulating macroeconomic policy. It should be noted that revisions to data are not a short-term phenomenon but continue for many years. This is brought out clearly in an article by Balacs (1972) which shows continuing and fluctuating revisions over the whole of the period 1953-69 to which his study relates.

Even if a published series 'settles down' (that is, no further revisions are forthcoming), this does not guarantee that the final figure is accurate. Because of the way the data are collected, some margin of error inevitably remains — though its magnitude varies from series to series. For example, the Central Statistical Office estimates that its figures for GNP are accurate only to within ±3%, while the figures for stock changes may show a margin of error of up to 10% either way.

The inevitable delays in the publication of key economic variables mean that it is often difficult to assess how the economy is behaving at any particular point in time. However, some insight may be gained by the study of proxy variables, or of other economic indicators whose publication is faster or more frequent than that of the variables of direct concern. Indeed, heavy reliance is placed on such indicators by the National Institute in forecasting the past. Thus, before the figure for consumers' expenditure for a particular quarter has been published, the Institute makes use of the published monthly figures on the volume of retail sales and the figures on new car registrations to provide an estimate. Similarly, an estimate of GDP is obtained with the use of the monthly figures on industrial production (and with the help of an equation showing the relationship between GDP and industrial production that held in the past). Such indicators may also be used to provide forecasts of the future; for example, housing starts in one month give some measure of investment in housing in subsequent months, while data on new orders placed with contractors and with engineering firms also give indications as to the future movement of capital formation. Information from investment intentions surveys (as carried out by the Department of Trade and Industry and the Confederation of British Industry amongst others) also provides evidence in this direction; both the Treasury and the National Institute make use of such surveys.

Although the use of indicators reduces the margin of uncertainty as to the behaviour of the economy in the recent past, some error inevitably remains. As with mistakes in forecasting the future, macroeconomic policy can be blown off course by mistakes in forecasting the past. Here again, errors in spotting turning points are likely to cause the most serious problems. A recent example is provided by the mini-budget in the closing stages of the 1970-74 Conservative administration. This budget, in December 1973, introduced heavy deflationary measures (mainly via cuts in public expenditure) in the belief that, in the absence of such measures, the economy would overheat (that is, grow at too fast a rate). However, on the subsequent publication of the relevant figures, it was realised that by the final quarter of 1973 the economy had already begun to turn down of its own accord, so that (at least some of) the deflationary measures had been unnecessary.

Conclusions

The inaccuracies of forecasting and the inadequacies of economic data pose problems for the successful implementation of macroeconomic policy; this suggests that the full potential welfare gain may not be realised. If the problems are sufficiently small, so that at least some of the potential gain is realised, then macroeconomic policy is worthwhile. If, however, the problems are so large that economic management actually reduces welfare rather than increases it, then it may be preferable to play down the role of macroeconomic policy.

In an examination of post-war UK experience, it is easy to come to the trite conclusion that full attainment of the objectives of macroeconomic policy has rarely been achieved. However, it is considerably more difficult to identify the reasons why policies did not achieve their full potential. It is more difficult still to conclude whether or not the operation of macroeconomic policy has led to higher welfare than would have been achieved in the absence of such policies.[12]

While it may be difficult to assess the degree of success of macroeconomic policy, and to disentangle the reasons for its

[12]This is because it is difficult to determine precisely how the economy would have performed in the absence of government intervention. For references to investigations into this problem, and for some insight into the differing conclusions reached, see Brittan (1971, p.450).

failures, certain broad conclusions do emerge. First, assuming that society does not wish to repeat the experience of the Great Depression, some government intervention at a macroeconomic level is necessary. Second, such intervention can clearly be beneficial, as a comparison of the post-war with the pre-war situation indicates. Third, because of the present deficiencies of forecasting and of economic data, there is inevitably some margin of uncertainty over the precise effects of macroeconomic policy and thus care should be taken not to expect too much from, or to place too much reliance on, such policies. For instance, the manifest absurdity of policy changes which attempt to alter the rate of growth of GDP by one or two percentage points should be recognised, since it is impossible to measure, let alone forecast, the rate of growth of GDP this accurately. Clearly we need to walk before we can run; while our ability to explain economic phenomena remains imperfect, we must keep our ambitions in this field appropriately modest.

In the meantime the tools of macroeconomic policy can be sharpened. The quality and speed of publication of economic data can continue to be improved. New generations of empirically-trained and scientifically-oriented economists can continue the process of refining our knowledge of the economy and of economic relationships. With the science of economics maturing through time, the future holds the promise of an improved understanding of the formulation and implementation of macroeconomic policy, with consequent increases in the welfare of nations.

References

Ash, J. C. K., and Smyth, D. J., *Forecasting the United Kingdom Economy*, Saxon House 1973.

Balacs, P. D., Economic Data and Economic Policy, *Lloyds Bank Review*, 104, April 1972, pp.35-50.

Brittan, S., *Steering the Economy*, Penguin Books 1971.

Dow, J. C. R., *The Management of the British Economy 1945-60*, Cambridge University Press 1964.

Hey, J. D., *Statistics in Economics*, Martin Robertson 1974.

Kaldor, N., Conflicts in Policy Objectives, *Economic Journal*, 81, March 1971, pp.1-16.

Kennedy, M. C., How Well does the National Institute Forecast?, *National Institute Economic Review*, 50, November 1969, pp.40-52.

Keynes, J. M., *The General Theory of Employment, Interest and Money*, Macmillan 1936.

Lipsey, R. G., *An Introduction to Positive Economics* (3rd edn), Weidenfeld and Nicolson 1971.

Lipsey, R. G., and Parkin, J. M., Incomes Policy: A Re-Appraisal, *Economica*, NS, 37, May 1970, pp.115-38.

Maurice, R. (ed), *National Accounts Statistics: Sources and Methods*, Central Statistical Office, HMSO 1968.

Phillips, A. W., The Relation between Unemployment and the Rate of Change of Money Wage Rates in the United Kingdom, 1861-1957, *Economica*, NS, 25, November 1958, pp.283-99.

Polanyi, G., *Short-term Forecasting: A Case Study*, Background Memorandum 4, Institute of Economic Affairs 1973.

Shaw, G. K., *An Introduction to the Theory of Macroeconomic Policy* (2nd edn), Martin Robertson 1973.

Surrey, M. J. C., *The Analysis and Forecasting of the British Economy*, National Institute of Economic and Social Research Occasional Paper 25, Cambridge University Press 1971.

Ministry of Reconstruction, *Employment Policy*, Cmnd 6527, HMSO 1944.

Treasury, *Financial Statement and Budget Report 1974-75*, HMSO 1974.

Suggestions for Further Reading

For an elementary introduction to the theory of macroeconomic policy see:
Lipsey (1971, Chapter 50).

For a fuller discussion see:
Shaw (1973).

Some aspects of the nature of conflicts between policy objectives can be found in:
Kaldor (1971).
Shaw (1973).

An introduction to modern forecasting methods is provided by:
Surrey (1971).

For a comprehensive analysis of the accuracy of forecasts see:
Ash and Smyth (1973).

A description of the methods used in collecting and processing economic statistics at the CSO is given in:
Maurice (1968).

Criticisms (of perhaps a rather biased nature) are listed in:
Balacs (1972).

For analyses of the operation of macroeconomic policy see:
Brittan (1971).
Dow (1964).

10. Inflation and its control: a monetarist analysis

DAVID LAIDLER
Professor of Economics,
University of Manchester

Inflation[1] is a process of generally rising prices. This is not to say that, as inflation proceeds, all prices rise at the same rate. In any economy the relative prices of different goods and services will change as conditions of supply and demand for individual items change over time. However, during an inflation prices rise on average. The cost in terms of money of a representative bundle of goods and services, such as might be consumed by an average household, continually goes up; or to put the same point another way, the purchasing power of money, its value, steadily declines. Inflation is usually regarded as undesirable, a state of affairs to be avoided; but what harm does it do if prices in general rise over time? The answer here depends critically upon whether inflation is anticipated or not. Many of the adverse effects that are usually

[1] Inflation is a problem which impinges on all aspects of economic life, and about which there are many points of view. In one chapter it is simply impossible to give a full account of all aspects of the problem or all alternative viewpoints, and then to assess all sides of all the questions. Thus I have concentrated on setting out my own views on what I regard as the most important aspects of the problem. So-called 'monetarist' analysis of inflation is not readily available in elementary economics texts and this chapter is designed to fill what I regard as an important gap in the literature at this level. However the reader is warned that many of the views expressed here are matters of controversy among economists. This chapter is intended to provide a basis for debate on the problem of inflation, not to provide an analysis of the problem that anyone should simply read and accept as definitive.

associated with inflation arise not as a result of a rising price level *per se*, but rather because the people affected by that rising price level did not anticipate that it would rise at the time when they took certain decisions. Indeed effects analytically identical to those of unanticipated inflation occur whenever the price level follows a different time path from that which people had expected it to follow.

These effects are on the distribution of income and wealth, and their nature may be illustrated with a simple example. Suppose that a man borrows £100 from another with the promise to repay the sum at 5% interest at the end of the year. Suppose, furthermore, that both expect the price level to remain stable over the year in question. If instead the price level rises at, say, 10% per annum, the wealth positions of both the borrower and the lender are affected by their transaction in a way they did not foresee. The lender receives £105 at the end of the year, but it will buy for him goods that would have been worth about £95 at the prices prevailing at the time he made the loan. He has earned a real rate of interest on his loan of minus 5% when he expected to earn plus 5%; he has been made unexpectedly worse off. The borrower, by exactly parallel reasoning, has gained unexpectedly. These effects are the result of disappointed expectations about the behaviour of the price level rather than of inflation *per se*. Suppose the 10% rise in prices had been anticipated. In order to get a real return on his loan of 5%, the lender would have asked for £115 to be repaid at the end of the year, the extra £10 to take care of rising prices. Furthermore the borrower, provided that he too expected prices to rise at 10% a year, would have acquiesced in this.

The matter is of course far more general than an affair between an isolated borrower and lender. Anyone who holds any asset denominated in money terms, or any claim to an income — a pension say — whose value is fixed in money terms, loses if the price level rises unexpectedly. Similarly, any debtor, the value of whose debts is fixed in money terms, gains. On the other hand, if debtors and creditors correctly anticipate inflation, then they allow for these expectations in the interest rate at which they strike their bargains, or, in the case of pension rights and such, in the terms of the pension contracts into which they enter.

While unanticipated inflation redistributes wealth from

creditors to debtors it should be clear that unanticipated deflation just as surely redistributes wealth from debtors to creditors. There is a general rule here: if the price level rises faster than anticipated (and this phrase includes situations in which the rate of fall of prices is smaller in absolute terms than the expected one) then debtors benefit, while if it is smaller they lose. A zero rate of change of prices when a 10% rate of fall is expected discriminates against creditors in just the same way, and to just the same extent, as does a 10% inflation when a constant price level is expected. A zero rate of change of prices when 10% inflation is expected, on the other hand, works in favour of creditors just as much as 10% inflation when constant prices are expected.

Now the redistribution we have discussed so far takes place between private individuals, or at least between institutions and individuals in the private sector of the economy. But one of the most important characteristics of inflation is its capacity for redistributing income and wealth between the private sector and the government. The most obvious way in which this happens is through the effect of price level changes on the real level of taxes. Tax laws, as they relate both to individuals and companies, are usually written on the assumption of a constant price level. Thus individuals are allowed to claim certain allowances fixed in money terms against their income before they become eligible for tax; thereafter the higher their money income the higher their marginal rate of income tax. Inflation erodes the real value of tax allowances, and by increasing money income pushes individuals into higher and higher tax brackets, even though, in real terms, their incomes are not increasing. Thus inflation increases the revenue accruing to the government from income taxes without the need for unpopular legislation to increase tax rates. Dealings between taxpayer and government are not automatically subject to renegotiation, even when both sides recognise and come to anticipate inflation; it is only if the government decides to adjust tax allowances and rates automatically and regularly in order to keep the real burden of taxes the same — if it decides to 'index' the income tax structure — that this redistributive effect of inflation may be avoided.

Inflation has similar effects on the revenue that arises from capital gains taxation. This is levied on the difference between the price at which individuals purchase and later sell a wide variety of assets. To the extent that with inflation the prices of certain assets rise in money terms, but not in real terms, nominal gains made in this way reflect no real accretion to the wealth of the person who holds assets. Nevertheless, because capital gains taxation is levied on gains measured in money terms, a tax liability is generated by the sale of an asset at a higher money price than that at which it was purchased, even if the gain in question is purely the result of inflation.

Inflation also affects company taxation. Here the key factor is its effect on the market value of inventories of goods held by companies. To see what is involved, consider the simple example of a grocery shop that must keep its shelves stocked with goods in order to carry on business. When prices are rising such goods will appreciate in money terms while they remain on the shelves; this rise in nominal value shows up as part of the shop's profit and is subject to taxation. But when goods are sold they must be replaced at a new higher price. Appreciation in the money value of inventories brings no real gain to the shop. Although the original stock of goods was sold at an increased price, that stock must be replaced at the same high price if business is to be carried on. But the shop is taxed as if the gain was a real one and wealth is redistributed from its owners to the government. Again, it is possible for tax laws to be rewritten in order to avoid the type of redistribution implicit in this example; but there is no automatic mechanism that can ensure that it will happen even if both taxpayer and tax collector are fully aware of what is happening. It is up to the government, if it so desires, to change its regulations. (Note that steps to take account of the effects discussed here were taken in the November 1974 budget.)

The real value of government debt held by the public falls with inflation, just as does the real value of private debt, and unless inflation is anticipated by both lenders and borrowers, in this case the government, this fall in real value will not be compensated for by the interest paid by the borrower. The redistribution implicit here is just like that between private borrowers and lenders which we have analysed above and there is no need to analyse it in any further detail.

Now the reader should be convinced by the foregoing discussion

that it is not inflation *per se* that has undesirable redistributive
effects within the private sector, but rather unanticipated
fluctuations in the time path of prices. The redistribution that
takes place between the private sector and the government as a
result of tax regulations is a somewhat different matter. However,
such regulations can be varied in order to offset the influence of
price level fluctuations if the government is willing to do so. To the
extent that one is worried about the redistributive effects of
inflation then, and desires 'price stability' to avoid them, the policy
objective implied by this phrase is not a zero rate of change of
prices, but a stable and predictable rate of change of prices with
taxation practices being adapted to take price level changes into
account.

However, there are also potentially important costs to
anticipated inflation; when these are considered, a zero rate of
change of prices comes to look more desirable than a positive one.
These costs arise from the fact that many assets used as money in
the United Kingdom, and in every other advanced economy for
that matter, bear a zero rate of interest. The rate of return on
holding them is given by the rate of change of their purchasing
power, that is by the rate of inflation. A positive rate of inflation
produces a negative real rate of return on money. It constitutes a
tax on holding money. This does not mean that no cash balances
will be held when inflation is anticipated, any more than the
imposition of a tax on any good will lead to people ceasing to
consume it altogether. However, if they expect inflation, people
will hold less cash than they otherwise would, and inasmuch as
cash provides services to those who hold it, they will be that much
worse off as a result. The more money one holds either as currency
in the pocket or in the form of a deposit at a commercial bank, the
easier it is to design one's expenditure pattern in the way found
most convenient and the more independent it can be made of the
time pattern of receipts; moreover, the more cash one has on hand,
the easier it is to make unexpected but advantageous purchases
when the occasion arises; and so on. When anticipated inflation is
seen to be eroding the value of money kept on hand, people begin
to cut back on their money holdings, to sacrifice these advantages
rather than face the losses which holding money imposes. They
will devote more time and trouble to arranging their affairs in

order to economise on cash than they would in the absence of anticipated inflation. Thus real costs are imposed upon the community even by an anticipated inflation.

These costs of anticipated inflation are not limited to inefficiency in financial arrangements; there are other costs too. When prices are rising, even if everyone expects them to rise, producers still have to notify their customers about the timing and extent of particular price changes; shops still have to change the price tags on the specific goods they have for sale. All this activity takes time and trouble, and consumes resources which might otherwise have been devoted to more productive uses.

Now these arguments suggest that, on balance, a stable price level is to be preferred to a rising one, even if its rate of rise is fully anticipated; but this would only be the case if there were no benefits to be had from rising prices, and it is often argued that such benefits do exist. In particular it is argued that rising prices enable the economy to be run at a higher level of employment and with more efficiency in the use of productive resources. This argument is of dubious validity, although it stems from the plausible proposition that money wages and prices are relatively sticky downwards, that it is easier, in any particular industry, for these to rise than for them to fall.

In any well functioning economy the pattern of output is going to change over time in response to changing patterns of consumer expenditure, changes in technology, and so on. Such a changing pattern of output, however, requires that resources, including labour, be re-allocated between sectors of the economy. Such re-allocation is accomplished by having relative prices and wages vary; by having them rise in the expanding sectors and fall in those areas where a contraction of output is needed. Now if some particular prices are going to rise against a background of an overall stable price level, then some others must fall. If it is difficult to get any wages and prices to fall, then it is going to be difficult for the allocative mechanism to work efficiently. However, if the overall price level was permitted to rise, the required changes in the pattern of relative prices could be brought about by permitting the prices of some goods, and wages in some industries, to rise faster than those elsewhere, but without actually trying to force any absolute falls in wages and prices on any sector of the economy.

Thus, it is argued a steady rate of inflation might actually be conducive to the more efficient working of the economy and might produce a lower overall level of unemployment.

Now the key to this argument is the proposition that there are downward rigidities in wages and prices. But why should wages and prices be downwardly rigid? The answer usually given has to do with the reluctance of wage earners in particular industries to take cuts in real income. When dealing with an economy in which a zero rate of change of prices has been the norm, and hence has come to be expected to continue, it makes a good deal of sense to argue that individual wages and prices will tend to downward rigidity and that this tendency will to some extent interfere with the effectiveness of the price mechanism in re-allocating resources in response to a pattern of demand that changes over time. It equally makes sense to argue that a rising general price level will then help to make the allocative process work smoothly, *but only so long as a zero rate of increase of prices is anticipated.*

If it is the case that prices and wages tend to be downwardly sticky because of the desire of wage earners to protect the level of their real wages, then a process of rising prices that lasts long enough to persuade them that rising prices rather than stable prices are to become the norm must inevitably lead them to attempt to ensure that their money wages, and hence the price of their output, rise at least as fast as the general price level. The result of this will be that wages and prices will become sticky relative to the new expected rate of change of prices. Any tendency for a particular wage or price to rise less rapidly than the overall expected rate of inflation will be resisted. If this is the case, then it follows that the benefits in terms of the smoother functioning of the allocative mechanism and of an associated lower unemployment rate that one might get from inflation will be shortlived. These benefits will persist only so long as the inflation in question remains unanticipated. Anticipated inflation, in other words, will do relatively little harm, but it will not do any good either as long as downward stickiness in wages and prices is itself the product of wage earners' expectations about inflation.

There is no reason to suppose that wage earners are not at least as adept as their employers in anticipating inflation, though for a long time quite contrary beliefs were held by many economists.

Indeed, a theory of the inter-relationship of inflation and economic growth, first introduced by David Hume, and given considerable prominence by Keynes, was based on the proposition that wages lag behind prices in inflationary situations. Were this the case, then the resulting fall in real wages would lead to an increase in profits and the incentive to accumulate capital would be greater. Hence inflation would lead to more rapid capital accumulation. This 'wages lag' hypothesis, in one form or another, was part of economics for close on two hundred years before anyone took any serious steps to find out if it was true or not. The result of testing it has been to show that there is no systematic tendency at all for real wages to fall during inflation, suggesting then that the labour force is just as adept at predicting inflation as any other part of the population. Thus the proposition that inflation leads to more rapid capital accumulation than would occur in its absence is probably false.

To summarise then, if inflation is unanticipated it redistributes income and wealth from creditors to debtors, with the government being prominent among the debtors who gain. When it is anticipated, however, contracts can be made in such a way as to avoid any redistribution arising from rising prices. However, whether it is anticipated or not, inflation distorts the effects of taxation and increases government revenue. This is an effect that can be avoided by adjusting tax regulations to take account of cost of living changes, but it requires conscious action on the part of governments to do this. Even though the main effects of inflation occur when it is unexpected, fully anticipated inflation still has its costs. Where money bears no interest it leads to people taking more time and trouble over arranging their trading activities in order to economise on their holdings of depreciating cash balances. Moreover, the very process of changing prices and informing customers of the fact uses up resources that could be devoted to more productive uses.

Inflation has its drawbacks then, and seems to yield no lasting benefits. It is therefore worth avoiding. If it is to be controlled and cured, we must understand what causes it. The key to such understanding lies in the very meaning of the word inflation: a sustained fall in the value of money. Supply and demand analysis tell us that, given a stable demand function for anything, its price will fall continuously only if the supply of it increases continuously. There have been inflations for as long as there is recorded history, and there has never been a sustained inflation in any country without a sustained increase in the supply of money in that country; nor has there ever been a sustained increase in the supply of money in any country without inflation. Both elementary economic theory and an immense body of evidence point to an increasing quantity of money as a key factor in the inflationary process.

The actual process whereby monetary expansion drives up prices is indirect and complicated. Also, once it has started, the process generates its own momentum; this makes it both difficult and painful to stop. A simplified, but, it is to be hoped, not over-simplified, example will help here. Consider an economy in which there is no economic growth and no foreign trade, and in which, initially, there is full employment with a stable price level and a constant quantity of money. Now let the government of that country take measures that lead to the quantity of money, that is the volume of currency in circulation and of bank deposits, increasing by, say, 10%. Before the increase, all the firms and households in the economy would be holding enough money to satisfy their desire for the convenience in carrying on their trading activities, a matter we have already considered earlier in this chapter. Once the quantity of money increases, people find that they have more cash on hand than they really want to hold, given that it can be used by them to purchase other assets or even goods and services. Different economic agents will spend their excess cash in different ways. One man may buy a bond, another may pay off a debt, another may purchase a new car, another may take an extra holiday, but one way or another they spend their excess cash. But when it is spent by one person, cash does not disappear. It passes on to another person who accepts it in exchange for whatever it is he is selling, not because he wants cash to hold, but because he in his turn could use it to buy something. Thus an increase in the supply of money leads to an increase in the overall level of demand for goods and services.

Producers, faced with this increase in demand for their output, try to meet it by increasing output, but in an already fully employed economy there is virtually no scope for this. They bid against one another for a supply of labour and other productive services that can only be increased marginally and succeed not so much in increasing their output as in driving up wages and other costs of production. Hence the price of output also rises. Now with a once-and-for-all increase in the quantity of money, this process comes to an end soon enough. As prices rise, people find they require more money to finance their day-to-day economic activity; indeed the amount of money so required rises in proportion to the level of prices at which such activity is being carried on. Once a 10% increase in the quantity of money has led to a 10% increase in prices, there will be no excess cash holdings left to bid up prices further and prices will stabilise at a new higher level.

If, instead of a once-and-for-all increase in the money supply, we have a continuous expansion of the quantity of money, the price level will be driven up continuously and will not come to rest at any new higher level. Continuous inflation will be set in motion. Now the mechanism whereby excess demand leads to rising prices is a key one in the early stages of inflation, but as the process continues over time another vital element comes into play. We have already argued that once prices and wages begin to rise people come to expect that they will continue to do so. Such expectations get built in to the pricing policies of firms and into the wage bargaining that takes place between firms and members of the labour force — whether or not they are represented by trade unions. Wages increase because prices are expected to increase and, because wages increase, prices do indeed increase. Though in the early stages of inflation it is an increasing quantity of money that drives up prices and wages, in the later stages, when inflation becomes anticipated and a wage spiral of the type just described gets under way, monetary expansion plays a permissive role. It allows people to have sufficient cash on hand to carry on their economic life without being inconvenienced by rising prices. Hence monetary expansion becomes something that allows inflation to continue rather than something which drives it along.

What would happen to the course of a wage-price spiral if it was not supported by an expanding money supply is something that we will come to in a moment. We must first deal with an important extension to the foregoing argument.[2] How would our analysis be affected if we applied it to the more relevant (particularly to

Britain) case of a relatively small economy linked to the rest of the world through foreign trade? The answer here depends upon whether the economy operates a fixed or a flexible exchange rate for its currency. Under a fixed exchange rate, the analysis would be considerably modified. Such an arrangement has the central bank of the country concerned standing ready to buy and sell its currency in exchange for foreign currencies in unlimited amounts at a fixed price. As we shall see, the ultimate effect of this is to ensure that any one country cannot for long sustain an inflation rate that differs substantially from that prevailing elsewhere.

Consider what would happen if prices in one particular economy did indeed begin to rise more rapidly than those in the rest of the world as a result of domestic monetary expansion. Potential and actual exporters in that country would begin to find it less and less profitable to sell their goods abroad instead of selling them at home. The price available to them in terms of their home currency from selling abroad would not rise as quickly as that available from selling at home and so they would begin to divert some of their output to the home market. Foreigners selling to the more rapidly inflating country would also begin to find the practice increasingly attractive. The volume of already existing imports would tend to increase, while goods that previously could not compete successfully with domestic products would also begin to be imported. This tendency for goods to come onto the home market in increasing quantities of course works against whatever forces there might be that were making domestic prices increase more rapidly. Implicit here is a tendency for the balance of payments of the more rapidly inflating economy to go into deficit. To keep the exchange rate stable, its central bank would have to act as a net purchaser of its own currency on the foreign exchange market and would have to carry out its purchases with its reserves of foreign currency.

In a fully employed closed economy monetary expansion must

---

[2]The reader should compare the section that follows with Chapter 12 on the International Monetary System. He should also note that, in order to keep the exposition simple here, I have set aside the complication that arises when the capital account of the balance of payments is analysed. These complications do not alter the basic outlines of the analysis.

be absorbed in rising prices. In an open economy it can also spill over into a balance of payments deficit which puts domestic currency into foreign hands, thus ensuring that it is not available to support a rising domestic price level. If the central bank, after buying up this currency from foreigners, puts it back into circulation domestically, it does of course become available again. In this case the balance of payments deficit persists and the central bank must continue to use its foreign exchange reserves to support the exchange rate. Since its stocks of reserves are finite it can only do so for a limited period, and if the value of the exchange rate is to be maintained, domestic policy actions must be taken to bring prices into a relationship with those ruling in the rest of the world that will permit balance of payments equilibrium. This must involve having a domestic rate of change of prices that is very much the same as that ruling elsewhere.

It is worth considering how the process described above might work out if the inflation in the rest of the world were to accelerate relative to that ruling at home. Domestic producers of export goods would respond to a widening of the gap between the world and domestic prices of their goods. They would divert goods from home markets and increase prices there to keep pace with those available abroad. The price of imports would also begin to rise and so the domestic inflation rate would begin to accelerate. But where would the monetary expansion come from to support this? A balance of payments surplus would be generated and the central bank of our relatively small open economy would find itself buying up foreign exchange from its own nationals with domestic currency, hence generating the monetary expansion needed to support the new inflation rate. This process would be permanent only if the central bank was willing to acquire foreign exchange reserves indefinitely. If it was not, then the authorities would have to set in motion the policies necessary to make domestic prices and their rate of change behave in such a way as to keep the balance of payments in equilibrium. As before, this would involve having an inflation rate very much like that ruling in the rest of the world.

As must be evident from the preceding pages, when an economy is open to the rest of the world and small in relationship to it, *and operates a fixed exchange rate*, the inflation rate is in the long run very much an imported item. Prices can rise in response to domestic excess demand and purely domestic expectations only for so long as it takes those involved in the import and export of goods to adjust to, and, in adjusting to, eliminate discrepancies in the behaviour of prices in various parts of the world. If the economy operates a flexible exchange rate, however, things are very different, because in such circumstances the exchange rate that operates is fixed by the supply and demand for the country's currency on foreign exchange markets — in the limiting case, with no central bank intervention at all.

If domestic monetary expansion leads to a relatively fast inflation rate, we have already seen that a tendency to an outflow of domestic currency is the result. Under a flexible exchange rate, this tendency drives down the price of domestic currency on foreign exchange markets. Domestic currency prices received by exporters increase, as do the domestic currency prices of imports. Thus the stabilising forces that are at work when there is a fixed exchange rate are nullified by a flexible rate. Such a rate will fall for just so long as domestic policies lead to a more rapid inflation rate than that ruling in the rest of the world and ensure that prices behave very much as they would in a closed economy. Conversely, as the reader will surely be able to see for himself, any tendency for the world price level to rise more rapidly than that at home will tend to drive the exchange rate up and hence to insulate the domestic price level from inflationary pressures originating elsewhere.

We have seen that there are good reasons for regarding inflation as undesirable and we have argued that it requires monetary expansion to get inflation going and to keep it going, but once an inflation is under way, there may be costs involved in bringing it under control.

Debtors gain from inflation and the government is a prominent debtor. Government, uniquely among debtors, has the power to generate the monetary expansion that brings about and sustains inflation. It is always easier for an elected government to provide state-financed benefits for the community than it is for it to increase the taxes that might pay for such benefits. There is always an incentive for governments to borrow to finance some of their expenditure. If such borrowing is from the public at large there is no real problem because, in order to raise its funds, the government must bid against would-be private borrowers. In doing so, it drives up rates of interest and causes some private borrowers to go out of the market and to give up the expenditure which they planned to finance by borrowing. Thus, as government expenditure goes up, private expenditure is squeezed down by higher interest rates to make room for it.

However, the private sector of the economy is no fonder of cancelling expenditure plans in the face of higher interest rates than it is of cancelling them in the face of higher taxes. Hence the government is under pressure to find somewhere else to borrow and it alone has the power to borrow at will from the central bank. When a government borrows from the central bank, that bank creates deposits for the government which are then spent and hence put into circulation. The effect on the money supply is exactly the same as if the government had literally printed the notes with which to finance its expenditure. As long as the government continues to finance expenditure by borrowing from the central bank in this way, the money supply continues to increase. If it increases more rapidly than the real output of the economy then we get inflation.

When inflation first starts, we have seen that it brings certain benefits in terms of an apparently smoother functioning of the economic system. Initially inflation is relatively tolerable. However, these benefits last only as long as inflation is not anticipated; when inflation becomes anticipated, it also becomes costly to stop. The reason for this is inherent in the nature of the wage-price spiral described earlier. There is a strong element of the self-fulfilling prophecy about anticipated inflation. Prices are expected to rise and so wages rise; therefore prices do in fact rise.

Suppose that attempts are made to stop this spiral by reducing the rate of monetary expansion. Initially firms and households will begin to find that they have insufficient cash on hand to support comfortably their usual transaction patterns. They will all try to restore their cash positions by temporarily cutting down expenditure. Firms will face a fall in the demand for their output, but will be unsure as to whether it is temporary or permanent.

Moreover, because they are tied into particular wage contracts, they will be unwilling to cut prices below levels originally planned. They will plan temporarily to cut back on output and employment, but this cutback sets up a tendency towards further such falls as a downward multiplier process gets under way. In short, the initial effect of the monetary slow-down is not on the inflation rate at all, but on output and employment. Firms will eventually revise their planned prices downwards, and the labour force will moderate its bids for money wages in the face of unemployment. The inflation rate will begin to slow down and, as it does so, the expected inflation rate will also begin to fall. As long as there exists unusually high unemployment the inflation rate will fall, and eventually it will reach levels at which, given the rate of monetary expansion, there is room for income and employment to get back to full employment levels again with a rate of inflation lower than originally. Thus, the cost of significantly reducing the inflation rate, in an economy where inflation has become anticipated, seems to be a period of unemployment and stagnation that might better be measured in years rather than in weeks or months.

The policy dilemma implicit here is a harsh one, and it is hardly surprising that so many governments in so many countries have resorted to direct controls upon wages and prices in order to find a way out of it. There is not space here to chronicle the series of failures that have resulted, or to assess the reasons for them. Suffice it to say that, in the current state of our knowledge of how the economic system works, it is becoming increasingly apparent that the painful cure for inflation outlined above is the only sure one available. The more slowly is the inflation rate brought down, the less unemployment and stagnation must be endured in the process. This is because unemployment arises from the cuts in expenditure plans made as the community tries to maintain the level of its money holdings. The more slowly is a cash shortage generated, the smaller will be the expenditure cuts in question. However, the slower is this monetary slow-down, the longer will the community suffer from the costs of inflation in the meanwhile.

There is quite a lot that can be done to mitigate the costs imposed by inflation. Inasmuch as there is redistribution between the public and the government as a result of inflation, this can be offset by the government gearing the tax system to changes in the price level. Inasmuch as creditors of the government lose because the real value of their assets falls with inflation — and this is a particularly important factor for poorer members of the community, for whom government savings bonds are one of the few ways of holding wealth — then the government can agree to pay interest rates at a level that will compensate for these losses. As far as redistribution with the private sector is concerned, problems are not so widespread because, as we have seen, once inflation becomes anticipated, private contracts adjust to take account of it. Some problems do remain: certain types of contracts — for example for private pensions — made long in the past, cannot now be revised, even though the expectations upon which they were based have long been shown to be false. In such cases, there is perhaps room for government intervention to iron out the redistribution that inflation brings about, even within the private sector.

Such actions as these of course would not remove all the costs that inflation imposes. There would still be some loss in the efficiency of the financial system; the extra costs involved in administering the pricing policies of firms when the price level is rising would still have to be borne. It would still be worthwhile to cure inflation then, but, by mitigating some of its costs, the government could make it less urgent to do so. Thus, the type of 'gradualist' cure outlined above, designed to minimise the costs of curing inflation by spreading them out over time, would be made more viable. The solution to the problem of inflation that derives from the foregoing analysis is thus very much one of trading off one set of costs against another. In the current state of knowledge, it is not really possible to quantify these costs and there should be no presumption that they will be negligible. However, unless some unforeseen breakthrough in our knowledge of inflation occurs, they are costs that, sooner or later, are going to have to be incurred.

234   DAVID LAIDLER

Suggestions for Further Reading

See the papers by Blackaby and Laidler in:

Robinson, Joan (ed), *After Keynes: Papers presented to Section F at the Annual Meeting of the British Association for the Advancement of Science 1972*, Blackwell 1973.

See also:

Parkin, Michael, *United Kingdom Inflation: the Policy Alternatives*, National Westminster Economic Review, May 1974.

11. Economic growth: policies and constraints

G K SHAW
Reader in Economics,
University of St Andrews

The Importance of Growth

The pursuit of economic growth has dominated much of the discussion concerning the appropriate mix of policies for securing macroeconomic objectives, especially in the post-war years. Growth has been sought partly for its political and strategic implications, but also because it is recognised that attaining a growth rate of GNP in excess of the pace of population expansion implies a rising level of income per capita permitting greater consumption of both goods and leisure and a wider degree of consumer choice. In brief, enhanced economic growth is seen to hold the key to increased economic welfare.

Moreover, it is generally conceded that it is only through a raising of the growth rate that the problem of poverty, both in advanced and less advanced economies, may be readily overcome. In contrast, policies to redistribute income and wealth, whilst they imply a once-and-for-all improvement in the lot of the very poor, have but a minor impact upon the existence of poverty *per se*. This is not, of course, to argue that there is no case for redistribution: redistribution may be desired upon grounds of equity and a concern with narrowing the gap between the rich and the poor. Nonetheless, the fact remains that redistribution will have a minimal impact upon absolute poverty levels compared to the impact of sustained increases in the level of income per capita.[1] In addition, economic growth permits redistributive policies to be implemented without necessarily diminishing the absolute living standards of the comparatively better off. To this extent economic growth increases the political acceptability of such policies.

Apart from the implications for increased welfare implicit in the cumulative nature of the growth process, economic growth may also make possible the attainment of other policy objectives. With an expanding population, economic growth becomes a prerequisite for the maintenance of full employment. Particularly with regard to the developing economies the 'employment through growth' strategy has taken on renewed significance in the light of modernisation programmes which have been accompanied by a decisive movement from labour-intensive to capital-intensive techniques. In a similar way, the pace of economic growth may have relevance to the problem of inflation in that the greater the rate of growth of output in relation to the growth of the money supply the greater are the chances that 'demand-pull' inflation may be avoided. Likewise, many economists advocate that the way to overcome the tendency towards persistent balance of payments deficits lies in the adoption of a policy of export-led growth.

Economic growth is not without costs. These costs may include the costs of pollution and congestion, the tensions and stresses associated with living in a highly technical and urbanised environment and also possibly in some cases an actual decrease in the area of choice confronting consumers. The latter situation may derive from the adoption of a highly efficient and cost-saving production process which produces a standardised product with which the more varied output of handicraft manufacture can no longer compete. Inevitably, growth achieved through the exploitation of economies of large-scale production implies a certain standardisation of the final product.

The costs associated with economic growth, particularly those arising from technology and generating significant external costs (including hazards to life, noise, pollution etc.), suggest the need for governmental intervention and control. In addition, the

[1] A 3% increase in real per capita income per annum implies an eight-fold improvement in real living standards over the course of the biblical life of three score years and ten.

welfare implications of economic growth have entailed government intervention to ensure that the fruits of economic growth are distributed in accordance with society's standards of equity. Almost paradoxically, the concern with redistributive policies reflected both in government transfers and direct government expenditures has increased with increasing income per capita. Both influences do much to explain the observed correlation between the government/GNP ratio and the level of income per capita (Musgrave 1969).

Although there exists a general consensus upon the importance of growth, and with very few exceptions (Mishan 1967) upon its desirability, there remains wide disagreement concerning the causes of growth. As a consequence, there remains a decided division of opinion over optimal growth strategies and measures to overcome the constraints which might otherwise impede the attainment of the growth objective. In part, this disagreement springs from the empirical difficulty of quantifying the various contributions to growth performance, but it also stems from the wide gulf between economic theory and growth policy. In no other branch of economics is the discrepancy between theory and policy more marked than in the area of economic growth. The theoretical contributions are derived from extremely esoteric model building and the emphasis is very largely directed to the stability and permanence of the indicated long-term growth path far removed from the short-run considerations which occupy practical policy makers.

Nonetheless, there have been notable attempts to identify the sources of growth. In particular, Denison, in his influential volume *Why Growth Rates Differ* (1967) indicated no less than twenty-three distinct sources of economic growth, ranging from such factors as variations in pressures of demand, improvements in education and learning, the changing hours of work and sex composition of the labour force, to fundamental re-allocation of resources. Denison's study was important in stressing that most economies were confronted with a relatively inelastic growth potential; accordingly policy measures should be judged in terms of deviation from the potential growth path and not by reference to arbitrary inter-country comparisons.

Conceptually it is convenient to group the sources of growth

into two distinct categories. On the one hand we may identify the
factor inputs — land, labour (allowance being made for changes in
its quality) and capital — and estimate their contribution to the
growth process. The relationship between the increase in factor
inputs and the resultant increase in output indicates *ceteris paribus*
whether increasing, diminishing or constant returns to scale apply.
On the other hand we have a residual component which takes
account of all increases in economic growth not accounted for by
the augmentation of factor inputs. In this latter component we
would undoubtedly include such major influences as innovation
and technical change as well as a host of cultural and sociological
factors, such as attitudes to work effort, trade union behaviour
and so forth, which may assist or impede the growth process.

It follows that we may adopt the same conceptual framework to
appraise growth policies, since the latter will attempt to influence
actual growth rates either by augmenting factor inputs, or by
influencing the residual component, or by some judicious
combination of the two. In what follows we will briefly review the
case of the principal claimants to growth contribution and in so
doing we may suggest possible explanations for Britain's
disappointing post-war growth performance. We will then be able
to evaluate specific policies for economic growth in the light of the
peculiar constraints which confront the British economy.

The Importance of Capital Accumulation

The belief that capital accumulation may hold the key to economic
growth is widely held and springs partly from the observed
correlation between high growth rates and high investment/GNP
ratios (Hill 1964). However, correlation need imply nothing about
causation; a high level of investment to national income may be
the consequence of rapid growth which creates a continuously
expanding demand for increased capacity. Moreover, the issue of
correlation is bedevilled by the fact that the crucial relationship is
between economic growth and *net* productive investment. That is
to say, for example, that if two countries were investing 15% of
GNP annually but in one case 10% of it was to meet depreciation
needs whilst in the other only 5% was required, then the latter

would have twice the net productive investment rate. Consequently, small variations in the aggregate investment/GNP ratio may conceal large variations in the net investment/GNP ratio. This issue is complicated by the fact that it is no simple matter in practice to distinguish between gross and net investment. Replacement of equipment seldom involves the identical asset; usually as capital assets are depleted they are replaced by improved and superior assets, so that it becomes difficult to distinguish the net from the gross investment.[2]

The theoretical basis for the advocacy of capital accumulation is closely related to the elementary Harrod-Domar growth model, which equates the increase in capacity income in any period to the volume of net investment divided by the capital-output ratio. Symbolically

$$\Delta Y = \frac{I}{C}$$

where Y refers to capacity income, I to net investment and C is the capital-output ratio. As stated, the equation is merely a tautology summarising the impact of net investment in extending the capacity income level of the conventional Keynesian national income model. It is not, however, without significance. If we allow for the capital-output ratio to differ between sectors of the economy, then it follows that the aggregate growth rate can be increased by transferring available investment resources from sectors of high capital-output ratios to sectors possessing comparatively low capital-output ratios. Our growth equation for an n-sector economy is now written

$$\Delta Y = \frac{I_1}{C_1} + \frac{I_2}{C_2} + \frac{I_3}{C_3} + \cdots \frac{I_n}{C_n}$$

$$= \sum_{j=1}^{n} \frac{I_j}{C_j}$$

[2]Witness for example the striking advances in the electronics industry.

where $I_1, I_2 \ldots I_n$ indicate the extent of net investment in various sectors and which when summed equal the total investment within the economy. It follows that a comparatively poor growth performance can spring from two distinct causes; either from a low investment/GNP ratio or from a relatively high aggregated capital-output ratio,[3] or indeed from some combination of the two. Critics of British growth performance have pointed to both factors, arguing that the incentive to invest has not been sufficiently strong to motivate the private sector. The incentive has been lacking, so it is alleged, primarily owing to the frequent recourse to 'stop-go' policies which have exerted an adverse impact upon business profit expectations. At the same time investment in the public sector and in the nationalised industries has been maintained, and these sectors are typically the declining sectors of the economy or sectors characterised by higher than average capital-output ratios.

Thus far we have discussed the concept of the capital-output ratio without specifying whether we are dealing in average or marginal terms. This is very much in keeping with the spirit of the Harrod-Domar model, since it assumed constancy — and thus equality — between average and marginal capital-output ratios. If the capital-output ratio is indeed a constant, then the logic of capital formation as a means to economic growth is unassailable. If, however, the capital-output ratio is not constant, then clearly it is the marginal concept or the incremental capital-output ratio which is crucial for policy prescription. Should increasing the amount of capital, relative to other co-operative inputs, encounter the onset of diminishing returns as neo-classical theory would predict, then clearly the incremental capital-output ratio will rise and the anticipated increase in productive capacity will not be forthcoming. This is broadly the line of argument taken by those economists who are sceptical of the claim of capital formation to be crucial to the growth process. In their view capital formation is the consequence of growth, since growth enlarges demand and broadens the scope of profitable investment opportunities offsetting the tendency towards diminishing returns. It may be

[3]When weighted by the investment undertaken within each sector.

noted that this controversy cannot readily be settled by reference to the available empirical findings. Whilst the evidence, such as it is, indicates a broad constancy in the average capital-output ratio over time, this is precisely what one would expect from the existence of diminishing returns to capital investment — a rising incremental capital-output ratio — assuming profit maximising behaviour. For as diminishing returns set in, the incentive to undertake new investment ceases and investment comes to a halt, leaving the average capital-output ratio virtually unaffected. Later, when new investment opportunities have emerged, investment recommences until the next onset of diminishing returns. Such a cyclical view of the investment process would then reveal virtual constancy in the average capital-output ratio.

Despite these arguments the virtue of capital accumulation as a means to growth commands great respect. Perhaps the most extreme example of this view has been voiced by the celebrated economist Paul Samuelson (1956) who claimed:

> With proper fiscal and monetary policies, our economy can have full employment and whatever rate of capital formation and growth it wants.

The proper monetary and fiscal policies which Samuelson had in mind have been aptly referred to as the strict-fiscal easy-monetary policy for economic growth. The essential idea is that taxes can be used to force down consumption spending and the budget surplus so obtained be diverted to investment usage, either by the government spending the proceeds directly or by transferring them to the private investment-oriented sector by the purchase of government bonds. In the act of purchasing outstanding government bonds, the money supply is increased and the interest rate lowered, thus providing further stimulus to investment activity. To quote Samuelson (1963) again:

> A strong growth-inducing policy of monetary ease, if it succeeds in producing overall employment, can be combined with an austere fiscal policy, in which tax rates are kept high and/or expenditure rates low enough, so as to remove inflationary pressures of the demand-pull type and succeed in increasing the net capital formation share of our full-employment income at the expense of the current consumption share.

Unfortunately, such a policy prescription implicitly presupposes a closed economy in which national income is represented by $Y=C+I+G$, where the symbols represent consumption, investment and government spending respectively. Taxation is used to force down C, whilst compensating adjustments in I and G maintain aggregate demand at a level to provide full employment. If the analysis is extended to the sphere of international trade, however, then even forgetting any reservations about diminishing returns to capital investment, sizeable constraints emerge with regard to the external deficit. If the full employment income level is maintained, then *ceteris paribus* so too will be the level of imports, and the lowering of the interest rate will worsen the capital account and hence *in toto* the overall balance of payments. It is for this reason that recent advocacy of the monetary-fiscal mix for enhanced growth has been accompanied by attempts to direct investment into the export sector (export-led growth), or by permitting the exchange rate to float in order to overcome the balance of payments constraint. Such requirements to the underlying doctrine are not easily effected. International trading obligations (such as GATT) specifically prohibit favourable fiscal assistance to the export sectors, whilst the automatic adjustment response of floating exchange rates predicted by elementary trade theory may involve a sizeable and unbearable time lag.

The Importance of Technical Change

As we have already indicated, one can mentally decompose growth into two components, the one resulting from augmentation of factor inputs and a residual element encompassing all other contributing factors. In the latter category one would undoubtedly wish to emphasise the importance of technical change and innovation. Many economists have argued the latter to be the major cause of growth and far more important than the role of capital accumulation.

A pioneering work emphasising the importance of technical change was published by Robert Solow (1957). In this article Solow attempted to segregate observed variations in output per head due to technical change from those due to the increase in capital per head. Applying US GNP non-farm data for the period

1909-49 and adopting a constant returns to scale production function exhibiting neutral technical change (not inconsistent with the evidence), Solow was able to obtain an estimate of the marginal productivity of capital and consequently a measure of the increased output due to increased capital formation over a specific period of time. The excess of increased output not so explained provides a measure of economic growth arising from all other factors described in the catch-all technical change. There are all sorts of difficulties and objections (Hicks 1960) involved in this approach[4], but nonetheless Solow's conclusion was startling, indicating that of the doubling of gross output per man which occurred over the forty-year period no less than 87½% stemmed from technical change with the remainder arising from capital formation.

If technical change is the major factor in economic growth then there are clearly important implications for policy. In particular, it would suggest that more encouragement be given to research and development and perhaps more emphasis in the educational framework should be given to science and technology, especially upon the applied side. However, the role of capital accumulation should not be dismissed lightly. As Solow was quick to emphasise, much if not all technical change is in fact embodied in new plant and equipment. It is through the inflow of new investment that the impact of technical change is transmitted to the economy. Thus the policy implication which appears to emerge is not that any less attention be given to capital formation; but perhaps attempts should be made to direct new investment towards the more innovating sectors. One consequence of incorporating technical progress into the act of investment was the development of the so-called vintage growth model, whereby capital is looked upon not as one homogeneous commodity but rather as a series of past

---

[4]Not least, the assumption that capital is paid its marginal product. Furthermore, the relevant variable to test the contribution of capital is not the change in the capital stock as such, but the change in the effective utilisation of the capital stock. Solow did indeed attempt to deal with this question by assuming an equal percentage unemployment of capital as of the labour force; an admittedly arbitrary assumption which highlights some of the difficulties encountered in empirical work of this nature.

investments, each series being unique in itself and with later series being the more efficient in terms of productivity per man. In the early post-war years the apparent superior growth performances of the West European nations *vis-à-vis* Britain was largely explained in the light of this thesis, since the former were compelled to rebuild much of their capital stock from scratch. As an explanation of Britain's continued comparative poor growth performance, however, it is clearly of less explanatory power.

The Importance of Labour and Labour Allocation

The preceding argument has emphasised the importance of technical change. However, it should be stressed that the meaning of technical change employed above is that of a residual factor which explains any upward shift of the production function — in short, anything not accounted for by increased capital per capita. Once this is recognised then it is clear that consideration must be given to the labour input and in particular to any factor which accounts for increased labour productivity not embodied in increased investment.[5]

There are two factors which specifically need to be taken into account. The first has become known as the learning process which relates the impact of job experience to labour productivity. Stated simply, this thesis maintains that the amount of labour input per unit of output declines as the total volume of output increases for any given product. The learning process is not of course without limit and the limit in many cases arises through a change of product: nonetheless, it remains an example of a peculiar economy of scale which raises overall productivity exogenously and is therefore independent both of capital accumulation and advances in technology.

Secondly, a change in aggregate productivity per capita may be achieved merely by the transfer of labour from low to high

[5]The quality and hence productivity of labour is enhanced by education. The resulting upward shift of the aggregate production function may thus be best described as technical advance embodied in investment in human resources.

productivity occupations, without any augmentation of the total factor input and without any technological advance. Such a change is closely related to the transfer of resources out of agriculture and non-agricultural self employment into manufacturing. Indeed, in the case of less advanced economies some of the labour employed within the agricultural sector may possess zero or near zero marginal product and its transference into more productive usages is often looked upon as a prerequisite for continuing development. There is no doubt that the ratio of agricultural output to GNP is closely correlated (inversely) with the level of income per capita and indeed such a ratio is sometimes looked upon as a useful index of the development process. This increased productivity through labour re-allocation is sometimes looked upon as being especially significant in accounting for the comparatively poor growth performance of both the United States and the United Kingdom *vis-à-vis* Western Europe. What is alleged is that this source of economic growth has become virtually exhausted for the former two countries; their ability to contract the agricultural sector is severely constrained in comparison to the economies of Western Europe.[6]

It is important to note what exactly is implied in this argument. There are two distinct issues involved. On the one hand differences in the pace of inter-sector resource transfer between countries will account for differences in productivity increases between countries — assuming that the sectors differ in their productivity per head. However, the evidence suggests that such static once-for-all effects would be limited and would not account for more than a comparatively small amount of the observed differences in actual growth rates. It is for this reason that Kaldor's restatement of the argument in dynamic terms (Kaldor 1966) involving differences in economies of scale between sectors, takes on great importance for it greatly reinforces the weight of the differential effect.

To paraphrase Kaldor's argument, the economy may be thought of as comprising three sectors, the primary (agriculture),

[6]For example, the agricultural population of the UK is currently put at 3.1% compared to an average of 11.5% for the original six EEC countries (European Commission 1974).

the secondary (manufacturing) and the tertiary (mainly services). They are characterised in general by diminishing, increasing and relatively constant returns respectively. The transference of labour from agriculture into manufacturing not only generates a once-and-for-all increase in total output, but it also implies induced productivity changes in response to the increment in total output. The fundamental relationship is thus between the rate of change of productivity and the rate of change of output and Britain's misfortune stems from being first in the field: "it has reached a high state of 'maturity' *earlier* than others, with the result that it has exhausted the potential for fast growth before it had attained particularly high levels of productivity or real income per head" (Kaldor 1966). This is indeed a disturbing conclusion for the British reader and suggests that the scope for policy-induced changes in the UK growth rate may be decidedly limited. Nonetheless, there will remain some scope for productivity increases arising from the re-allocation of labour within the manufacturing sector. The argument is perfectly analogous to that of directing investment into sectors possessing low capital-output ratios; in the present case productivity is increased by directing labour into areas with relatively low labour-output ratios. The greater the degree of competition in factor markets, the greater the likelihood of the efficient allocation of factor inputs. Policies to increase the mobility of labour, including policies to increase labour's awareness of market conditions, are conducive to the growth process. Conversely, influences which restrict labour mobility, as for example many non-transferable occupational pension schemes, must be judged harmful to the cause of economic growth.

British Growth: Performance and Policy

Although we have warned against attaching too much importance to inter-country comparisons of growth upon the grounds that different countries will possess different potential growth paths, there can be little doubt that Britain's post-war growth performance has been disappointing, averaging approximately half that of the original six EEC countries. Table I indicates some

Table 1. *Average annual rates of growth of GDP at constant prices by type of expenditure (%) 1960-70*

Country	GDP	Per capita GDP	Government consumption expenditure	Private consumption expenditure	Gross domestic fixed capital formation	Exports	Imports
UK	2.8	2.2	2.2	2.4	4.9	4.9	4.4
France	5.7	4.6	3.5	5.6	8.7	9.2	10.9
W. Germany	4.6	3.5	3.8	4.7	4.5	9.1	9.3
Italy	5.4	4.5	4.0	5.8	3.9	12.1	10.3
Switzerland	4.0	2.4	4.3	4.3	4.6	7.3	7.1
USA	4.6	3.3	4.9	4.6	4.5	6.6	8.6
Canada	5.5	3.6	5.1	5.0	6.3	9.4	8.6
Japan	10.9	9.7	6.5	9.1	13.9	15.4	13.3

comparative growth performances and also suggests some interesting relationships, especially that between the growth rate of GNP and the growth rate of exports. Perhaps even more significant in highlighting the impact of disparate growth rates is the information summarised in table 2, which emphasises the compounding nature of economic growth.

In assessing growth performance it is important to emphasise that the crucial factor is the long-term trend in productive capacity and not any short-term fluctuation in actual output. The latter is influenced not just by the extent of productive capacity, but also by its degree of utilisation which will vary with the changing pressure of demand. The two are of course closely connected; a sustained period of unemployment due to demand deficiency will inevitably slow down the growth of productive capacity. Yet nonetheless, if attention is focussed upon short-run changes in actual output, it can give rise to misleading impressions of performance. In the period 1972-73, for example, the United Kingdom attained an actual growth rate of output in the region of 5%, but this was largely due to the rapid decline in unemployment under expansionary monetary and fiscal policies and was not sustainable over time.

Growth policies in the United Kingdom are perhaps most aptly described within the context of the differing philosophies of alternative governments, with the Labour Party favouring more

Table 2. *Index numbers of per capita GDP at constant prices 1960-70*

	1960	1963	1970
Austria	90	100	151
Spain	78	100	145
France	88	100	138
Italy	84	100	135
Belgium	88	100	134
West Germany	91	100	132
Norway	88	100	130
Sweden	89	100	127
UK	96	100	117

direct intervention and control and the Conservatives relying generally, but not entirely, upon the market mechanism, with the latter subject to fiscal and monetary influence. Labour governments have tended to direct resources whilst Conservative administrations have emphasised the importance of incentives.

The Labour administration of 1945-51 faced the enormous task of post-war reconstruction in the face of a chronic dollar shortage and committed to an extensive and far-reaching programme of social reform and nationalisation. In these circumstances it is hardly surprising that they did not pursue a conscious growth policy as such. Moreover, the economic climate of the time still conceived the main economic problem to be maintenance of a high level of employment especially in the earlier post-war years.

More attention was accorded the growth process in the 1950's which coincided with the long period of Conservative rule 1951-64. If it is at all possible to summarise policies for economic growth extending over a decade, the underlying philosophy would appear to be as follows. Growth depends upon investment; for investment to be maintained at a high level, business must be given the incentive to invest; to provide such incentive, consumer demand must be high, and this can be achieved by progressively lowering the fiscal burden and cutting taxes to offset the tendency towards fiscal drag.[7] Unfortunately this high level of consumer demand sucked in imports which tended to expand at a faster rate than exports. Given recurring balance of payments deficits, the government was repeatedly called upon to adopt deflationary policies and in particular to rely upon increases in Bank Rate to assist the capital account of the balance of payments and maintain the exchange rate. Generalising over the period 1951-64 therefore, one might argue that the authorities adopted policies in direct contradiction to the strict-fiscal easy-monetary prescription; they relied on lowering taxes to promote consumption-led growth and they were compelled to raise interest rates and restrict increases in the money supply to maintain the fixed exchange rate of the pound.[8] The repeated checks upon expansionary policies became known as 'stop-go' and it has been contended that it was responsible for a disappointing investment record on the part of British industry. The key to investment, it is alleged, lies in the expectation of profits; industry will not invest if it expects the force of the payments constraint to lead to periodic deflationary cutbacks in demand. In turn, the disappointing investment record was often looked upon as the cause of Britain's disappointing growth rate.

It was partly in an effort to overcome the stop-go dilemma that Britain applied for membership of the European Economic Community in 1962. The arguments, of course, were not all economic and even on the economic side there was widespread disagreement about the reasons why membership of the EEC would benefit Britain's growth rate. Some economists stressed the importance for British competitiveness of economies of scale which could be obtained by access to a market of over 250 million people. Others emphasised the psychological impact that membership would have in transforming attitudes on both sides of industry, namely that in the face of competition industry would be compelled to become much more dynamic and that, perceiving the benefits of a more dynamic economy, labour would rid itself of

[7]Fiscal drag refers to the tendency for tax revenues to grow at a faster pace than government expenditures, partly owing to the progressive nature of the tax system, with the consequence that the budget surplus gradually increases over time and if not offset would act as a drag upon the economy.

[8]Attempts were made to influence saving — witness the introduction of premium bonds — but comparatively little emphasis was placed upon capital formation as such. Discriminatory tax treatment in favour of retained earnings by companies was abolished.

restrictive practices. Whatever the arguments, the eventual vetoing of Britain's application for membership was looked upon as a blow to her growth prospects and the alternative of the Free Trade Association was viewed as inadequate compensation.

In many respects the Conservative government of 1970-74 could be said to have followed similar policies as its Conservative predecessor, introducing substantial tax cuts to promote demand and pursuing Common Market membership which it successfully negotiated. However, there was one important distinction which many observers thought of as being crucial to the success of the growth policy, namely that the government was no longer dogmatically committed to maintaining a fixed and overvalued exchange rate for the pound. Indeed, in the pursuit of growth the pound was allowed to float and depreciate quite substantially; no longer was the balance of payments constraint able to dictate the permissible rate of economic growth by necessitating stop-go policies. Moreover, when the automatic adjustment implicit in the concept of a freely floating exchange rate failed to materialise, the policy of consumption-led growth was still adhered to even in the face of alarming payments deficits, primarily in the belief that sustained growth would generate the corrective increase in exports as Britain's competitive position improved. What the outcome of this policy *would* have been, had it been allowed to continue, is a matter of conjecture; in the event the policy had to be abandoned in the wake of the Middle Eastern war and its aftermath of fuel crisis and large price increases in oil which placed an intolerable burden upon the balance of payments.

The Labour administration of 1964-70 sought the solution to growth policy in economic planning and launched the so-called National Plan in 1965 (HMSO 1965) under the newly created Department of Economic Affairs. The purpose of the plan was primarily to indicate the potential growth path that the economy could attain and identify areas where bottlenecks might otherwise develop to impede the fulfilment of the plan. On the basis of a consistent set of projections for the various sectors of the economy, it was one purpose of the plan to create the set of expectations which would induce the appropriate response from the private sector so as to meet the projections. However, whilst committed to the aim to increase national output by 25% over the period 1964-70, the national plan was conceived of within the context of the existing rate of exchange and its initial task was seen as that of eliminating the sizeable payments deficit and building a surplus as a basis for faster economic growth. In the event the overvalued exchange rate proved unsustainable and generated severe speculative movements against sterling, but in the attempt to maintain it severe deflationary measures were imposed, necessitating the abandonment of the plan.

The period of the Labour government 1964-70 also witnessed specific fiscal actions designed to influence the overall growth rate. Whereas Conservative governments had resorted to fiscal policy mainly in the context of controlling the aggregate level of demand, the Labour government sought to influence resource allocation directly by discriminatory tax treatment. One example of such a policy was the adoption of the Selective Employment Tax in 1966. This tax owed much to the influence of Professor Kaldor who, as we have previously noted, was an exponent of the view that the re-allocation of labour from agriculture to industry was a major source of economic growth; and one which had been virtually eliminated in the case of the United Kingdom. The real purpose of the tax was to find a substitute for this depletion of labour supply from the primary sector. By taxing service activities heavily whilst effectively non-taxing or even subsidising manufacturing activities, the attempt was made to effect a 'shake-out' of labour from the tertiary to the secondary sector, since it was the latter which was characterised by increasing returns to scale. Moreover, it was the latter sector which was responsible for the majority of British exports. The attempt therefore was to influence the allocation of resources towards export activity whilst simultaneously raising the growth rate — a policy of export-led as opposed to consumption-led growth (Kaldor 1971). This ingenious fiscal device did appear to have some beneficial impact on labour productivity (HMSO 1970), although it was undoubtedly also a factor in increasing the problem of short-term unemployment. Moreover, such an innovation conflicted with the proposed plans for fiscal harmonisation within the countries of the EEC and to that extent jeopardised British prospects of entry, which for many observers offered the only real solution to Britain's long-term growth rate. Finally, it is extremely dubious whether any policy of export-led growth could have been successful as long as the government was committed to the maintenance of a fixed rate of exchange which clearly overvalued sterling.

This brief review of post-war measures to promote economic growth has highlighted one overriding fact: the importance of the balance of payments constraint. Regardless of the specific policies adopted, which in turn spring from the diverse views about the ultimate causes of economic growth, the payments deficit has repeatedly intervened to dictate the growth pattern. The problem has been intensified by the peculiar role of sterling in the world's economy, by the sense of commitment to the extensive holders of sterling balances and also, perhaps, by a mistaken view of Britain's future international status. One cannot resist the temptation to conclude that the exchange rate has on occasion been mistaken as an end in itself, rather than a policy tool to be used to obtain other desirable goals.

Given the absence of surplus reserves of potentially productive agricultural labour and the political infeasibility of large-scale immigration, together with the external payments constraint on increased investment expenditure incentives, the most that can be expected is an increased productivity arising from the re-allocation of existing resources. In turn this would in all probability require an increase in the degree of competition and the elimination of restrictive practices on both sides of industry and the termination of essentially uneconomic activities. Yet such a fundamental re-allocation would certainly involve conflict with other ends of macroeconomic policy; especially with employment and regional policies, which specifically seek goals other than increased output per capita and which permit a certain resource misallocation in order to achieve them. We are left with the conclusion that whether it is the augmentation of factor inputs, or the power of technological advance and innovation, which is ultimately responsible for economic growth, it must remain extremely dubious for Britain to accelerate her growth performance without simultaneously overcoming the constraint of the balance of payments deficit.[9]

[9]This chapter has benefited from helpful comments by Professor Alan Peacock.

References

Denison, Edward F., *Why Growth Rates Differ: Postwar Experience in Nine Western Countries*, Brookings Institution 1967.

Hicks, J., *Thoughts on the Theory of Capital: The Corfu Conference*, Oxford Economic Papers, Oxford University Press 1960.

Hill, T. P., Growth and Investment According to International Comparisons, *Economic Journal*, June 1964.

Kaldor, N., *Causes of the Slow Rate of Economic Growth of the United Kingdom*, Cambridge University Press 1966.

Kaldor, N., Conflicts in National Economic Objectives, *Economic Journal*, March 1971.

Mishan, E. J., *The Costs of Economic Growth*, Staples Press 1967.

Musgrave, R. A., *Fiscal Systems*, Yale University Press 1969.

Samuelson, Paul A., Fiscal and Financial Policies for Growth in *Proceedings: A Symposium on Economic Growth*, The American Bankers Association 1963.

Samuelson, Paul A., The New Look in Tax and Fiscal Policy, *Federal Tax Policy for Economic Growth and Stability*, US Government Printing Office 1956.

Solow, Robert M., Technical Change and the Aggregate Production Function, *Review of Economics and Statistics*, August 1967.

Effects of the Selective Employment Tax: First Report -- The Distributive Trades, HMSO 1970.

Report on Social Development in the Community, European Economic Community Commission 1974.

The National Plan, Cmnd 2764, HMSO 1965.

Suggestions for Further Reading

Beckerman, Wilfred (ed), *The Labour Government's Economic Record 1964-70*, Duckworth 1972.

Cairncross, Sir Alec (ed), *Britain's Economic Prospects Reconsidered*, George Allen & Unwin 1971.

Caves, Richard E., *et al.*, *Britain's Economic Prospects*, Brookings Institution 1968.

Henderson, P. D. (ed), *Economic Growth in Britain*, Weidenfeld & Nicolson 1966.

Lipton, Michael, *Assessing Economic Performance*, Staples Press 1968.

Maddison, Angus, *Economic Growth in the West*, The Twentieth Century Fund 1964.

Peaker, Antony, *Economic Growth in Modern Britain*, Macmillan 1974.

12. The international monetary system: retrospect and prospect

G ZIS
Research Fellow in Economics,
University of Manchester

International trade allows countries to specialise in the production of those goods in which they enjoy a comparative cost advantage. If the world economy is to derive all the gains that follow from trade, there must exist a set of international monetary arrangements conducive to a system of multilateral payments. The rules and regulations governing the operations of the International Monetary Fund (IMF), and through it specifying the norms of conduct for member countries, are such a set of international monetary arrangements. During the post-1945 period a system of multilateral trade and payments was firmly established. The importance of the contribution of the IMF system to this achievement is generally accepted. However, recurring international monetary crises have exposed weaknesses in the original system, and have led governments to seek an alternative, more enduring, set of international monetary arrangements.

This chapter describes the objectives of the IMF system and the means by which these objectives were to be achieved. In evaluating the performance of the system, the causes of its breakdown are considered and the options currently discussed with respect to the future international monetary system are examined.

The IMF System

Countries viewed the establishment of the IMF system in 1944 as an important instrument in achieving the objectives of full employment and high rates of growth. The IMF was to provide a forum for consultations among member countries aiming at the promotion of international monetary cooperation, the lack of which was seen as an important cause of the ills of the inter-war period. International cooperation was seen as the necessary precondition for the monetary arrangements embodied in the IMF system to form the basis of a multilateral system of payments which would be conducive to the rapid expansion of trade. In order to ensure that there existed a set of international monetary arrangements which would promote the expansion of trade, while recognising the possibility that the interests of the world community may diverge from those of an individual economy, the IMF was envisaged as a source of aid to countries facing balance of payments difficulties. Such assistance, aimed at harmonising international and national interests, would facilitate the correction of external disequilibria without necessarily involving the sacrifice of domestic economic objectives.

The central feature of the IMF system was the commitment of member countries to maintain fixed exchange rates; these were thought of as necessary if countries were to enjoy the benefits of full employment, growth and specialisation. The main argument for a system of fixed exchange rates is that it so links economies with each other as to promote trade among them, just as the establishment of an individual currency within a country facilitates transactions between regions of that country. If such a system is to have the desired effects, certain conditions must be met.

Let us analyse these conditions by examining how a system of fixed exchange rates would ideally function. British importers, for example, are willing to supply sterling in exchange for goods from abroad. On the other hand, importers in the rest of the world wish to exchange their respective currencies for British goods. However, foreign importers need sterling to pay British exporters. Thus the demand for British goods implies a demand for sterling, while the British demand for foreign goods implies a supply of sterling. Private demand for, and supply of, sterling can therefore determine its price in terms of the other currencies. If the international price of sterling is thus determined, whenever excess demand for or supply of sterling emerges, the equilibrium exchange rate, i.e. the price of sterling equating demand and supply, will alter. A system whereby exchange rates are freely determined in this way in the foreign exchange market has been advocated by some economists; however, there is widespread scepticism about the advantages of such a system. Flexible exchange rates are rejected on the grounds that such a system is unlikely to promote the exchange rate stability required for the rapid expansion of international trade.

If governments decide that it is undesirable for the exchange rate to be freely determined by private demand and supply, then they must be able to offset any excess supply or demand for the national currency. For governments to maintain a fixed exchange rate, there must exist some internationally acceptable money which a government can use to purchase the excess supply of its currency, or be prepared to accept in exchange for its currency whenever there exists excess demand for the latter at the agreed exchange rate. This internationally acceptable money can either be a commodity, e.g. gold, or a national currency, e.g. sterling or dollars, or an asset created by an international institution, e.g. IMF Drawing Rights, which all countries are prepared to use. Exchange rates can, therefore, be maintained fixed by central monetary authorities making purchases and sales of this international money.

As trade expands it is not unreasonable to suppose that the fluctuations in the discrepancy between the private demand for and supply of a currency may become larger. Governments will therefore require a greater volume of international liquidity for their foreign exchange market operations. Thus if fixed exchange rates are to be maintained, there is need for provisions ensuring a rate of growth of international liquidity in line with the expansion of world trade.

Suppose that the UK, for example, decides to increase its rate of monetary expansion with the aim of reducing the level of unemployment; UK citizens will now find themselves holding money balances in excess of the desired level. They will attempt to eliminate these excess money balances by exchanging them, among other things, for goods, some of which are produced abroad. The balance of payments provides a channel through which excess money balances can be eliminated; but as UK citizens attempt to restore their money balances to the desired level, they increase the supply of sterling in the foreign exchange market. If the private foreign demand for sterling has not correspondingly increased, and there is no reason to suppose that it will have done so, in order to maintain the international price of sterling unchanged the UK authorities will have to purchase the excess supply of sterling in exchange for that asset which is internationally acceptable. Assuming that the UK originally had a balance of payments equilibrium, we conclude that the increase in the rate of growth of the money supply leads to a balance of payments deficit, i.e. an excess supply of sterling in the foreign exchange market.

If the UK authorities maintain the rate of growth of the money supply at this higher level, the balance of payments deficit will persist. Consequently, the UK's foreign exchange reserves, i.e. those assets which are internationally acceptable, will be run down. However, no country has an unlimited amount of international liquidity at its disposal. If the UK is to maintain its exchange rate, sooner or later it will have to initiate such measures as to eliminate its balance of payments deficit. Given that the deficit did emerge as a result of an expansionary monetary policy, the remedy most likely to succeed in restoring balance of payments equilibrium is a reduction in the rate of growth of the money supply. However, a reversal in the monetary policy of the UK will lead to an increase in the level of unemployment in the short run. This may be regarded, for various reasons, as undesirable. Instead the UK policy makers may opt for imposing barriers to the movement of goods and capital in the form of tariffs, quotas, exchange restrictions, etc. But the adoption of such measures as a means of curing a balance of payments disequilibrium is totally at variance with the main argument for a system of fixed exchange rates, which is that it facilitates international trade.

We can, therefore, conclude that if countries pursue divergent monetary policies, balance of payments disequilibria will emerge which, unless eventually corrected, will render a system of fixed exchange rates unworkable. If the world economy is to derive all the advantages of such a system, there exists a need for an effective mechanism of adjustment whereby countries initiate corrective measures before balance of payments disequilibria get too far out of hand.

Let us now examine the inter-relationship between the two requirements for a smoothly functioning fixed exchange rate system: an adequate rate of growth of international liquidity and an effective mechanism of adjustment. Suppose again that Britain decides to increase its rate of monetary expansion. This leads to a balance of payments deficit and a loss of foreign exchange reserves. The UK, for whatever reason, is reluctant to take immediate measures to eliminate its balance of payments disequilibrium. How long, then, can Britain delay initiating corrective policies? The answer to this question depends on the volume of foreign exchange reserves at the disposal of the UK. The larger the volume of UK foreign exchange reserves, the longer the UK can delay taking such steps as to correct its balance of payments disequilibrium. Thus, in a system of fixed exchange rates, a rapid rate of growth of international liquidity can be a substitute for an effective mechanism of adjustment. If international liquidity grows at a low rate, then a system of fixed exchange rates is not viable without a mechanism of adjustment that works effectively and speedily.

Consider what will happen if countries adopt divergent monetary policies. Countries which attach high priority to price stability might be expected to pursue a moderate rate of monetary expansion, while those whose prime objective is the maintenance of a low level of unemployment are likely to allow their money supply to increase at whatever rate will ensure the achievement of their main economic goal. Under such circumstances large balance of payments disequilibria will emerge, the former countries accumulating, and the latter losing, foreign exchange reserves. If the stock of international liquidity and its rate of change are such that countries are not put under pressure to take corrective measures as soon as disequilibria emerge, and if they persist with their divergent monetary policies, payments imbalances will become larger. Thus countries will sooner or later encounter the need to eliminate their deficits or surpluses. One way that this could be achieved is by surplus countries accelerating their monetary expansion and thus allowing their rate of inflation to rise, and by deficit countries sacrificing their objective of maintaining a low level of unemployment and thus initiating deflationary policies. If such a situation were to prevail, a conflict between the internal and external objectives of countries would emerge: surplus countries would have to endure inflation and deficit countries relatively higher levels of unemployment, if external disequilibria were to be eliminated. If countries are not willing to abandon the domestic objectives to which they attach highest priority, then the only option available to them for restoring balance of payments equilibrium is to change their exchange rates. Deficit countries will devalue, i.e. lower the price of their currencies in terms of other currencies, while surplus countries will revalue, i.e. increase the price of their currencies in terms of other currencies.

No set of international monetary arrangements can ensure the irrevocable fixity of exchange rates if countries pursue different economic objectives, some attaching higher priority than others to achieving price stability. But if complete certainty in the international value of a currency is lacking, then economic agents will attempt to anticipate changes in exchange rates. A country running a persistent balance of payments deficit will come to be expected to devalue its currency. Such expectations will induce economic agents to move their funds into a country whose currency is expected at least to maintain its international value. If the expected devaluation does materialise, then economic agents can repatriate their funds and thus make a profit. If, on the other hand, the national authorities of the deficit country do succeed in maintaining the exchange rate, then people who acted on their expectation will have suffered no loss above the costs of transferring their funds from country to country.

We may, therefore, conclude that divergent monetary policies not only lead to balance of payments disequilibria, but also that they are not conducive to the promotion of confidence in the international value of currencies.

In summary, the three requirements that must be fulfilled for a system of fixed exchange rates to operate smoothly are: provisions must be made for an adequate rate of growth of international liquidity; the system must ensure a speedy and effective mechanism of adjustment; and the system must promote confidence in the international value of currencies, particularly of the major ones.

The next set of questions that needs to be considered relates to the means by which the IMF system was to meet the three requirements of a smoothly operating fixed exchange rate system.

The liquidity requirement was to be fulfilled by the IMF making available international credit facilities to the member countries. These IMF Drawing Rights were to supplement national gold holdings, thus ensuring that the liquidity needs of a growing world economy would be met. Also, under IMF rules the price of gold could be increased, which would be equivalent to an increase in the world stock of international liquidity.

Briefly, the IMF was to contribute to the solution of the liquidity problem in the following way. A quota subscription was specified for each member country; usually the member country subscribed 25% of its quota in gold and the rest in its own currency. The size of the quota determined the country's voting strength and drawing rights. Member countries could purchase currencies from the IMF in exchange for their own currency, the limit being determined by the country's quota and the level of the IMF's holdings of the currency of the country. Member countries could automatically borrow from the IMF an amount equal to their gold subscription. If they wished to borrow more, which would imply that the IMF would hold balances in excess of the quota of the borrowing country's currency, the approval of the IMF Executive Board was required. For most countries the upper limit of drawings was reached when the IMF's holdings reached 200% of the quota.

The pool of currencies with the IMF was to be made available to member countries facing balance of payments difficulties. Increases in international liquidity were to be provided by increases in member countries' quotas and in gold holdings.

Member countries were requested to define the price of their currencies in terms of gold and were obliged to maintain a 1% margin on either side of the declared parity. Given that all countries' currencies were tied to gold, the price of any individual currency in terms of the other currencies was thus automatically determined. Countries were committed to defend their declared exchange rates and under the IMF rules they could devalue or revalue their currency only if confronted with a 'fundamental disequilibrium' in their balance of payments and after they had secured the agreement of the IMF. What precisely is meant by 'fundamental disequilibrium' is something that has never been clarified, though a country with a persistent and increasing surplus or deficit in its balance of payments would be thought of as facing fundamental disequilibrium.

By incorporating rules, albeit ill-defined, under which countries could alter their exchange rates, the IMF was hoping to provide some solution to the adjustment problem which would not inevitably lead to a conflict between the external and internal objectives of a country. Further, in order to contribute towards easing the adjustment problem, provisions were made under which the IMF could declare a currency 'scarce'. In such an event, countries would be permitted to discriminate against trade with the country whose currency was declared scarce.

Finally, under IMF rules, countries were to be allowed to impose controls on short-term capital movements, if such controls were deemed necessary by the national authorities for the maintenance or restoration of confidence in the international value of the country's currency.

Having considered the objectives of the IMF and the means by which they were to be achieved, we shall now turn to examine how the IMF system did operate in practice.

The IMF System in Practice

A complex of reasons led to recurring international monetary crises during the 1960's, which culminated in the breakdown of the IMF system in August 1971. Failure by the IMF to solve the liquidity problem could be argued as being the most important reason, creating uncertainty and doubt about the ability of governments to sustain the degree of monetary cooperation required for the viability of any set of international monetary arrangements.

As already indicated, a prime function of the IMF was to provide international liquidity to supplement gold holdings. A role, but only a minor one, for reserve holdings in the form of

Table 1. *Volume and composition of world monetary reserves ($ billion)*

Year (end):	1951	1956	1961	1965	1969	1970	1971	1972	1973	1974†
Gold*	33.9	36.1	38.9	41.9	39.1	37.2	29.2	38.8	43.1	43.1
	66.9%	62.7%	60.9%	59.1%	50.0%	40.2%	30.0%	24.4%	23.4%	21.6%
Foreign exchange	15.1	19.2	20.8	23.6	32.4	44.6	78.2	103.6	123.1	137.9
	29.8%	33.3%	32.6%	33.3%	41.4%	48.2%	59.9%	65.3%	66.8%	69.2%
Reserve position in IMF	1.7	2.3	4.2	5.4	6.7	7.7	6.9	6.9	7.4	7.8
	3.4%	4.0%	6.6%	7.6%	8.6%	8.3%	5.3%	4.3%	4.0%	3.9%
SDRs	—	—	—	—	—	3.1	6.4	9.4	10.6	10.6
						3.3%	4.9%	5.9%	5.8%	5.3%
Total reserves	50.7	57.6	63.9	70.9	78.2	92.6	130.6	158.7	184.3	199.4

*Gold valued at $35 an ounce until December 1971; $38 between 1971 and
 January 1973, and thereafter at $42.22.
†June figures for 1974.
Source: International Financial Statistics, IMF.

sterling and dollar balances was envisaged, but the emphasis was
on gold and IMF Drawing Rights as the main components of
international liquidity. However, the IMF failed to provide the
international liquidity that an expanding world economy needed.
The implications of the IMF's failure were accentuated by the fact,
not surprising in retrospect, that increases in gold production were
not sufficient to meet the expanding demand for international
liquidity. The vacuum thus created was filled by the emergence of
the dollar as a key currency, US deficits becoming the main source
of additional international liquidity. Table 1 presents figures
relating to the world monetary reserves and the percentage of the
total volume represented by each component.

The failure of the IMF to provide the additional international
liquidity is illustrated by the fact that, while during the period 1951
to June 1974 world monetary reserves rose by nearly $150 billion,
countries' reserve positions in the IMF increased by only $6.1
billion. In terms of the contribution towards the aggregate volume
of world liquidity, IMF reserve positions represented less than 4%
in 1974 and never exceeded 10%.

If we now turn to the contribution of gold, we see that this
component of international liquidity has been steadily declining in
importance throughout the period; by June 1974 gold holdings
amounted to just over one fifth of total world reserves. Indeed,

after 1965 gold holdings fell in absolute terms and the increases registered for the period 1971-74 were only the result of the small rises in the official price of gold.

Given the almost insignificant contribution of IMF credit facilities and of gold holdings in the increases of international liquidity, the figures in table 1 provide striking evidence of the growth, in relative as well as absolute terms, of foreign exchange holdings. World aggregate reserves increased by $148.7 billion between 1951 and June 1974, of which $122.8 billion was due to the expansion of foreign exchange reserves. In 1951 foreign exchange reserves amounted to approximately 30% of the total international liquidity, but to nearly 70% by 1974. The major component of countries' foreign exchange has been held in dollar balances. Some countries chose to hold their reserves in sterling balances; however, the steady decline of the UK comparatively to the rest of the world, and perennial balance of payments problems, have implied a decreasing role for sterling as an international currency. In contrast to the UK, the dominance of the US economy and its large gold holdings were the main factors which led to the supremacy of the dollar as an internationally acceptable currency. Countries were willing to accumulate dollar balances, confident that they could be converted to gold if desired — an attitude which lasted until the mid-1960's.

US deficits, by providing the required additional liquidity, were important in creating an environment conducive to the expansion of the world economy. Be that as it may, the failure of the IMF to solve the liquidity problem, combined with the inadequate increases in gold production and the emergence of the dollar as the main key currency, was the basic cause of the instability and ultimate breakdown of the IMF system.

The holding of dollar balances as a form of international liquidity allows countries to economise in the use of gold whilst obtaining interest income. However, an international monetary system which operates on the basis of gold and a national currency as the main components of international liquidity is inherently unstable. This instability arises from two sources: firstly, from fluctuations in the demand and supply of gold, and secondly, from the contradiction inherent in a national currency being used simultaneously as international money — its acceptability as such being dependent on the volume of gold at the command of the reserve currency country.

The world economy experienced high rates of growth during the post-1945 period. Not surprisingly this growth led to an increase in private demand for gold. The fact that the price of gold was fixed in an inflationary period, when the prices of all other commodities were rising, reinforced the increase in the demand for gold. However, on the supply side, the fixed price of gold and the resultant change in relative prices implied that the production of gold became less profitable. The emergence of private excess demand for gold may well lead to the expectation that the central monetary authorities will raise the price of gold; such an expectation would further stimulate private demand. If central monetary authorities are reluctant to raise the price of gold, then their position will change from being net buyers to net sellers. Indeed, this is what did happen after 1965, when central authorities' gold holdings had to be reduced in order to maintain the fixed price of gold at $35 per ounce.

The willingness of countries to accumulate dollar balances rested on the confidence that they could convert any excess dollar balances in their portfolio of international reserves, there being no serious doubts that the US could honour its commitment to convert dollar balances into gold at the fixed price. However, the fact that US balance of payments deficits became the main source for additional international liquidity inevitably led to the ratio of US gold holdings to US liabilities becoming increasingly smaller. But the implied deterioration of the reserve position of the key currency country gradually led the rest of the world to suspect that the US would not be able to maintain the dollar price of gold. The fear that the US might be forced to devalue the dollar in terms of gold, and thus in terms of all other currencies not linked to the dollar, resulted in countries becoming increasingly reluctant to accumulate further dollar balances. Indeed, from the early 1960's certain European countries, especially Germany and France, sought as a matter of policy to restrict increases in their international reserves in the form of dollar balances. To this end they converted sizeable amounts of dollar balances into gold holdings. Table 2 presents data relating to the gold reserves of certain major countries for selected years. The most notable

Table 2. *Gold reserves of major countries* ($ billion)*

Year (end):	1958	1964	1967	1970	1971	1972	1973	1974†
Belgium	1.3	1.4	1.5	1.5	1.7	1.6	1.8	1.8
France	0.8	3.7	5.2	3.5	3.8	3.8	4.3	4.3
Germany	2.6	4.2	4.2	4.0	4.4	4.5	5.0	5.0
Italy	1.1	2.1	2.4	2.9	3.1	3.1	3.5	3.5
Japan	0.1	0.3	0.3	0.5	0.7	0.8	0.9	0.9
Netherlands	1.1	1.7	1.7	1.8	2.1	2.1	2.3	2.3
UK	2.8	2.1	1.3	1.3	0.8	0.8	0.9	0.9
US	20.6	15.5	12.1	11.1	11.1	10.5	11.7	11.7

†June figures for 1974..
*Gold valued as described in footnote to table 1.
Source: International Financial Statistics, IMF.

features of the developments in gold holdings are the pronounced fall in US gold reserves and the large increase in the gold reserves of Germany, Italy and France during the decade 1958-67, a trend exhibited in the gold holdings of most European countries.

By the mid-1960's, therefore, the co-existence of gold and dollars as the main components of international liquidity was becoming a source of instability. Confidence in the dollar was rapidly decreasing, generating speculative flows of short-run capital in the expectation that major countries would not be able to maintain their exchange rate. The failure of the IMF system to provide a solution to the liquidity problem was leading directly to the emergence of a confidence problem, engulfing not only individual currencies' international prices but also the prevailing international monetary arrangements. The world economy had three options: to raise the price of gold and stimulate its production, to move on to a dollar standard system, or to create a new international asset.

The international role of the dollar was at the centre of the controversy of what the solution to the liquidity problem required. The emergence of the dollar as a reserve currency permitted the US to run balance of payments deficits without being under the pressures that other deficit countries were under to eliminate their external disequilibria. Similarly, surplus countries were resentful of the position of the US, as they were open to inflationary impulses emanating from the American economy. Thus a number of countries argued for the elimination of US deficits, some of them — France being the most vociferous — advocating an increase in the price of gold. The US opposed any rise in the price of gold, this having become a symbol of American supremacy which no government was willing to abandon. It was further argued that an increase in the price of gold was politically unacceptable as this would benefit the Soviet Union and South Africa, these being the major producers of gold. At the same time, the US argued that the elimination of its balance of payments would be detrimental to the world economy, if it preceded the establishment of a new scheme guaranteeing the adequate growth of international liquidity. While agreement could not be reached the international monetary system became increasingly unstable, especially after 1965.

The US, taking advantage of its position as a reserve currency country, decided to finance its domestic social programmes and the escalation of the war in Vietnam by expansionary monetary policies rather than by increasing taxes. The increase in the rate of growth of the US money supply resulted in a rise of the American rate of price inflation and, because of the size of the US economy, in an acceleration of the world rate of inflation. US deficits increased after 1965, leading to an expansion in the money supply of the surplus countries which thus were importing the effects of the inflationary policies of the US. Free from any balance of payments constraint, given their balance of payments surplus, certain countries pursued more vigorously the objective of full employment. This reaction added fuel to the acceleration of world price inflation which had begun as a result of American policies. Divergent monetary policies, combined with increasingly large transfers of short-term capital from country to country, led to countries developing balance of payments disequilibria of dimensions that had no precedent in the post-war years. Half-hearted attempts to effect adjustment were not particularly successful, as they took the form of restrictions in the movement of goods and capital and neglected the main cause, i.e. divergent national monetary policies. Thus by the mid-1960's the IMF system was not adequately meeting any of the three requirements of a well functioning system of fixed exchange rates.

Prolonged international negotiations on the most desirable

means of solving the international liquidity problem culminated in an agreement, in 1967, to create a new international asset, the Special Drawing Rights (SDR's). Any member of the IMF has the right to participate in the SDR scheme. SDR's are allocated on the basis of countries' quotas; participating countries undertake to provide their currency, when so instructed by the IMF, in exchange for SDR's. A country cannot refuse to accept SDR's unless its total holdings reach three times its allocation. Any country using SDR's is charged a rate of interest, set originally at 1.5% and raised to 5% during 1974, while the country providing its currency in exchange for SDR's receives a payment at the same rate of interest. Countries are obliged to maintain their average holdings of SDR's over a period of five years to a level equivalent to at least 30% of their average cumulative net allocations. Thus, if a country uses more than 70% of its SDR allocation, it has to reconstitute its holding by providing its currency for other participating countries. Countries using SDR's are not obliged to submit their policies for the approval of the IMF, this being a major difference between SDR's and IMF Drawing Rights.

The SDR scheme was greeted with widespread scepticism. Doubts regarding the suitability of the scheme as a solution to the liquidity problem rested on the view that policy makers had reached the wrong diagnosis with respect to the causes of the crisis of the IMF system. It has already been argued that the co-existence of the dollar and gold as the main components of international liquidity was the prime reason for the instability being exhibited by the system during the mid-1960's. In other words, the essence of the problem was the composition of the existing stock of world reserves and therefore the rate of growth of each separate component. Negotiations, however, over the SDR scheme concentrated to a large extent on the issue of whether or not there was a shortage of international liquidity at that period. Posing the problem in such a manner is nonsensical, as it is nonsensical to debate whether or not there is a shortage of money in an economy at any particular moment of time, given the price level. In specifying the purpose of the scheme as a means of providing the world economy with additional liquidity, the implication was that there was a shortage of international liquidity. Indeed, the IMF, in explaining how it arrived at the volume of SDR's to be created when the scheme was activated in January 1970, argued that there was evidence suggesting a shortage of liquidity in the world. In deciding the volume to be allocated in the period 1970-72, the IMF first estimated the amount that the world would need. Then it proceeded to estimate the extent to which world reserves were likely to increase as a result of US deficits. The difference between the world 'needs' and the likely increase in dollar balances was to be made up by SDR's. Thus, an implication of the SDR's scheme was that a third international asset was to be introduced alongside gold and dollars, accentuating rather than solving the difficulties stemming from the availability to countries of alternative methods of holding their foreign assets. That countries are not allowed to use SDR's to change the composition of their reserves does not detract from the force of the criticism that policy makers, in establishing the SDR scheme, were at fault in not fully appreciating the importance of the distinction between problems relating to the composition of world reserves and problems stemming from their level. That the stipulation regarding the use of SDR's and a country's composition of reserves is of dubious relevance can be seen if we consider the case of a deficit country. Nothing prevents such a country from financing its balance of payments deficit by running down its dollar balances. By abstaining from using SDR's, deficit countries can easily alter the composition of their reserves.

Not unrelated to the composition problem, interest payments were thought of as a means of making SDR's more attractive than gold. Given that the interest rate was originally fixed at only 1.5% and the capital gains which would result from an increase in the price of gold in line with what the demand and supply of gold would imply, it was hardly likely that SDR's would become acceptable as a substitute for gold and thus permit a decrease in the international role of the latter.

Further, the SDR scheme was criticised for not taking into consideration the special needs of developing countries in its provisions of how a given volume was to be allocated among participating countries. That the allocation was to be determined on the basis of countries' quotas implied that the industrial countries would receive the major share of SDR's.

The emerging lack of confidence in the prevailing set of exchange rates during the 1960's led to movements of short-term capital in anticipation of devaluations and revaluations. To counteract the effects of these short-term capital flows, countries developed certain *ad hoc* arrangements, e.g. the swap arrangements. Under a swap arrangement a central bank agrees to lend balances to another and to accept the other's currency up to some agreed level. Swap arrangements are operational for a limited period and a number of them were agreed during the 1960's.

The 1968 Basle Agreement was another measure taken in response to the increasing lack of confidence in the international prices of major currencies. This agreement related to sterling and, significantly enough, was concluded after the devaluation of sterling in 1967. Holders of sterling balances continued with their efforts to reduce this component of their foreign exchange reserves, demonstrating a lack of confidence in the new exchange rate for sterling. Thus, in September 1968 the UK agreed to guarantee the dollar value of official sterling balances, in exchange for an undertaking by sterling area countries to hold a specified minimum proportion of their foreign exchange reserves in the form of sterling balances. At the same time, the UK reached an agreement with the major industrial countries and the Bank for International Settlements for $2 billion to be made available to the UK for use in support of sterling, if sterling balances declined below an agreed level. The Basle Agreement was for a period of three years and it was renewed for a further two years in September 1971. Towards the end of 1974 the UK government announced that the sterling guarantee arrangements were to be terminated.

Divergent monetary policies were rapidly undermining confidence in the international value of currencies in terms of each other. US deficits were creating large volumes of short-run funds, the holders of which exhibited increasing willingness to move them from country to country in anticipation of exchange rate changes. But perhaps even more significant for the IMF system was the acceleration of inflation rates throughout the world from the mid-1960's. The price of gold was fixed at $35 per ounce while the prices of all other commodities began to rise at an increasing rate, leading to an increase in the demand for gold additional to that resulting from the real growth of the world economy. Central monetary authorities began to sell gold from their stocks in order to maintain the official price of gold; but the ability of the major countries to maintain the price of gold at $35 per ounce in face of the increasing demand was widely questioned. Expectations that the price of gold would be increased in terms of all currencies led to a further rise in the demand for the metal in anticipation of profits to be made from such a revaluation. These expectations were further encouraged by certain countries, particularly France, pronouncing themsemselves in favour of an increase in the price of gold. Under the impact of these pressures, in March 1968 the major countries announced that they would cease to operate in the gold market with the aim of maintaining the gold price at $35 per ounce. Thus the price of gold in the private market was freed to vary as demand and supply forces dictated. However, the price of gold was to stay at $35 per ounce for transactions among central monetary authorities.

The devaluation of sterling, the agreement on the SDR scheme, the Basle Agreement, the increasing use of swap arrangements and the freeing of the price of gold in the private market, were not sufficient to restore confidence in the IMF system. Individual currencies came under increasing speculative pressures, while expectations regarding a rise in the official price of gold gathered momentum. In 1969 the French franc was devalued and the German mark revalued, and in August 1971 the US, facing a large and deteriorating balance of payments deficit largely reflecting outflows of short-run funds in anticipation of a dollar devaluation, announced that it was suspending the convertibility of its currency into gold. The dollar was to float, its price in terms of other currencies being determined by demand and supply in the foreign exchange market.

The crisis that followed the US decision was 'resolved' in December 1971 when the countries comprising the Group of Ten agreed on a new set of exchange rates, the US devaluing the dollar in terms of gold from $35 to $38 per ounce. Further, the IMF announced that member countries would be allowed to move within margins of 2.25% instead of 1% on either side of the newly agreed parities.

Any hopes that the new set of exchange rates was to last were proved unfounded by June 1972, when the UK authorities announced that sterling would be allowed to float. In January 1973, when the US trade figures were announced, the whole international monetary system was thrown into turmoil. These figures showed the US as having the largest-ever deficit and its first deficit with Europe in the post-1945 period. Speculation against the dollar rapidly gathered momentum and general uncertainty over exchange rates intensified when it was revealed that the US was to continue to have a large budget deficit. Germany and Japan experienced particularly heavy capital inflows. The decision in that month to devalue the dollar by a further 10% in terms of gold, raising its price from $38 to $42.22 per ounce, was not sufficient to curtail speculation. In March the EEC countries decided to maintain fixed exchange rates among their currencies but not *vis-a-vis* other currencies. The UK and Italy did not participate in the joint float; instead they let their currencies move independently. Thus, after March 1973, the world moved to a system of fluctuating exchange rates, central monetary authorities abstaining from systematic intercessions in the foreign exchange markets.

With the breakdown of the IMF system, the need for reforming the rules governing international monetary arrangements became urgent enough to attract the continuous attention of policy makers. In June 1972 the Committee of Twenty was formed, with the task of presenting a set of proposals which would form the basis for the radical reform of the international monetary system. In September 1973 the *First Outline of Reform* was presented at the Annual Meeting of the IMF.

The views set out in this document reflected a large measure of agreement among countries regarding the principal features of the future international monetary system. There was optimism that remaining disagreements could be resolved without undue delay. Countries appeared to favour a system of fixed exchange rates, with only occasional adjustments, the failure of the IMF system not having shaken confidence in the principles on which it was established. Flexible rates were opposed, particularly by developing countries, on the grounds that such a system would lead to undesirable uncertainties in the foreign exchange markets which could obstruct the expansion of international trade. However, the *Outline*, in recognition of the fact that the reluctance of countries to effect adjustment combined with fixity of exchange rates was a major cause of the large disequilibria that emerged during the late 1960's, accepted the desirability of increased exchange rate flexibility and suggested that countries should be allowed to float their exchange rates under particular circumstances for a limited period of time, provided that the IMF authorised such action. That much was generally agreed; but disagreements did arise in defining the circumstances under which a country would have the right to float its exchange rate, and whether each individual case was to be treated separately or whether IMF authorisation would be automatic once certain well-defined circumstances prevailed. Further, with the aim of providing greater flexibility, the *Outline* declared the desirability of margins of 2.25% on either side of the parity.

Still on the adjustment mechanism, there was agreement that the burdens of eliminating balance of payments disequilibria should be shared by both deficit and surplus countries. Thus countries would be expected to pursue such policies as would keep their reserves within internationally agreed limits. Towards this goal, a reserve indicator was advocated. Movements of this indicator would activate IMF examination, with the aim of determining whether or not the country under consideration needed to alter its policies. In order to ensure both symmetrical and speedy adjustment, an objective on which there was general agreement, the *Outline* suggested that provisions should be made "for graduated pressures to be applied to both surplus and deficit countries in cases of large and persistent imbalance". However, there is disagreement as to the way in which these pressures should be activated as well as about their precise nature. One form of financial pressure advocated is that countries with net creditor or net debtor positions in the IMF should be subjected to penalty rates of interest. An alternative suggestion is that if a country's reserves rise to a predetermined level, that country should be required to deposit any further accrual of reserves with the IMF at progressively increasing negative rates of interest. Also, trade restrictions against countries with persistent balance of payments surpluses are suggested as a form of pressure.

There is widespread disagreement among the major countries about the pressures and the way that they will be activated. The EEC countries oppose the adoption of an automatic indicator and prefer a set of arrangements that would permit each case to be assessed on its own merits before sanctions are activated. On the other hand, the US is in favour of automatic indicators and automatic sanctions. The argument for automatic sanctions rests on the belief that discussions are likely to delay adjustment, which was the case in the past, so that once again the burden of adjustment will fall mainly on deficit countries.

On the liquidity problem, the *Outline* recommended that SDR's become the principal international asset and that the role of both gold and reserve currencies be gradually reduced. Thus there appears to be recognition that any set of international arrangements that permits the existence of alternative international reserve assets is not viable. However, there is still disagreement on what precisely will be the role of gold in the reformed system. France and Germany are favourably disposed towards the retention of gold and its valuation at market prices, while the US argues that if gold continues to play a significant role that would undermine the position of SDR's.

Finally, the *Outline* recommended that an important feature of the reformed system should be provisions ensuring "an increasing flow of real resources from the developed to the developing countries". One way suggested for achieving this is to link development aid and the allocation of SDR's.

The negotiations over the future international monetary system were running parallel to efforts to achieve monetary union among the EEC countries. It was accepted that the two sets of negotiations were inter-dependent, the course of each likely to influence the developments in the other. European monetary integration was defined as the irrevocable fixity of exchange rates among EEC countries, with or without the establishment of a European currency. The creation of a unified European monetary bloc would directly impinge on questions relating to the desirable flexibility of exchange rates, the role of gold, and the method of assessing the international liquidity needs of the world economy.

Efforts to resolve the remaining disagreements over the new international monetary system and progress towards European monetary unification were brought to an abrupt halt when, in the winter of 1973, the oil producing countries increased the price of oil by nearly 400%. It was immediately evident that oil consuming countries were going to face large balance of payments deficits. Nationalistic tendencies emerged, especially among industrialised countries, as these countries sought to minimise the fall in their real standard of living concomitant with the increase in the relative price of oil.

One of the immediate consequences of the oil crisis was a renewed demand for gold to be retained and its price increased. Countries argued that if their gold holdings were to be valued at market prices, which by February 1974 had passed the $180 per ounce mark, that would facilitate the financing of their deficits. Such considerations led to the decision of December 1973 allowing countries to sell gold in the private market, thus reversing the 1968 agreement.

A further implication of the oil price increase is that a few relatively small countries will accumulate large balances. The fact that these balances may be switched from currency to currency, as particular countries show signs of weakness or strength in their balance of payments position, implies that movements of short-run funds may well turn out to be a source of continuing instability.

In the aftermath of the oil crisis, negotiations for a reformed monetary system made little progress, emphasis being placed on required measures to meet immediate short-run problems arising from the increases in the price of oil. Indeed, the IMF in its 1974 Annual Meeting concluded "that it will be some time before a reformed system can be finally agreed and fully implemented". In its efforts to ease the strains of the 'oil deficits' the IMF created a new facility, available to member countries for a limited period of time, with the specific aim of assisting them to finance deficits arising from the increase in oil prices. By October 1974 countries had made purchases totaling SDR 383.97 million under the oil facility.

Conclusions

Exchange rate stability is required if countries are to derive the benefits of international trade. The architects of the IMF system were of the opinion that this exchange rate stability could best be achieved by a system of essentially fixed exchange rates. Flexible exchange rates were considered as undesirable, on the grounds that such a system would not promote exchange rate stability if countries were free to pursue divergent monetary policies.

The IMF system was undermined by the co-existence of gold and dollar balances as the major components of international liquidity. The very emergence of a national currency, the dollar, as international money was a significant cause of the divergent monetary policies in the 1960's which accentuated the problems relating to the composition of the stock of international liquidity. There is evidence that these lessons have been learnt: that the international community will aim, once the ephemeral oil crisis has been overcome, for an international monetary system to promote international monetary coordination by penalising persistent balance of payments disequilibria; and to rely on the existence of a single international asset, the SDR, so that the rate of growth of international liquidity will be determined at an international rather than a national level.[1]

Suggestions for Further Reading

Johnson, H. G., *Further Essays in Monetary Economics*, George Allen & Unwin 1972, Chapters 7, 8, 11 and 15.

Machlup, F., *Remaking the International Monetary System: The Rio Agreement and Beyond*, Johns Hopkins University Press 1968.

Mundell, R., Towards a Better International Monetary System, *Journal of Money, Credit and Banking*, August 1969.

[1]The author is indebted to Professor D. J. Coppock, Professor David Laidler and Mr M. Sumner for valuable comments on an early draft of this chapter and to Mr R. Ward for research assistance.

13. Regional policy in the UK: the effect on employment

R R MACKAY
Lecturer in Economics,
University of Newcastle upon Tyne

Introduction

In a reference to regional development policy, the Expenditure Committee Report *Public Money in the Private Sector* claims: "There must be few areas of government expenditure in which so much is spent, but so little is known about the success of the policy" (HMSO 1972). A subsequent Report *Regional Development Incentives* states: "We are far from satisfied that the continuing search for a viable regional policy has been backed by a critical economic apparatus capable of analysing results and proposing alternative courses . . . Much has been spent and much may well have been wasted. Regional policy has been empiricism run mad, a game of hit-and-miss, played with more enthusiasm than success. We do not doubt the good intentions, the devotion even, of many of those who have struggled over the years to relieve the human consequences of regional disparities. We regret that their efforts have not been better sustained by the proper evaluation of the costs and benefits of policies pursued" (HMSO 1973).

As the Expenditure Committee implies, sympathy and assistance will only be effective if they are based on a sound understanding of the problems involved in bringing employment opportunities to the depressed areas. In the absence of reliable evidence, exaggerated and misleading claims of imminent salvation are circulated and the very real problems involved in notably improving the performance of regions that are heavily dependent on declining industries are disregarded. The lack of constructive criticism militates against the emergence of an effective regional policy. Policy changes depend on short-term political considerations, rather than on the true interests of the economy.

Regional Development Incentives lists ten 'areas of uncertainty'. The first and most important refers to "the effectiveness of regional policy over the last 10-15 years in terms of increased employment ... compared with what would have occurred otherwise" (HMSO 1973, p.73). There are considerable problems in attempting to quantify this effect.

The first difficulty is to identify important changes in regional policy. Over the last 10-15 years[1] mentioned by the Committee, regional policy changes have been all too frequent. The sheer volume of change means that the commentator has to simplify and select, in order to make a clear distinction between a limited number of policy periods where policy differs significantly.

The second difficulty is to provide an accurate account of what has happened in the different regions. Unfortunately, consistent and accurate statistical series are the exception rather than the rule. Definitions of employment, unemployment, industrial building, firm movement etc. change over time, as do industrial classifications and regional definitions. This makes comparison difficult and explanation tedious.

The task of providing an account of what has happened is by no means simple, but it pales into insignificance when compared with the third problem: assessing what would have happened if regional policy had not changed. In the counter-factual situation we inevitably enter the realm of speculation. Such dependent variables as regional employment, industrial building, firm movement, are strongly influenced by factors other than changes in regional policy. The strength of some of the more important

[1] In this chapter I concentrate on the actual, as distinct from the expected, effect of regional policy. It is too early to try and assess the impact and importance of the Industry Act of 1972, so the analysis, evidence and argument relates to the major changes in approach from 1956 to 1972.

relationships may be approximately measurable, but relationships change over time and even the direction of some cause-and-effect associations remain difficult to identify. Using accurate, consistent statistical series that were simple to interpret and available over a large number of years, the economist would ideally take each of the infrequent policy interventions and compare the actual subsequent course of the economy with what could have been expected to occur in the absence of any policy change. In the real world of *non ceteris paribus*, the gap between what has happened and what would have happened can only be approximately measurable. Estimates of regional policy effect are given in this paper, but they are inevitably somewhat speculative and there is considerable margin for error.

Even if precise estimation is impossible, we can look to the evidence to distinguish between those circumstances where the impact of change is obvious and considerable and those where it is doubtful and disappointing. This is in fact possible in the case of regional policy. The evidence shows that the policy innovations of 1960 and 1963 have had a clear and appreciable impact on Development Area employment. The impact of the Regional Employment Premium, now the most important item of regional assistance in expenditure terms, is not so obvious.

The Changing Nature of Regional Assistance

In the 1950's expenditure on regional assistance was low, industrial development certificates were readily attainable in all parts of the country, and the regional problem was not an important area of government concern. The increasing problems of the less prosperous areas in the late 1950's led to renewed emphasis on regional differences in prosperity and opportunity, and the Local Employment Act of 1960 marks the return to active government intervention in influencing the location decision. In the 'active period' of regional intervention, the years 1960-62, Local Employment Act assistance (building grants, loans, expenditure on advance factories, grants for unusual initial expenses) was the only important form of regional subsidy to industry. Local Employment Act (LEA) expenditure was at the discretion of the Board of Trade, which would refuse assistance if a project was not considered viable, or if the cost per job was unreasonable; most of the assistance went to firms new to the assisted areas (Development Districts 1960-66, Development Areas from 1966) and was designed to reduce costs (and raise liquidity) in the early problem years of expansion in a new and unfamiliar location. The Finance and Local Employment Acts of 1963 amended and added to the 1960 measures and the years 1963-66 can be termed the years of 'intensive' regional policy. Easily the most important innovation was the introduction of regionally differentiated non-discretionary investment incentives, which were available to firms established in Development Districts as well as incoming firms. As a result of the Finance and Local Employment Acts of 1963, differential expenditure increased substantially. In the four financial years 1963-64 to 1966-67 differential expenditure[2] on regional assistance came to approximately £240m, as compared with a total of only £180m for the seventeen previous financial years 1946-47 to 1962-63.

Until 1963 assistance was concentrated on firms new to the assisted areas. Given the importance of capital investment to the new firm, regionally differentiated investment incentives were not entirely inconsistent with the infant-industry version of regional aid. However, with the introduction of the Regional Employment Premium (REP)[3] in 1967, all pretence of temporary subsidy designed to provide protection for the incoming firm vanishes. REP goes to all manufacturing firms, whether established in or new to the Development Areas, whether expanding or declining. Indeed, a wage subsidy related to existing employment levels is more attractive to the established firm, which is at or near its 'target' employment level, than it is to the incoming firm, which in the early years will be expanding towards its intended employment level. Instead of concentrating on the introduction of new firms

[2]Total cost of special regional assistance to industry over and above that available nationally (HMSO 1973). The figures exaggerate the drain on the Exchequer because they do not allow for loans repaid and factory rent payments, or for the impact of assistance in reducing taxable allowances and raising tax receipts.

[3]REP was set at £1.50 for each man employed in manufacturing (75 pence per woman) and was introduced for a minimum period of seven years.

and new industries, regional policy turned to subsidisation of existing manufacturing employment. The change in emphasis is considerable and important.

Expenditure on regional policy rose substantially and the total for the single financial year 1968-69, approximately £266m, was above the total for the four years of intensive regional policy, 1963-66. The years from 1967 can be described as the years of 'intensive' regional policy plus REP. The REP years can be split into phase one 1967-69, and phase two 1970-72. Regional assistance was more effective in phase one. The value of the fixed grant of £1.50 per man was progressively reduced by inflation and the investment grant system was replaced in 1970 by a system of free depreciation, which gave the Development Area firms little differential advantage over firms in other parts of the country. More important still is the steady deterioration in the health of the national economy, since rising unemployment and recession considerably reduced the impact of regional policy. Relatively few firms contemplate expansion in depression conditions and those that do grow have little difficulty in finding the required labour force at their existing location.

In spite of the considerable increase in expenditure on regional assistance, the value of the protection provided to the new project increased only marginally when REP was introduced, and for most firms was lower in phase two of REP than in the years 1963-66. For example, taking a project new to a Development District in 1963 with capital costs 25% and labour costs 30% of total cost,[4] the total anticipated cost reduction over the first five years of development is estimated to be 5.1% of total costs.[5] Identical calculations for projects new to a Development Area in September

[4]For the established firm capital and labour costs of 15% and 40% may be taken as reasonably representative. 25% and 30% are adopted to allow for the tendency for capital expenditure to be unusually high in the early years.

[5]Considerable simplification is required in order to arrive at the approximate value of assistance. Attention is confined to those forms of assistance which have the most important effect on the cost of production: wage subsidies, investment grants (or free depreciation) and building grants (it is assumed that the firm receives the maximum building grant). The reduction in capital and labour costs come to 20.3% and nil in 1963, 17.2% and 3.9% in 1967 and 11.4% and 2.0% in September 1971. Cash flow is discounted at 10% per annum.

1967 and September 1971 give cost reductions of 5.5% and 3.5% respectively. Thus introduction of REP slightly raised the assistance available to the new firm, but the assistance available to the new project was less generous in September 1971 than in 1963. The additional expenditure on regional assistance went to firms already established in the Development Areas, and was spread over a wide range of firms and industries rather than concentrated on the major sources of employment growth.

Quantitative Analysis of the Effects of Regional Assistance

The three sets of statistics employed to show a regional policy effect are: employment anticipated to result from Industrial Development Certificate (IDC) approvals, employment created as a result of the movement of manufacturing firms, and actual employment in the Development Areas compared with employment 'expected' if each manufacturing industry expanded or contracted at the national rate. All three sets yield important information, but there are problems of interpretation.

The great advantage of the approval statistics is that the decision to expand will normally be taken in the year the approval is granted. Thus the figures for any given year give a direct guide to the effect of regional assistance currently available. There is little or no time-lag problem. The approval statistics can be directly related to the five different phases of regional policy (see figure 1). There are two important disadvantages. One is a tendency to exaggerate expected employment in the Development Areas, since the more 'jobs expected' there are the more likely it is that firms will receive the assistance applied for. Secondly, there is an incomplete account of employment creation, since the statistics only record employment additions in factory extensions of 5,000 sq. ft. or over and so do not detect movements into existing industrial premises, small additions to employment, which involve little or no factory building, or situations where regional assistance (e.g. Regional Employment Premium) helps to preserve employment.

The firm movement figures avoid one of the problems of the approval statistics — the temptation to exaggerate future growth

Figure 1 *Development Area share of employment anticipated* from IDC approvals*

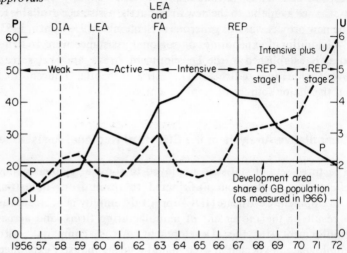

*Anticipated employment in the Development Areas has been reduced by 30%.

— because they measure actual employment. However, like the approval statistics, they provide only a partial measure of employment creation, since they do not measure the effect of assistance on industry established in the Development Areas.

The third measure, the comparison of actual with expected employment, allows for differences in industrial structure by comparing Development Area employment with the employment expected if each industry expanded or contracted at the national rate. In theory at least, the actual-expected employment comparison provides a total measure of the impact of regional policy. All additions to employment in existing or new factories raise actual employment, which is also influenced if regional policy helps to preserve jobs in declining industries. But in practice the measure gives only an approximate indiction of the impact of regional intervention on manufacturing industry in the Development Areas. Problems of interpretation are created by the existence of a complex and variable time-lag between the implementation of a policy and its effect upon employment, and by the influence of the general macroeconomic situation of the country on the impact of regional policy.

Given the timing problem, it is extremely difficult to relate the firm movement and actual-expected employment series to the five phases of regional policy. These two sets of statistics will therefore only be used to concentrate attention on the contrast between the pre- and post-REP years.

Employment Anticipated from IDC Approvals

Figure 1 shows the Development Area share of anticipated employment.[6] The results are given year by year for the five distinct regional policy periods. The Development Area share of anticipated employment rose from 14.5% in 1957 to 49.4% in 1965 before falling to 20.1% in 1972. There was a slight rise in 1958, the year of the Distribution of Industry Act, and a notable improvement in 1960 and 1963 when the more important Local Employment Acts (and the Finance Act of 1963) were passed.[7] The results for the pre-REP years are consistent with a strong positive relationship between additional expenditure on regional assistance and greater success in the Development Areas; but the results for the post-REP period are not.[8]

Regional assistance is not the only important factor influencing the location decision. A high level of national demand and a tight labour market encourage the natural and desirable adjustment

[6]The employment statistics have been modified to reduce anticipated employment by 30% in the Development Areas. This exaggeration factor is adopted because it is consistent with the experience of a group of firms interviewed by the Department of Economics at Newcastle University and also because it is similar to the unofficial adjustment made by Department of Trade and Industry officials when allowing for exaggeration in Development Area estimates.

[7]The improvement over 1959-60 and 1962-63 was greater than the change for any other two consecutive years.

[8]The approval statistics on the number of industrial buildings and the area of industrial buildings provide a check on anticipated employment figures. The development Area share of expected employment, number of projects and area of industrial building all rose in the years of active regional policy (1960-62) and again in the intensive period (1963-66). The three series reach a peak in 1965 and fall in REP years.

predicted by theory — the movement of industry to, and expansion in, those areas where labour is more readily available. In order to allow for alteration in the labour market situation, P (the Development Area share of anticipated employment) can be related to U (national male unemployment), as in figure 1; here P is expressed as a percentage of employment expected from IDC approvals in Great Britain (there are no figures for Northern Ireland).

There is a strong inverse relation between P and U in the years 1963-72. In every year that U falls P rises, and when U rises P falls. The correlation coefficient between P and U is -0.93. In statistical terms 87% of the variation in P is 'explained' by alteration in the level of male unemployment. The fall in the Development Area share of anticipated employment is attributable to changes in economic circumstances. Recession, restraint and rising unemployment are thus seen to be serious obstacles to an effective regional policy.

There is, however, no indication that the introduction of REP improved the relationship between unemployment and the Development Area share of anticipated employment. Change in unemployment is the only obvious factor influencing P from 1963 to 1972. In order to test for the effect of REP, the premium is introduced as a dummy variable with R = 0 in the years 1963-67 and R = 1 in 1968-72. The result is $P = 56.7 - 5.7U - 3.8R$. The effect of R is not statistically significant, but the negative sign suggests that the introduction of REP had no appreciable effect on the Development Area share of employment anticipated from industrial building.

On the other hand, the earlier changes in regional policy notably improved the relationship between P and U. P rose slightly over 1957-58 (Distribution of Industry Act) and more notably and significantly over 1959-60 (20% to 35%) and 1962-63 (27% to 39%). The increases in P over 1957-58 and 1962-63 were achieved in spite of substantial increases in male unemployment. An indication of the strength of the shift in the relationship is given by comparing two years with identical levels of male unemployment: in 1961 and 1965 male unemployment was 1.7%, but P was 29.8% in 1961 as compared with 49.3% in 1965. The evidence suggests that if the government had not operated a policy of control and inducement,

Table 1. *Net gain or loss in employment ('000) by period when inter-regional moves took place.*

Moves undertaken in:	1945-51[1]	1952-59[1]	1960-65[1]	1966-71[2]	1945-71[3]
Development Area regions[4]	+213.5	+67.0	+120.8	+80.5	+481.8
Other regions[5]	-162.7	-23.6	-96.9	-66.5	-349.7

[1]Employment as measured at end of 1966.
[2]Employment as measured at mid-1971.
[3]1945-65 moves measured at the end of 1966; 1966-71 moves measured at mid-1971.
[4]North (100% of insured employees within Development Areas in 1967), Scotland (89%), Wales (65%), North-West (28%) and South-West (10%) and Northern Ireland (not strictly speaking a Development Area, but covered by separate and more generous legislation).
[5]West Midlands, East Midlands, East Anglia, South-East, Yorkshire and Humberside. Taking all regions together there is a net gain. This is the result of movement from abroad.

the Development Area share of industrial building would have been considerably lower over the last 'ten to fifteen years'. It also suggests that the changes introduced in 1960 and 1963 had more impact than REP.

Movement of Firms

Firm movement into the Development Areas rose absolutely and as a proportion of national movement in the late fifties and early sixties. Brown (1972) claims that the innovations of 1960 and 1963 "can safely be regarded as effective ... there was a massive diversion of moves to the peripheral areas,[9] which ... is almost certainly to be associated with the series of administrative and legislative changes of the time — each of which probably produced some effect quite quickly and further effects cumulatively over a period of two or three years."

The Green Paper on the REP (HMSO 1967) claimed that the 'intensified regional policies' had had a marked effect on industrial movement to the assisted areas and predicted that the introduction

[9]Geographical areas similar to, but more extensive than, the Development Areas (see Howard 1968, para 48, pp.15-16).

of the REP would encourage further diversion. Table 1 shows that improvement was not maintained in the post-REP years.

Comparing the six-year periods 1960-65 and 1966-71, the net gain to the Development Area regions is approximately one-third lower in the later years. The years of notable success are the immediate post-war years and 1960-65.

The contrast between the obvious response to the innovations of 1960 and 1963 and the lack of reaction to REP would probably be even more marked if Special Development Area assistance had not been introduced in November 1967. The important point about this assistance,[10] introduced to help coalfield districts with particularly severe unemployment problems, was that it would only be available for new projects brought into a Special Development Area (SDA) and would substantially reduce costs in the early problem years in a new location. The cost reduction for the 'representative' new project is calculated at approximately 9% over a five year period — as compared to 5.1% in a Development Area.

Forty-two of the forty-seven employment exchanges given SDA status in November 1967 were in Wales or Northern England. Comparing 1966-71 with 1960-65, the net employment gain rose by 7.4 thousand in the Northern region and 5.1 thousand in Wales; the fall for the other four Development Area regions was 52.8 thousand, suggesting that the SDA measures diverted a substantial proportion of new projects to the Northern region and Wales. In the eighteen months before November 1967 the SDA's accounted for 19% of employment expected from new projects in the Development Areas, and in the eighteen months immediately after for 56%[11] — a remarkable degree of success for mining areas, which had few obvious attractions for industrialists and contained only 8% of the Development Area population.[12] It is possible, even probable, that the SDA measures had a favourable impact on the total movement into the Development Areas, thus emphasising more strongly the lack of response to REP.

[10]An operational grant allowed firms moving to a SDA to claim, during the first three years of a project, 10% of the cumulative expenditure incurred each year on the acquisition of new eligible buildings, plant and machinery.

[11]The Tenth Report on the Local Employment Acts (HMSO 1970).

[12]Subsequent changes in legislation have introduced new SDA's, but the operational grant has been withdrawn. The SDA's remain special only in name.

Actual and Expected Employment

According to the Green and White Papers, the premium was expected to provide 'an additional inducement' to move to the Development Areas and 'stimulate the need for more factories' in those areas. As we have already seen, the movement and approval statistics suggest that REP has had remarkably little effect on firm movement or factory expansion. It is, however, possible that the REP could avert decline, or encourage further utilisation of existing capacity — effects that would not show up in the movement and approval statistics.

In order to test for the total effect of regional policy, actual and expected employment can be compared. Expected employment is calculated by applying the national rate of change for each industry to actual employment for the base year; it is claimed that the changing relationship between actual and expected employment gives an indication of the effect of innovations in regional policy. Using this method, Moore and Rhodes (1973) showed that there is little divergence between actual and expected Development Area employment in the years 1951 to 1963, but discovered a large and growing divergence in the post-1963 years. They provided convincing "evidence . . . to support the contention that this difference between actual and expected employment which emerged after 1963 was in fact caused by the strengthening of regional policy rather than by chance or any other factor" and took the divergence to be an approximate measure of the direct effect of regional policy on manufacturing employment.

The purpose of this adjustment to the shift-share approach is to discount differences in industrial structure by comparing the national and Development Area record for similar groups of products. Moore and Rhodes used the industrial order level of classification to calculate expected employment. However, it is difficult to accept that satisfactory allowance has been made for differences in structure, when a wide range of products with considerable variation in performance (e.g. textiles) is regarded as a single industry. A finer industrial classification, the Minimum List Heading Level, is available, which divides industries into a hundred and one product groups. Most of the firms in a product group are sensitive to similar movements in demand and supply.

Table 2. *Actual and expected employment ('000) in manufacturing industry in the Development Area regions.**

	1963 (1959 base year)	1967 (1963 base year)	1971 (1967 base year)	1971 (1963 base year)
Actual employment	3332.3	3362.1	3297.1	3297.1
Expected employment	3328.3	3274.0	3209.3	3119.0
Divergence	+4.0	+88.1	+87.8	+178.1
Index: actual/expected	100.1	102.7	102.7	105.7

*As specified in table 1.

In columns 1, 2 and 3 of table 2, expected employment is calculated by applying the UK growth rate over four-year periods to actual employment in 101 Development Area industries in the base years 1959, 1963 and 1967. In column 4, expected employment is calculated by applying the UK growth rates over 1963-71 to actual employment in 1963.

Column 1 shows that actual employment in the Development Area regions in 1963 was marginally above expected employment. In 1967 (column 2) actual employment was 88,000 above expected employment. There is a marked change in the relationship. The results given in columns 1 and 2 are reasonably consistent with the IDC approval and firm movement statistics. Improvements in industrial building and firm movement occurred before 1963, but it took time before permissions to expand and firm openings notably influenced actual employment. The differential shift (the gap between actual and expected employment) once again stood at approximately 88,000 in 1971. By itself this suggests that REP had remarkably little effect. In order to calculate the effect of regional policy on manufacturing employment, we assume that the change in differential shift, after 1963, was entirely the result of renewed interest in regional intervention. On the basis of this heroic assumption, the regional policy effect was 84,000 for both 1963-67 and 1967-71.

The results suggest that REP was surprisingly ineffective, but this conclusion must be heavily qualified. There are great problems in comparing the results for two four-year periods showing very different general economic conditions. Unemployment was low and generally falling over 1963-67, but rose steadily during the period 1967-71. Growth and low levels of unemployment are the most important prerequisites for an effective regional policy.

The differential between actual and expected employment might have been smaller in the absence of REP, but assessment is complicated by the change in 1966 from Development Districts to Development Areas. Even if no additional assistance had been provided, the change to Development Areas should have encouraged movement to an expansion in the Development Area regions.

Even greater problems are posed by the inconvenient and variable time-lag. The gap between the initial response to assistance and employment creation depends partly on the nature of assistance. Regional assistance designed to reduce the cost of movement takes time to influence employment. Additions to employment in the years 1967-71 partly reflect the high levels of industrial building and firm movement in the pre-REP years. Assistance designed to raise employment in existing premises and to strengthen the general economy of the Development Areas should have a more immediate effect. Thus the results for 1967-71 show the combined effect of the premium and employment gains resulting from decisions to expand taken in earlier years. This is an additional reason for believing that there was no substantial response to REP.

Conclusions

There are still 'areas of uncertainty' in estimating the effect of regional policy, but some issues are beyond dispute. Without the incentives and controls of regional policy, the level of employment in the Development Areas would now be considerably lower. Given the problems with the statistics, the variation in economic circumstances, the sheer volume of change in regional legislation, the alterations to the definitions of assisted areas and the difficulties in measuring the time-lag, there are obvious problems in identifying a total regional policy effect and in measuring the importance of individual changes in regional policy. But there is sufficient evidence to indicate that there was an important and obvious response to the intensification of regional policy in the early sixties. The success of the SDA measures in diverting mobile industry to the coalfield areas confirms that pump-priming had a positive effect on the location decision.

The attempt to provide a rapid solution to regional unemployment by extending assistance to all manufacturing firms has not been notably successful; aid to the mobile firm has been much more effective. When a firm is encouraged to move to a Development Area, there is a marked and obvious gain for the favoured region. There is first of all a displacement effect: employment is created in the Development Area rather than a non-assisted area. There may also be an acceleration effect: as a result of assistance, the firm may be encouraged to expand more quickly than it would otherwise have done. Once the firm has moved to a Development Area the natural tendency to expand in, or close to, a known location should have a cumulative effect, the area receiving benefit not only from the initial move but also from subsequent expansion. By assisting mobile firms, the Development Areas can encourage the establishment of new industries — the first priority in the permanent solution of the regional employment problem.

A substantial proportion of any non-selective subsidy will go to declining firms and there are powerful *a priori* reasons for believing that arresting a decline in employment will be a more expensive process than encouraging expansion. Blanket subsidies go to firms without the ambition, organisation or will to expand. In extreme circumstances the receipt of a windfall gain may actually reduce production, by making it easier to achieve 'target' profit or revenue levels.

A subsidy related to existing levels of employment has only a marginal effect on the cost of expansion and is therefore unlikely to encourage notable growth. A subsidy which is sensitive to, or is allocated according to, *additions* to employment, output or investment is more likely to evoke a response. Such a subsidy could substantially reduce the cost of expansion and raise the rate of return on additional investment. According to an OECD study (1970), the original intention was to relate REP to alterations in employment rather than pay a flat rate according to the number employed, but practical difficulties ruled out this more effective approach. In 1970 the then Minister for Industry admitted that "REP has been disappointing in the effect it has had in raising the prosperity of the Development Areas and we shall be looking for something more effective to put in its place" (HMSO 1971), but there has since been a change of heart. Just prior to the October 1974 election REP was doubled to a weekly payment of £3.00 for each man employed in manufacturing industry in the Development Areas. This action is contrary to the main thrust of this chapter, namely that more effective assistance is more important than more assistance.[13] It is difficult to disagree with Nevin's claim (1972, p.64) that "the implicit hypothesis that the economic weakness of a region could be eliminated by making the inefficient use of labour within it a charge on the Exchequer was always one which testified more to the desperate *ad hocery* of the British approach to the regional problem than to its economic expertise." More important and more effective than assistance is growth and a lower level of unemployment. Regional policy cannot act as a substitute for a solution to the basic macroeconomic problems of the UK.[14]

References

Brown, A. J., *The Framework of Regional Economics in the UK*, Cambridge University Press 1972.

Castelbajac, P., *Les Aides a l'Expansion Industrielle Regionale dans les Pays du March Common*, La Documentation Francaise no. 3917, 1972.

Howard, R. S. (ed), *The Movement of Manufacturing Industry in the UK*, Board of Trade, HMSO 1968.

[13]According to a French survey of regional aid programmes (Castelbajac 1972), the United Kingdom accounted for over half of the total expenditure on regional aid to industry in the nine countries of the Common Market. This estimate was made before REP was doubled. It is extremely difficult to compare expenditure rates, but it is safe to claim that regional assistance to industry is more generous than in any of the other Common Market countries.

[14]The author wishes to thank Professor D. I. MacKay for helpful comments and to acknowledge his considerable debt to Mrs L. Segal.

Moore, B., and Rhodes, J., Evaluating the Effects of British Regional Economic Policy, *Economic Journal*, March 1973.

Nevin, E. T., Europe and the Regions, *Three Banks Review*, June 1972.

Department of Economicc Affairs, *The Development Areas: A Proposal for a Regional Employment Premium*, HMSO 1967 (Green Paper).

Department of Economic Affairs, *The Development Areas: Regional Employment Premium*, Cmnd 3310, HMSO 1967 (White Paper).

Local Employment Act Report, HMSO 1970 (annual).

Manpower Policy in the UK, OECD 1970.

Public Money in the Private Sector, HC 347, HMSO 1972.

Regional Development Incentives Report, HC 85, HMSO 1973.

Trade and Industry, HMSO 1971, p.500.

Suggestions for Further Reading

Brown (1972), Chapter 11.

Cameron, G. C., Regional Economic Development: The Federal Role, in *Resources for the Future*, Johns Hopkins University Press 1970, Chapters 1 and 2.

Cameron, G. C., The Regional Problem in the US: Some Reflections on a Viable Strategy, *Regional Studies*, 1968.

Luttrell, W. F., *Factory Location and Industrial Movement* (vol. 1), National Institute of Economic and Social Research 1962, Conclusion.

MacKay, R. R., Evaluating the Effects of British Regional Economic Policy: A Comment, *Economic Journal*, June 1974.

Moore (1973).

Nevin (1972).

Robinson, E. A. G. (ed), *Some Old and New Issues in Regional Development*, Macmillan 1969, particularly chapters by Hoover and Robinson.

Wilson, T., Finance for Regional Development, *Three Banks Review*, September 1967, pp.3-23.

Wilson, T., *Policies for Regional Development*, University of Glasgow Social and Economic Paper no. 3 1964.

HMSO (1973).

Statistical appendix

S DONOVAN
Research Assistant in Econometric Methods,
Imperial College, University of London

ECONOMIC TRENDS IN THE UK

Growth of Output and Population

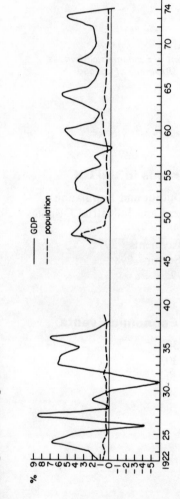

Figure 1. *Rates of growth of population and real GDP at factor cost (1922-74).*

Unemployment and Industrial Disputes

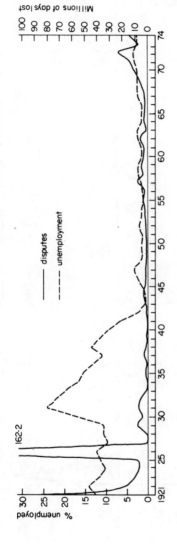

Figure 2. *Registered unemployed as a percentage of the labour force, and working days lost through industrial disputes (1921-74).*

Inflation

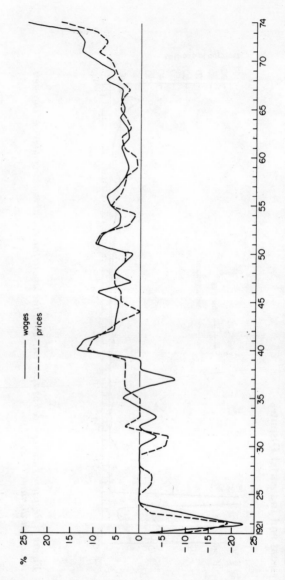

Figure 3. *Rates of growth of retail prices and the average weekly wage (1921-74).*

Balance of Payments

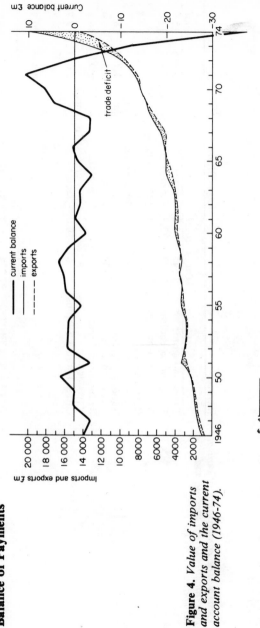

Figure 4. *Value of imports and exports and the current account balance (1946-74).*

Figure 5. *The rate of exchange: US dollars per pound sterling (1946-74).*

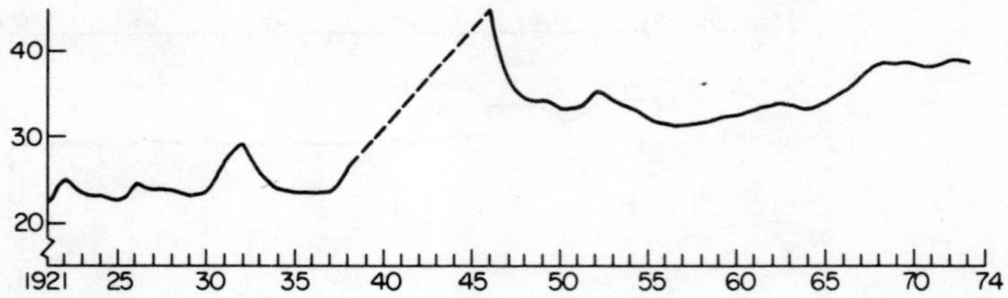

The Public Sector

Figure 6. *The growth of public spending: public authorities current expenditure as a percentage of GDP at factor cost (1921-74).*

Table 1. *The composition of central government current income and expenditure (1973).*

Income	£m	% of total
Taxes on income	9,143	41.2
Taxes on expenditure	7,389	33.3
NI contributions	3,636	16.4
Rent, interest and dividends	1,740	7.8
National Health payments	237	1.1
Redundancy Fund payments	53	0.2
Gross Trading Surplus	6	0.0
TOTAL RECEIPTS	22,204	100.0

Expenditure	£m	% of total
Defence	3,316	15.6
National Health Service	2,497	11.8
Agriculture, fishing and food	82	0.4
Other expenditure on goods and services	1,758	8.3
Subsidies	1,351	6.4
NI benefits	3,927	18.4
Other grants to personal sector	2,073	9.7
Debt interest	1,801	8.9
Current grants to local authorities	4,446	20.9
TOTAL EXPENDITURE	21,251	100.0

298

Finance

299

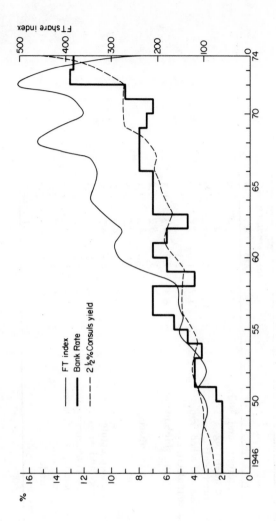

Figure 7. *Bank Rate,[1] the yield on 2½% Consuls[2] and the Financial Times Industrial Ordinary Share Index[2] (1946-74).*
[1]Maximum annual levels; after October 1972 the Bank Minimum Lending Rate is shown.
[2]Average annual values.

FT share index

500
400
300
200
100
0

%
16
14
12
10
8
6
4
2
0

1946   50   55   60   65   70   74

FT index
Bank Rate
2½% Consuls yield

Finance *(cont.)*

Table 2. *Employment by industry.*

	% of total employment			
	1923	1938	1952	1974
Agriculture, forestry and fishing	7.5	5.1	3.4	1.9
Mining and quarrying	10.9	6.5	4.3	1.6
Manufacture (total)	46.6	43.0	41.4	34.2
chemicals and allied trades	1.7	1.6	2.4	1.9
metal manufacture	2.9	2.3	2.7	2.7
engineering and shipbuilding	8.8	7.0	9.3	9.4
vehicles	2.2	3.1	5.2	3.4
food, drink and tobacco	4.0	4.0	4.0	3.4
paper and printing	2.8	3.0	2.5	2.5
textiles	10.6	7.6	4.4	2.5
Building and contracting	6.8	9.3	6.3	5.9
Gas, electricity and water	1.4	1.5	1.8	1.5
Transport and communication	6.4	6.1	8.4	6.7
Insurance, banking and finance	1.8	1.8	2.2	4.7
Public administration	3.4	4.3	6.6	7.0
Distributive trades	10.9	14.1	10.4	12.1
Other services	5.3	8.3	15.1	23.8

Table 3. *Comparison of real growth rates of GDP, inflation and unemployment.*

	Growth of GDP (%)			Growth of consumer prices (%)			Unemployment (%)
	1962-72 (average annual)	1973	1974	1965-73 (average annual)	1973	1974[1]	1973
UK	2.7	5.2	-0.3	5.9	9.2	18.4	2.7
US	4.2	5.9	-2.0	4.1	6.2	12.1	4.9
Canada	5.5	6.8	4.0	4.1	7.6	12.0	5.6
Japan	10.4	11.0	-3.0	6.2	11.7	24.5	1.3
France	5.7	6.1	4.5	4.8	7.3	14.9	3.0
West Germany	4.5	5.3	1.5	3.9	6.9	6.5	1.0
Italy	4.6	5.9	3.1	3.7	10.8	23.7	3.8

[1] 12 months to November 1974.

Note: All figures for 1974 are either provisional or estimates.

Sources:

London and Cambridge Economic Service, *The British Economy: Key Statistics 1900-1970*, Times Newspapers 1971.

Department of Employment Gazette, HMSO.

Central Statistical Office, *Economic Trends*, HMSO.

National Institute Economic Review, National Institute of Economic and Social Research.

Main Economic Indicators, OECD.

Department of Employment and Productivity, *British Labour Statistics 1886-1968*, HMSO 1971.

CALENDAR OF ECONOMIC EVENTS 1964-1974

Budgetary, Monetary and Balance of Payments Policy	Industrial and Labour Policies and Issues	Other Events and Policies
	1964	
Feb. Bank Rate raised to 5%.	Mar. 'Beeching Plan' for rail rationalisation announced.	May GATT countries begin Kennedy Round trade negotiations.
Apr. Budget: duty on tobacco and alcohol increased; no increase in public expenditure.	Jul. Resale Price Maintenance Bill becomes law.	Oct. Labour government under Mr Wilson; Mr Callaghan becomes Chancellor and Mr Brown Minister for Economic Affairs.
Oct. Import surcharge imposed.	Dec. Joint statement of intent on prices and incomes policy signed by government, TUC and employers.	
Nov. Budget: taxes on incomes, companies and petrol increased. Bank of England requests lending restraint by banks and borrows abroad.		
	1965	
Jan. NI contributions and benefits increased.	Mar. National Board for Prices and Incomes established. 3-3½% norm for wage increases.	Feb. Prescription charges removed.
Apr. Deflationary budget: taxes on incomes, vehicles, tobacco and alcohol increased. Capital Gains tax introduced. Special Deposits and restricted bank lending called for.	Apr. White Paper on steel nationalisation.	Jul. President Johnson escalates Vietnam war.
	Dec. Redundancy Payments Act comes into operation. Government and trade unions take stake in Fairfields shipyard.	Sep. National Plan published.
May Further borrowing from the IMF.		Nov. Rhodesia declares UDI.
Jul. Public investment projects deferred.		

302

1966

Feb. Bank advances frozen.
Apr. Corporation tax set at 40%.
May Deflationary budget.
Jul. Bank Rate raised to 7%, Special Deposits doubled, public expenditure cut.
Sep. Further public expenditure cuts.
Nov. Travel allowances limited to £50.

Jan. Investment grants replace allowances. Industrial Reorganisation Corporation established.
May Seamen's strike.
Jul. Voluntary prices and incomes freeze introduced; becomes compulsory in October.
Sep. SET introduced.
Dec. Investment grants increased by 5%.

Mar. Labour government re-elected.
Aug. Mr Stewart takes over Department of Economic Affairs.
Oct. Oil found under the North Sea.

1967

Apr. Neutral budget.
Oct. NI benefits increased.
Nov. Cuts in public expenditure, Bank Rate from 6% to 8%, $3,000m credit sought, 14% devaluation of sterling.
Dec. Further cuts in public expenditure.

Jan. Six months severe prices and incomes restraint begins.
Jul. New prices and incomes policy; increases to be justified against stated criteria.
Sep. Regional Employment Premium introduced.

Mar. Decimal Currency Bill published.
May UK makes second application to join EEC.
Jun. Seven Day War in Middle East; Suez Canal closed.
Aug. Prime Minister takes over direction of DEA.
Sep. IMF announces creation of SDR's.
Nov. Mr Jenkins becomes Chancellor.
Dec. UK EEC application vetoed.

Budgetary, Monetary and Balance of Payments Policy	Industrial and Labour Policies and Issues	Other Events and Policies
	1968	
Jan. Further cuts in public expenditure. Mar. Increases in indirect taxation. Oct. Social security benefits increased. Nov. Restrictive monetary measures.	Jan. BMC and Leyland Motor Co. to merge. Apr. Restrictive Trade Practices Bill published. Jun. Donovan Commission reports.	Mar. Two-tier gold system announced. Jun. Prescription charges reimposed. Nov. Mr Nixon elected US President.
	1969	
Feb. Bank Rate raised to 8%. Apr. Budget: duty on petrol and wine increased; Corporation tax set at 45%. May Letter of intent to IMF promises limit on domestic credit expansion. Nov. NI contributions and benefits increased. Dec. Import deposits reduced to 40%.	Jan. Investment grants reduced. *In Place of Strife* published. Apr. Intermediate Areas established. Jun. Plans for Industrial Relations Bill dropped. Oct. Post Office becomes public corporation.	Mar. Maiden flight by Concorde. Aug. Franc devalued. Sep. Deutschmark floated, then revalued. Oct. SAYE scheme introduced.

1970

Jan. CIR issues first reports.
Sep. CBI announces voluntary price restraint.
Oct. Investment grants replaced by investment allowances.
Nov. Miners' strike.
Dec. Industrial Relations Bill published.

Jun. Conservative government under Mr Heath.
Jul. Mr Barber becomes Chancellor following the death of Mr Macleod.
Oct. Department of Trade and Industry and Department of the Environment established. BP discovers the 'Forties Field'.

Jan. UK travel restrictions lifted.
Apr. Reflationary budget: personal allowances increased; some stamp duty abolished. Bank Rate lowered to 7%, but growth of money supply restricted.
Jul. Additional public expenditure announced.
Oct. Cuts in Income tax, Corporation tax and public expenditure.
Dec. Import deposits abolished.

1971

Jan. Rolls Royce collapses.
Feb. Special Development Areas created.
Mar. NBPI wound up. IRC abolished.
Jul. 12 months of price restraint agreed by CBI. UCS 'work-in' commences.
Dec. Provisions of Industrial Relations Act implemented.

Jan. Post Office strike.
Feb. Decimalisation of currency.
Aug. USA introduces wage and price freeze and non-convertibility of the dollar. Family Income Supplement introduced. Sterling floats, followed by the yen.
Oct. Labour Party rejects EEC entry terms.
Dec. Dollar devalued following settlement by Group of Ten.

Mar. Budget: Corporation tax lowered; child allowances increased.
Apr. Bank Rate lowered to 6%.
Jul. Reduction in Purchase tax and SET. Increases in public expenditure.
Sep. More flexible system of control over banks introduced. 12½% eligible assets ratio imposed.
Oct. Clearing banks to compete on interest rates.
Nov. Increases in public expenditure.

305

Budgetary, Monetary and Balance of Payments Policy	Industrial and Labour Policies and Issues	Other Events and Policies
1972	**1972**	
Feb. Expenditure on NHS and social services increased.	Jan. Miners' strike.	Jan. EEC entry negotiations completed.
Mar. Budget: personal allowances increased; exemption limits for Surtax and Estate duty raised.	Feb. Expansion of training system announced. Three-day working week. Miners' strike settled following Wilberforce report.	Jun. Sterling floats.
Dec. Bank Rate raised to 9%. Increases in public expenditure.	Jul. National dock strike.	Jul. 3-year agreement by USA to sell wheat to USSR.
	Nov. Tripartite talks between government, TUC and CBI break down; 90-day freeze introduced (Phase 1). Manpower Services Commission established.	
	Dec. Fair Trading Bill announced.	
1973	**1973**	**1973**
Apr. Budget: introduces unified system of personal taxation, VAT and Corporation tax imputation scheme; SET abolished.	Jan. Phase 1 extended.	Jan. UK joins EEC.
	Apr. Phase 2 introduced. Pay Board and Price Commission established.	Feb. 10% devaluation of the dollar.
	May Protest strikes against Phase 2.	Mar. Joint float of EEC currencies.
		Oct. Arab-Israeli War. 70% rise in crude oil prices.

May   Cuts in public expenditure.

Jul.   Bank Rate raised to 11½%, ½% Special Deposits called for.

Dec.   Stringent monetary controls. HP controls reintroduced. Cuts in public expenditure.

Nov.   Phase 3 limits wage increases to 7% and introduces threshold agreements.

Nov.   State of Emergency declared following miners' overtime ban.

Dec.   Crude oil prices doubled.

1974

Feb.   Record trade deficit.

Mar.   Neutral budget: taxes and pensions increased.

Apr.   Government loan to building societies.

Jul.   Mini-budget lowers VAT and introduces food subsidies.

Nov.   Mini-budget offers relief for industry, increases social security payments and VAT on petrol.

Jan.   Department of Energy established.

Feb.   Miners' strike.

Mar.   Miners' strike and three-day week end.

Jun.   Statutory incomes control ended. Industrial Relations Court disbanded.

Jul.   Government stake in North Sea oil announced.

Aug.   White Paper announces extension of state ownership and planning agreements with industry.

Dec.   Sir Don Ryder appointed to head National Enterprise Board. Aid given to British Leyland.

Mar.   Labour government under Mr Wilson; Mr Healey becomes Chancellor. Rents frozen.

Apr.   Renegotiation of EEC entry conditions demanded.

May   General strike in Northern Ireland.

Aug.   President Nixon resigns, is replaced by Mr Ford.

Oct.   Labour government re-elected.

Index

308

UNIVERSITY LIBRARY LIVERPOOL